Setting Tile

Setting Tile

Michael Byrne

The Taunton Press

Cover photo: Kevin Ireton
Photos, pgs. 4, 22, 96, 112, 154, 172: Sloan Howard
Photo, p. 70: Dan McCoy
Photo, p. 136: Kevin Ireton
Photos, pgs. 196, 220: Carolyn L. Bates

Taunton
BOOKS & VIDEOS

for fellow enthusiasts

First printing: 1995

Printed in the United States of America

A Fine Homebuilding Book

Fine Homebuilding® is a trademark of The Taunton Press, Inc.,
registered in the U.S. Patent and Trademark Office.

The Taunton Press, 63 South Main Street, PO Box 5506,
Newtown, CT 06470-5506

Library of Congress Cataloging-in-Publication Data

Byrne, Michael.
      Setting tile / Michael Byrne.
         p.   cm.
      Includes index.
      ISBN 1-56158-080-5
      1. Tiles.   2. Tile laying.   I. Title.
   TH8541.B97   1995   95-947
      698 — dc20   CIP

For Virginia, George, Bill and Kathy, Tom, Jack and Pam,
Kevin and Suz, Kris and Eric, and all the little ones

Acknowledgments

There is not enough room here to thank by name all the readers of Setting Ceramic Tile *(the first edition of this book) and all the professional installers who have offered suggestions and passed along tips and techniques. The best way I can thank you is to continue to listen and observe.*

Many members of the tile industry have been generous with their time, enthusiasm and encouragement. Henry B. Rothberg of Laticrete International in Bethany, Connecticut, Harvey Powell of The Noble Company in Grand Haven, Michigan, and Craig Hamilton of Mapei Corporation in Chicago, Illinois, have always managed to find time to answer countless questions, provide sound advice and furnish lavish support. They would be a credit to any industry.

Anyone interested in tile owes a big thank you to the Tile Council of America. I'd personally like to thank everyone at the Tile Council for allowing me to reproduce parts of the TCA Handbook.

Setting tile always seems easier than writing about tile installation. I am indebted to Kevin Ireton of Fine Homebuilding *magazine, Steve Bliss of* The Journal of Light Construction, *Howard Olansky and Harold Arkoff of Specialist Publications and Carolyn Bates of Black Silver Photography for their support and for helping to keep my batteries charged.*

Writing is a solitary task, but producing a book requires help from many people. Barbara Sallick allowed me to take control of the Waterworks tile showroom in Danbury, Connecticut, for photographs. Her patience and good humor are greatly appreciated. Russ Gregory of American Tile Supply, also in Danbury, supplied the tiles for the videotape series and let me back into his shop to use the facilities for this revision (sorry for flooding the back of your shop, Russ).

Finally, a special thanks to my editor, Peter Chapman, and to all the folks at The Taunton Press who helped make writing this book a real adventure and pleasure.

Contents

Introduction

Over 20 years ago, unable to find any certified training in tilesetting and confused by conflicting information, I set out to find the best way to install ceramic tiles. Since boyhood, I had been attracted to the beauty of tiles, and as a young man, I would do whatever was necessary to learn the tricks and secrets of installing tile and mosaics over thick slabs of mud. No mastic jobs for me! I wanted sand, cement and tradition.

The creative exchange I had envisioned between the master and student quickly eroded when I took a job with a ceramic-tile repairman; with a mountain of damaged tiles, broken concrete and dry-rotted timbers to get through every week, I was not exactly basking in the glamour that some tilework can provide. But within a short time I learned my most important lesson about tile installations both plain and fancy: that the tiles were just a skin and not as critical to the durability of the installation as the selection and application of the materials and methods used to build it.

In removing and rebuilding thousands of damaged installations, I also learned that having the tiles installed over a mortar bed was by no means a guarantee of durability, and that not all tiles installed with mastic were doomed to certain failure. The important thing was to use materials and methods appropriate for the kind of use the installation would get. Working as a repairman may not have been glamorous,

but it taught me numerous techniques and exposed me to a wide range of materials and situations. This repair experience ultimately became my best tilesetting ally when I decided to test my skills on new construction and remodeling work.

Sometimes on my own and sometimes as an employee for other companies, I worked on residential, commercial, medical, food-processing, industrial and military projects, and learned that the various markets for tile application required many different kinds of tile installers—specialists—and many different kinds of installations from the simple to the exotic. In spite of the range of choices and the level of detail, however, I also learned that every installation required minimum levels of planning, specification, execution and maintenance, and that overlooking a detail at any stage could prove costly.

Some special applications require the very latest materials and the most skillful labor to produce, but at the heart of every ceramic-tile installation are the basic materials and skills that are required for even the most simple residential tile applications: a solid base, a strong adhesive, the right kind of tile and firm grout joints—all installed with care and understanding. These are the basic materials and skills that you will find discussed in this revision.

A modest training program I directed convinced me to write about ceramic-tile installations. My own work experiences, questions raised by seminar and workshop students, and requests from retailers and distributors led to a string of articles in *Fine Homebuilding* magazine and the publication of *Setting Ceramic Tile* in 1987.

Since then, my work as a consultant requires that I continue to learn about tile installations, observe different installation techniques and sift through the ever-changing array of tiles, tools and installation materials. The continuing search for the best materials and methods is what drove me to begin writing this revision. Not just to bring the words and the phone numbers up to date, but to approach tile installation from a different perspective.

As a professional tile installer, I knew that no book or videotape could substitute for practical experience. But as an author, I was determined to expose the interested reader to the same kind of selection and application processes that every professional must develop to produce durable, attractive, low-maintenance tilework. To help do that, I decided to base this revision more on materials and techniques than on specific installations or projects. Much of the text and illustrations that first appeared in *Setting Ceramic Tile* can still be found within these pages intact, but all has been scrutinized, some has been altered to conform to industry standards or thinking and some has been eliminated. My intent was to condense the core of information found in the original book, bring it up to date technically and add layers of additional techniques that would allow the reader enough flexibility and confidence to go far beyond basic installations.

All the techniques described in this edition are based on those used by professional installers to ensure consistent, high-quality results. And although there is nothing tricky or secret about the techniques, and most are relatively easy to learn, every installer (novice or professional) needs to put together the right combination of techniques and materials to complete a successful installation.

At one time, this meant installing tiles over a setting bed of fresh mortar—a process requiring considerable experience and training. Today, however, with reliable, ready-to-use cement backer boards (panels designed specifically for ceramic-tile installations) and other materials, the only special manual skills required for installing tiles are knowing how to cut backer boards to size and fasten them with screws or nails, knowing how to mix and spread adhesives uniformly with a notched trowel and knowing how to mix, spread, compact and clean grout.

Because only simple, basic skills are required for the thin-bed method, anyone in reasonable shape with a few tools and the *time* and *desire* can do the work. I emphasize time and desire because although the individual steps in most installations are quite simple, the entire installation must be orchestrated carefully, with a constant eye for details. Like any other handwork, tiling takes time and attention. (In my workshops and seminars, participants range from high school graduates to retirees, male and female, professionals and amateurs. By the end of the sessions, I hear the same comment over and over: "I never realized there were so many steps; the actual setting of the tiles took the least amount of time!")

Successful tile installations are the result of attention to detail from start to finish: building on a sound structure, selecting appropriate materials, cutting no corners, being observant and seeing each step through to the end. After reading this revision, you should understand the basic concepts enough to assess your own abilities and expectations. Then, whether you decide to tackle an entire installation alone, get help on a portion of the work or turn the whole thing over to a professional, you will be in better control of the results.

Chapter One

Ceramic Tile

All tile was once made of pure clay from the bed of a stream or river. Tile makers gathered the wet clay, crudely processed it to eliminate stones and debris, formed individual tiles by hand and let the pieces bake in the sun. Early in tile's history, which dates back at least 6,000 years, tile makers developed frames for shaping the body of the tile. And then, historians speculate, someone noticed that the fired clay inside the ovens used for baking bread was sturdier than the sun-dried clay and was also unaffected by water. This significant observation led tile makers to try baking their tiles in these ovens and, in turn, to create special ovens, or kilns, for firing tile. These kilns were probably reserved for special tile, while ordinary tile continued to be baked in the sun.

After these advances—or perhaps before them—another important development took place that changed the laborious task of gathering clay, a process that involved moving the tile maker's household each time a source of clay was exhausted. At some point, a weary tile maker must have realized that it was possible to extend raw clay by mixing it with ground shards of pottery and broken tile. This practice probably took hold quickly and set a precedent for later extending clay even further by mixing it with ground shale and eventually ground gypsum.

Modern Tile Making

Nowadays, while some commercially produced tile is made of pure clay or pure gypsum, the vast majority is made from a combination of clay, ground shale or gypsum, and other ingredients such as talc, vermiculite and sand. These latter materials serve both to extend the clay and to control shrinkage in the tile. After the clay has been refined and mixed with water and these additives, it's shaped into a bisque, or biscuit, which is the body of the tile.

Bisque

The green (unfired) bisque can be formed in several ways. It can be extruded through a die, like toothpaste squeezed from a tube, or it can be rammed into a die, in the same way that a piece of metal can be stamped. It can also be cut from a sheet, cookie-cutter style, or be formed by hand in a wooden or metal frame.

Manufacturers who produce tile in great quantity form the bisque in a die, which yields uniformly shaped and sized tiles. Most tile today is made by the dust-press method, in which the moisture content of the dry ingredients is so low that they hold together only when rammed into a die. Tile producers with smaller, less mechanized operations and makers who work by hand cut the bisque from sheets of clay or form the tiles in frames.

However the bisque is formed, it must leather-harden, or dry enough to lose its plasticity, before being fired in a kiln. Most tile, whether glazed or unglazed, is fired only once, though some tile is fired several times, and some highly decorated tile may even undergo five or more firings. The number of firings, as well as the purity of the clay, largely determines the eventual cost of the tile.

The temperature at which tile is fired ranges from as low as 900°F to as high as 2500°F, but, generally speaking, most tile is fired at temperatures between 1900°F and 2200°F. Low-temperature firing usually produces porous tile and soft glazes, whereas high-temperature firing yields dense, nonporous tile and hard glazes. The amount of time a tile remains in the kiln also contributes to the tile's porosity, and while some tile may be fired for only a few minutes, other tile may stay in the kiln for as long as a week.

The demand for commercial ceramic tile, efforts to control air and water pollution, and the need to conserve energy have led to the development of significant advances in kiln and production technology. With the latest equipment, ceramic tiles that used to linger for days within the kiln can now be formed, glazed, fired and packaged in less than two hours.

Glazes

Although the bisque may be the backbone of the tile, it's the glaze that gets all the attention. The earliest examples found of tile finished with colored glaze date to ancient Egypt, where copper particles formed the base of this glaze. Today most glaze consists of a transparent or opaque coating of silicates and pigment, which is brushed or sprayed on the surface of the bisque and fired. The glaze can be applied to the tile's green bisque and be fired along with the tile itself, or it can be added after the tile has undergone one or more firings. Either way, it serves both to decorate the tile and to protect its surface. While much of the tile produced today is glazed, some, like quarry tile and many Mexican pavers, is left unglazed and derives its color only from the clay from which it's made.

In some cases, a glaze is intended not only to color and preserve the surface of the tile but also to give it texture. Sawdust is one of several substances added to the glaze of some tile for this purpose. As the temperature in the kiln rises, the sawdust burns, leaving behind a bumpy covering that's not as slick as the traditional, smooth glaze. For another type of tile, particles of silicon carbide are sprinkled on the wet glaze before firing to produce a nonskid surface. (Some unglazed tile has carbide bits pressed into its surface before firing for the same purpose.)

When selecting tile for a particular installation, consider the use the tile will receive and how its glaze will hold up.

Depending on the temperature at which it's fired and the amount of time spent in the kiln, a glaze may be soft, easily scratched and unable to withstand the wear a floor or kitchen countertop receives. Or the glaze may be hard, quite durable and serviceable for any installation. (For a discussion of the various types of tile available, see pp. 9-16, and for suggestions on how to choose tile, see pp. 16-19.)

Water Absorption

Because tile sometimes has to coexist with water, determining how much water a particular tile can absorb is important. The amount of water a tile absorbs depends on the number of air pockets in the tile's bisque. The presence and number of these air pockets depends not only on the temperature at which the tile was fired but also on the amount of time it spent in the kiln and the composition of the clay. (The glaze on tile absorbs no moisture, regardless of the firing temperature or time in the kiln.)

The American National Standards Institute (ANSI) measures the permeability of various types of tile by comparing the dry weight of a finished tile with its weight after it's been boiled in water for five hours. The four categories of tile established by ANSI, as presented in its handbook of standard specifications (see the Resource Guide at the back of the book), are nonvitreous, semi-vitreous, vitreous and impervious. Knowing how permeable a tile is is important in deciding which kind of tile to use for a particular installation. Tile that absorbs little or no water, for example, is more suitable for a wet installation (a shower stall, for instance) than tile that really soaks up a lot of water.

Nonvitreous tile

Nonvitreous tile readily absorbs water, about 7% of its weight, meaning that air pockets make up about 7% of this tile's bisque. Because this type of tile is fired at relatively low temperatures for a comparatively short time, it requires less energy to manufacture and is usually less expensive than vitreous tile.

Since nonvitreous tile absorbs so much water, it's not a good choice for tiling wet areas or for exterior installations. In wet areas, this tile's porous bisque may not dry out completely between uses and may, in time, harbor bacteria. And because nonvitreous tile lacks what is termed freeze/thaw stability, when it's installed outdoors in cold climates, the water it absorbs in winter will expand as it freezes, causing the tile to crack.

That said, tilesetters install nonvitreous tile all the time in wet and exterior installations. And in areas with few tile

CROSS SECTIONS OF THE FOUR TYPES OF TILE BISQUE

Air pockets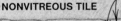

NONVITREOUS TILE

Fired at around 2100°F for up to 21 hours. Absorbs 7% water or more.

SEMI-VITREOUS TILE

Fired at around 2100°F for up to 22 hours. Absorbs between 3% and 7% water.

VITREOUS TILE

Fired at around 2200°F for up to 30 hours. Absorbs between 0.5% and 3% water.

IMPERVIOUS TILE
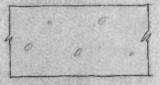
Fired at around 2500°F for up to 60 hours. Absorbs less than 0.5% water.

stores nearby, nonvitreous tile may be all that's readily available. Nonetheless, I don't recommend using this tile in these potentially problematic locations. For this reason, I would urge people without access to a fully stocked tile store to order the tile they need from a source listed in the Resource Guide. If you choose to use nonvitreous tile in these situations for whatever reason, at least upgrade the installation to minimize the problems. In addition to properly waterproofing the wet interior installation (see Chapter 6), install the tile with a thinset adhesive and mix a latex additive with the adhesive as well as with the grout. (To decipher this mysterious advice on adhesives, and for a full discussion of choosing setting materials, see Chapter 3.)

For setting nonvitreous tile in any installation, some adjustments should be made to accommodate this tile's high water-absorption rate. Set tiles immediately after the adhesive is spread (I prefer to use polymer-modified thinset mortars to ready-to-use mastics). And before any nonvitreous installation is grouted, the unglazed portions of the tile should be misted with water to prevent the porous bisque from sucking liquid out of the grout and causing the grout to cure prematurely. (This adjustment may not be required with a polymer-modified grout mixture.)

Semi-vitreous tile

Semi-vitreous tile is fired at about the same temperature as nonvitreous tile but usually for a little longer, which produces a somewhat less porous bisque. This tile has an absorption rate of from 3% to 7% of its weight and is, in effect, a transition tile between very porous nonvitreous tile and essentially nonporous vitreous tile. With proper waterproofing, semi-vitreous tile can be used for wet interior installations, but because it's not really freeze/thaw stable, it should not be used outdoors in

cold climates. Like nonvitreous tile, it can be set with an organic mastic or a thinset adhesive, though a polymer-modified thinset should be used for a wet installation. To ensure good results, semi-vitreous tile should also be misted with water before grouting to prevent its somewhat porous bisque from sucking water from the grout.

Vitreous tile

Vitreous tile is fired at temperatures of around 2200°F for up to 30 hours, which causes the ingredients in the bisque to fuse together like glass. Because of its very dense body, vitreous tile absorbs only from 0.5% to 3% water and is therefore an excellent choice for any installation, including those that will get wet or that will freeze. This tile's dense bisque also accounts for its high compressive strength (that is, it can withstand the compression of a heavy load without fracturing). Since it is able to bear considerable weight, vitreous tile is generally more suitable for floors than soft-bodied, nonvitreous tile. Because some vitreous tiles have relatively soft glazes, however, and because a few manufacturers of vitreous tile state that their products are unsuitable for floors despite high-temperature firing, it's a good idea always to check the tile maker's specifications when selecting tiles for a particular installation.

For setting vitreous tile in dry installations, either an organic mastic or a thinset can be used. In wet installations, only a polymer-modified thinset adhesive should be used. Before grouting, vitreous tile needs only to be sponged down rather than misted with water.

Impervious tile

Impervious tile, as its name suggests, is almost waterproof. This tile absorbs less than 0.5% water and for this reason is frequently used for sanitary installations in hospitals and pharmaceutical plants. Impervious tile is easily sterilized and can withstand repeated cleaning and

Unlike interior tilework, which is protected by the structure, exterior tilework is exposed to the extremes of nature and requires extra care in planning, constructing and maintaining the installation. The two major areas of concern are freeze/thaw cycling and the harmful effects of the direct rays of the sun.

Since a given volume of water expands about 8% as it freezes, only tiles warranted by the manufacturer to be freeze/thaw stable (i.e., vitreous or impervious tiles) should be used on exterior applications; otherwise, moisture absorbed by the tile can expand within the tile, causing all or part of the glaze to spall or the entire tile to part from the setting bed. In addition, all adhesives, grouts, sealants, caulks and backing materials used for exterior applications in cold climates must be freeze/thaw stable. Although there are plenty of materials that allow for sub-freezing installations, the actual application of the materials (and the tiles) must be done at normal room temperatures.

At the opposite end of the spectrum is heat, and, in particular, the rays of the sun. Most tile-installation materials are designed to be stored and applied at normal room temperatures. The sun's rays (even in winter) can drive necessary moisture from adhesive and grout mortars, rendering them powdery and useless. Excessive heat (with or without the presence of the sun's rays) can also accelerate the setup time of most mortars and epoxies, thereby reducing their workability.

Throughout the course of an installation project, whether exterior or interior, the tile installer must keep all parts of the installation protected from extremes of heat or cold. This means acclimating installation materials, the tile and the setting bed to room temperatures, shielding the work in progress from the direct rays of the sun and keeping the installation protected until all the materials have cured.

disinfecting. And since this tile absorbs practically no water, germs have little chance of finding a home in an impervious installation. Like other tile, impervious tile, too, can be installed with either an organic mastic or a thinset adhesive, though a polymer-modified thinset should be used for wet installations. Unless the weather is hot when the tile is installed, impervious tile does not need to be misted or sponged down before grouting.

None of the four types of tile is any more difficult to work with than another. With regard to cutting, all can be trimmed with the snap cutter, biters and wet saw (for a description of these tools, see Chapter 4), though because of their density, vitreous and impervious tiles are likely to require a bit more pressure and time to cut than soft-bodied tiles.

Ceramic Tile and Specialty Tile

This book is devoted primarily to ceramic tile. Yet because there are several types of nonceramic tile installed with ceramic methods, they, too, are included in the discussion that follows. Not included here are tiles made from natural stone. Although stone tiles are installed using the same basic methods and setting materials as ceramic tiles, the tiles are subject to cracks, fissures and other weak points and will be discussed in a separate chapter (see pp. 22-31). Not covered in this book are linoleum and vinyl tile, whose installation needs are quite different from those of ceramic tile.

Before looking at the various types of tile available, let's consider the several formats in which tile is sold and a side of tile that usually goes unnoticed—its back.

Loose tiles

Perhaps the most striking thing about visiting a tile store is the vast array of tile available. Produced in a wide spectrum of colors, sizes and shapes, tile is sold mainly as separate, loose tiles, all of which share a common requirement in setting: They must be consistently spaced. Setters installing loose tiles have used any number of devices to space them evenly—sticks, nails, string or rope, and, since their development in the late 1950s, tile spacers. The latter are small plastic devices sold in various shapes and widths (from $1/16$ in. to $1/2$ in.) that establish consistent grout joints between tiles (see the photo on p. 64). Some manufacturers resolve the problem of spacing by building spacing lugs into the sides of the tile or by packaging tile in sheet format.

Sheet-mounted tiles

Sheet-mounted tiles are individual tiles evenly spaced and mounted on a backing sheet, approximately 12 in. square or larger. Various kinds of tiles are packaged in sheet format, but most are vitreous, no larger than 4 in. square and mounted on paper, plastic mesh or a grid of rubber dots (see the photo below). The placement of the mounting material distinguishes the several types of sheet-mounted tile. As its name suggests, face-mounted tile has its mounting, a sheet of paper, adhered to the face of the tile. This paper is left in place during setting and is dampened and removed after the adhesive has dried. Back-mounted tile is held together by plastic or paper mesh applied to the back of the tile, which is left in place when the tile is set. Dot-mounted tile is joined by small rubber or plastic dots between the joints, which are not removed for setting. Wherever the mounting is positioned, the sheet of tiles can be easily trimmed to approximate size with a sharp utility knife, a razor knife or an X-acto blade.

The obvious advantage of placing the mounting material on the back of the tile is that the face is then visible during setting, making it easier to align the tile and grout joints. The disadvantage of this arrangement is that the backing material interferes with the bond of the tile and adhesive. In the case of dot-mounted tile, some setters also report installation problems caused by a thin film of oil deposited on the back of the tile when the dots were applied. (For a full discussion of how to handle the installation problems with sheet-mounted tile, see pp. 197-199.)

Tile backs

Although a tile's face gets most of the attention, its back deserves note, too, since it's often intentionally covered with raised ridges, dots or squares. The configuration of a tile back varies greatly from tile to tile, yet it's consistently designed either to expand the surface area of the back (and

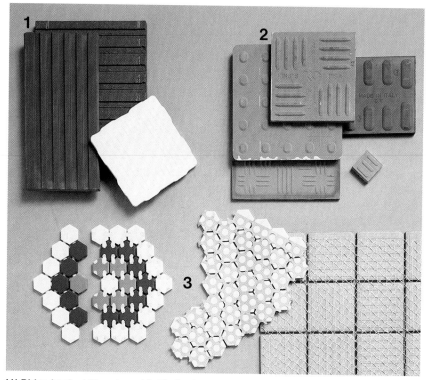

(1) Ridge-backed tiles alongside tile (at right) with spacing lugs and modified ridges; (2) button-backed tiles in a variety of configurations; and (3) sheet-mounted tiles, including (from left) dot-mounted tile and back-mounted tile with paper and plastic mesh backings.

Sloan Howard

thus increase the adhesive's bond strength), aid in the firing process or denote manufacturing information.

Ridge-backed tile is extruded tile whose back bears a series of elevations, which can effectively double, and in some cases even triple, the flat surface area of the back. Button-backed tile has raised dots or squares on the back, which separate the individual tiles when they're stacked in a kiln, allowing heat to pass evenly among them and ensuring a uniform firing. Finally, many tiles are embossed with identifying marks to denote a particular production run of tile or to record color and other manufacturing specifications. All of these various markings can be helpful when you need to find replacement tiles for restoration or remodeling work.

Glazed wall tile

Generally speaking, glazed wall tile is nonvitreous tile with a white gypsum or terra-cotta-colored bisque and a soft glaze, which makes it unsuitable for floor use. In contrast, floor tile is any nonvitreous, semi-vitreous, vitreous or impervious tile, whether glazed or unglazed, that is considered sturdy enough to be used for

floors. This tile could, of course, also be used for walls, as perhaps some of it should be—some tiles officially classified as floor tiles are not particularly durable, or they may have a tough vitreous bisque finished with a fragile glaze.

Most glazed wall tile sold in the United States is produced in this country by the dust-press method. Usually about ¼ in. thick, these tiles are most commonly made in 4¼-in. and 6-in. squares, though larger tiles up to 12 in. square are available. With a few exceptions, these tiles are intended for wall use, rather than for floor and countertop installations. With proper waterproofing, they can be used for wet installations, but they should be limited to interior use, as they are not freeze/thaw stable. Glazed wall tile requires no special setting bed and can be installed with either an organic mastic or a thinset adhesive for dry installations, but should be used only with a polymer-modified thinset adhesive for wet installations.

Paver tile

Pavers are clay, shale or porcelain tile, made by hand or machine, which are at least ½ in. thick, sometimes glazed, and

These unglazed pavers exhibit the individuality and texture inherent in the manufacturing process. Because they're nonvitreous, however, they shouldn't be used for wet or exterior installations in cold climates.

Sloan Howard

intended for use on floors. Machine-made pavers are produced both in the United States and in Europe. Sometimes they are extruded, but more often they are made by the dust-press method. Generally speaking, machine-made pavers are fired at high enough temperatures to produce semi-vitreous or vitreous tile. These tiles usually range in size from 4 in. by 6 in. to 12 in. square and are up to ¾ in. thick. The large pavers are sometimes paired with smaller squares called spots. These accent tiles have been used for centuries and were originally colored with various stains rather than glaze.

Whether used on floors or walls, machine-made pavers should be installed with a thinset adhesive. Because they are vitreous and thus freeze/thaw stable, these pavers can be used in both wet and exterior installations. They require no special setting bed, but because of their uneven surface, they may need to be back-buttered with adhesive (see pp. 144-145) to ensure complete contact with the setting bed.

Unglazed handmade pavers are generally produced in Mexico and in the Mediterranean. Those from Mexico are usually terra-cotta-colored, yellow or brown, while Mediterranean pavers are traditionally doe-colored. Glazed handmade pavers are produced mainly in Mexico, Portugal, Italy and France. All handmade pavers are nonvitreous tiles fired at low temperatures. (Sometimes in remote regions of Mexico these tiles are fired in jury-rigged kilns made from the bodies of automobiles, with the heat supplied by burning discarded tires!) About ½ in. to 2 in. thick, these pavers range in size from 4 in. square to 24 in. square. Because these tiles are often crudely made, a run of a particular dimension can vary widely in size from tile to tile, and individual tiles may bear fingerprints, animal tracks or other such "signatures."

Like machine-made pavers, these tiles are produced primarily for floors, though they are sometimes used for walls, especially when glazed. They are unsuitable

Carolyn L. Bates

This step detail shows tumbled green and white marble 'spots' paired with 8-in. Mexican paver octagons.

for countertops, though, because they are not flat and because, to be kept clean, they need to be finished with sealers that shouldn't be used around food. If you really want handmade pavers on a kitchen countertop, I suggest that you use them on the backsplash to accent a more practical choice of tile for the work surface. Finally, because handmade pavers are porous, they should not be used in wet interior locations or in exterior installations in freezing climates.

Before setting, the backs of handmade pavers should be cleaned of any debris and loose particles. They can be scraped or brushed and vacuumed or, if time permits, submerged in water, scraped clean with a knife or a margin trowel, rinsed with clean water and turned on edge to dry. Any handmade pavers that need to be cut for the installation should be trimmed on the wet saw rather than on the snap cutter. Like machine-made pavers, they should be installed with a thinset adhesive for floor or wall use. Since handmade pavers generally aren't flat, they too may need to be back-buttered with adhesive to ensure complete contact with the setting bed. Finally, unglazed pavers should be sealed to make grouting easier, and to protect the finished tiles and slow down the wearing process.

Traditionally, these pavers were sealed with hot oil and beeswax, but now they are often sent untreated to the tile retailer, who stains and seals them. If the pavers you select are unsealed, seal them before grouting with at least two coats of sealer made especially for tile (see the Resource Guide). Sealers may be glossy top-coat applications or satin-finished penetrating types. With either type, normal usage means that they may need to be reapplied after a year or so. If a top-coat sealer is used, the floor will need to be stripped and completely resealed each time the sealer is reapplied. With a penetrating oil, the worn spots alone can be refinished.

Quarry tile

Originally, quarry tile was quarried stone, cut, ground and polished to uniform dimensions. Now the term generally applies to semi-vitreous or vitreous clay tile, extruded and fired unglazed, which resembles the original quarry tile. The bisque of these hard-bodied tiles is available in a variety of colors and treatments.

Quarry tile is manufactured in 4-in. to 12-in. squares and hexagons as well as in rectangles, most commonly 3 in. by 6 in. or 4 in. by 8 in. The pieces range in thickness from $\frac{1}{2}$ in. to $\frac{3}{4}$ in. Because of their density, these tiles are excellent for floor and countertop use and could also serve for wall installations.

Quarry tile used for floors can be finished with a sealer or left unsealed. If you want to seal quarry tile after installing it, do so before grouting with a top-coat sealer especially made for tile (quarry tile is too dense for a penetrating oil). Depending upon usage, the tiles will need to be entirely stripped and the sealer reapplied from time to time. Because top-coating sealers should not be used around food, a quarry-tile countertop must be left unsealed. This may mean that the countertop will become stained with use and that another tile would make a more practical choice for this installation. (Quarry-tile surfaces are often found in food-processing plants, where staining is less of a problem. Here, the durability of these tiles means they may be repeatedly cleaned with steam or other methods not really suited for home or light commercial use.)

Because they are vitreous, quarry tiles are excellent for wet installations and can also be used outdoors. They need no special setting bed or unusual installation treatment. Whether used for floors or walls, they should be paired with a thin-set adhesive.

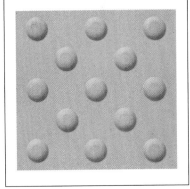

Porcelain tile

Small porcelain tiles (like the 1-in. by 1-in. tiles commonly seen on sloped shower floors) are relatively easy to produce and have long been an economical flooring choice for both wet and heavy-use areas. Large porcelain tiles, on the other hand, have traditionally been very difficult to produce, have always been somewhat fragile and have usually carried a very high price tag.

The demand for a tough yet fashionable tile suitable for both residential and commercial spaces has led to the development in Italy (the spawning ground for most ceramic-tile technology) of porcelain tiles in sizes up to 24 in. by 24 in. Referred to as *monopressatura,* these tiles are made by compacting a layer of dry bisque ingredients and a layer of dry glaze ingredients under extremely high pressure and speeding the resulting tile sandwich through a kiln.

As a group, porcelain tiles have excellent wear properties, stain resistance and high compressive strength, and are freeze/thaw stable. However, because they absorb virtually no moisture, porcelain tiles (especially those larger than 2 in. square) should be installed with a polymer-modified thinset mortar made specifically for porcelain tiles. Otherwise, installation is the same as for any other kind of ceramic tile (see Chapter 8).

Mosaic tile

The tile industry considers any tile 2 in. square or smaller to be mosaic tile. This tile can be made of either glass or vitreous porcelain or clay (though, traditionally, mosaic tile also includes chipped bits and pieces of tile, stone, pebbles and shells). When made of porcelain, mosaic tile is usually unglazed but colored by pigment added to the bisque. Most ceramic mosaic tile is produced by the dust-press method and is almost always packaged in sheet-mounted format to make it easier to handle. Some can be bought loose on special order.

Sold in a wide variety of colors, ceramic mosaic tile typically comes in ¼-in. to 2-in. squares, 1-in. by 2-in. rectangles, or small hexagons. Glass mosaic tile is usually available only in 1-in. squares, and both types of mosaic tile range in thickness from ³/₃₂ in. to ¼ in. Because of its density, mosaic tile is very tough and excellent for use on floors as well as countertops and walls. Since it's vitreous and freeze/thaw stable, it can be used for both wet and exterior installations. As with other back-mounted tile, the mounting material on mosaic tile may interfere with the bond of the adhesive. For this reason, mosaic tile should be installed with a thinset adhesive for extra grip. (For a full discussion of the problems involved in installing mosaic tile, see pp. 197-199.)

Brick-veneer tile

There are several types of brick-veneer tile, all of which simulate the appearance of real brick. Some of this tile is actually brick produced in thin cross section. Other brick-

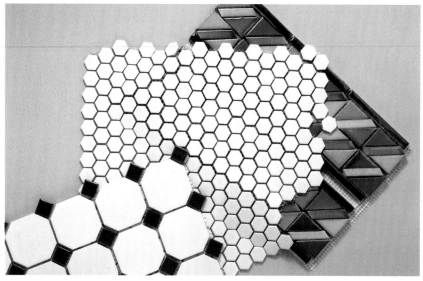

Sloan Howard

Most ceramic mosaic tile is sheet-mounted for convenience. The top sheet shown here is an adaptation of a classic design, the octagon and spot. The sheet of traditional 1-in. hex tiles illustrates the somewhat fragile nature of the netting that holds the individual tiles together. The bottom sheet contains two mosaic border strips mounted and shipped on a single piece of netting.

When time, creativity and budget are limitless, mosaics can be installed one piece at a time. For relative economy, the hand-cut stone mosaic borders set into the wall of glazed tiles shown here were factory-mounted on flexible sheets.

Sloan Howard

veneer tile is imitation brick, low-fired and made from ingredients similar to tile but with a coarser texture. A third type is made from colored mortar that is extruded like tile and dried, but not fired, in a kiln. Sometimes additional mortar is applied to this unfired tile to simulate antique brick.

Real brick-veneer tile can generally be installed wherever regular brick is used, both indoors and outdoors and in wet and dry installations. Remember, however, that brick is very porous, and if used for shower walls or tub surrounds, it will harbor bacteria and be difficult, if not impossible, to clean. Most imitation brick-veneer tile

should be reserved for wall installations because it's too soft to wear well under floor traffic. Some manufacturers do specify that their tile can be used for floors, however, so check the manufacturer's specifications. Similarly, before settling on this tile for exterior use, make sure that the tile you want to use is freeze/thaw stable.

No special setting bed is required for brick-veneer tile. If installed outdoors, it should be set with a thinset adhesive. An organic mastic can be used for an interior, decorative installation. Porous materials like brick are sometimes best grouted with a grout bag and striking tool, rather than with a grout trowel and sponge (see p. 66).

Cement-bodied tile

Cement-bodied tile is made of mortar rather than clay and is either extruded or cut from sheets. Because this kind of tile is only dried in a kiln, not fired at high temperatures, it is usually less expensive to produce than regular tile. Various surface textures are often stamped into the wet tile before it is dried, and instead of being glazed, the tile is stained after hardening with a colorant in one of a handful of earth tones. To improve wear, the manufacturer coats this tile with a protective sealer. Another coat of sealer may need to be applied after the tile is set and grouted, and will need to be reapplied occasionally as the tile wears.

Cement-bodied tile weighs no more than regular tile, has the look of stone or paver tiles and even develops a patina as it ages. Because its surface is very tough, this tile is excellent for floor installations and gives years of service when properly installed and maintained. This tile is not the best choice for wet installations, nor is it generally recommended for exterior installations in cold climates, because some brands may not be freeze/thaw stable (check the manufacturer's specifications). Since a selvage edge produced in the manufacturing process is occasionally left on the tile, this edge should be trimmed

Sloan Howard

Not all cement-bodied tiles wear the natural look. This distinctive tile owes its colorful design to polymers sandwiched to a mortar base.

with the biters or a grindstone before cutting on the wet saw (so the excess does not interfere with the fence when it is used for repeat cuts). Some cement-bodied tiles can be cut with a snap cutter, but I have fewer problems and neater results with the wet saw. This tile needs no special setting bed and can be installed on walls with an organic mastic adhesive and on floors with a thinset adhesive.

Choosing Tile

Whenever I'm asked how to choose tile, I always tell customers first to determine the kind of use the tile will get, and next to draw a sketch of the proposed installation, showing the outline of the area to be tiled, its dimensions and any special features to be taken into account. I then advise them to go to a tile showroom and simply pick a

tile they like. This tile may not be the one they select in the end, but it provides a place to start.

The tile in showrooms is organized in any number of ways, from color to intended use to pure whimsy on the part of the store manager. The one way tile is unlikely to be organized, however, is by density and porosity, that is, by nonvitreous, semi-vitreous, vitreous or impervious groupings. While it's important to know how permeable a tile is when making a selection for a given installation, the salesperson may or may not be able to tell you if a particular tile is vitreous or nonvitreous—some may not themselves be clear on the distinction. Nonetheless, the salesperson should have manufacturers' specifications on all tile in the showroom and should at least be able to tell you whether a given tile is rated for use on floors, walls or countertops. If the tile you like is not rated for the use you have in mind, the salesperson should be able to direct you to a similar-looking tile that's better suited to your needs.

Grading systems

You may also hear a tile retailer mention a tile's grade. This refers to the grading system established by ANSI for tile sold in the United States, whether made in this country or elsewhere. This somewhat arbitrary grading system classifies tile as standard grade, second grade or decorative thin wall tile.

So-called standard-grade tile, which accounts for about 75% of all tile sold in the United States, is that which meets all the minimum requirements for tile established by ANSI. Second-grade tile is tile that is structurally equivalent to standard-grade tile, except that its glaze may have minor imperfections or its sizing may be slightly off from the specifications

A design-conscious tile showroom can offer a dazzling array of colors, shapes and styles of ceramic tile.

Sloan Howard

For most of my career as a tile installer, I have been fortunate to do business with sales and service professionals who have supported my work, kept me abreast of new developments and been willing to go the extra mile when I needed help. Shop around until you see the tile you like or find a shop that seems to want your business. Shopping for a beautiful material like tile can be fun and exciting, so don't let an uncooperative salesperson spoil the experience.

Most retailers and distributors have a mix of customers that includes seasoned professionals, rank amateurs and everything in between. Regardless of where you fit on the ladder, look for tool loans or inexpensive rentals, seminars or workshops, personalized services and other signs that a retailer or distributor can support the customers' needs.

Installation materials are a matter of personal choice, or regional preference. Make sure your supplier carries only those materials that bear the quality hallmark of the Tile Council of America, or one of the organizations listed in the Resource Guide.

Many suppliers are willing to review your plans and recommend the right materials from their inventory. If not, their competition will be happy to oblige you.

---

for that tile. Second-grade tile is less expensive than standard-grade tile, with much of it created as a manufacturer starts up production on a new run or changes equipment in the plant. Decorative thin wall tile is tile whose bisque and glaze are so fragile that it should not be put to any functional use, but should rather be reserved for decorating walls.

In addition to graded tile, there is a broad spectrum of ungraded tile whose production standards don't match those established for standard-grade tile. This tile includes products of genuinely inferior quality as well as crudely made Mexican pavers and even Japanese tile of very high quality. Simply because a tile is ungraded, however, it should not be rejected out of hand.

For consumers in the United States, the PEI Wear Rating System (developed by the Porcelain Enamel Institute) offers a more practical approach to selecting tiles. The PEI system divides tile application into five groups:

GROUP I   Tiles suitable for residential bathrooms where soft footwear is worn.

GROUP II   Tiles suitable for general residential areas, except kitchens, entrance halls and other areas subjected to continuous heavy use.

GROUP III   Tiles suitable for all residential and light commercial areas.

GROUP IV   Tiles suitable for medium commercial and light institutional applications, such as restaurants, hotels and hospital lobbies.

GROUP V   Tiles suitable for heavy traffic and wet areas where safety and maximum performance are required, such as exterior walkways, food-service areas, building entrances and shopping centers.

I tell my customers in the end that, no matter what grade of tile they select, they can be the best judge of a tile's suitability by taking home samples of the tile they like and putting them through a few tests of their own to see how they hold up. It's only fair to tell the retailer of your plans first, though. Knowing this, the salesperson may or may not charge you for the samples, but will in any case be able to steer you away from tile that is fragile or inappropriate for your purposes.

To put a sample tile through its paces, I suggest first rubbing it with a favorite pot or frying pan to see how easily it's marked up and, in turn, cleaned off. I also recommend scuffing it up with junior's hiking boots and grinding your own heel into the glaze. If the tile resists marks, you're in business. If it scuffs easily, you may want to think twice—especially if the marks are difficult to clean off.

If you want to test the tile's permeability, turn it over and sprinkle a few drops of water on the back. If the water is absorbed, the tile is nonvitreous. If the water sits on the surface of the bisque, you have a vitreous tile. Alternatively, you can do as many setters do: touch your tongue to the back of the tile. If your tongue momentarily sticks to the tile, it is nonvitreous. If it doesn't, the tile is vitreous.

Cost

One important factor in selecting tile is obviously its cost. Most commercial tile ranges in price from about $1 to $30 per square foot, with a wide selection available between $5 to $10 per square foot. If cost is not an issue, exquisite art tile can be had for hundreds or thousands per square foot, although local artists, working through retailers or distributors, can usually supply custom work for considerably less.

Once you've established a price range, your choice of tile revolves around the questions of size, color and style. Although these decisions are highly subjective, a few guidelines may be helpful.

Size

With regard to size, begin by considering the dimensions of the entire installation. Generally speaking, small tiles look better in small installations, and large tiles in large installations. Yet this rule of thumb does not always hold true. One of the most attractive installations I've ever seen, for example, is the vast floor in the California State Capitol Building in Sacramento that is covered with more than a million 1-in. square tiles. And similarly, while I would generally advise reserving tiles 12 in. square and larger for sizable floors, I have tiled several countertops with 24-in. square tiles, with results that were streamlined and elegant. The point is to consider this

size guideline sound but not sacrosanct. Disregard it if you want to, but plan your design carefully.

While considering size, it's important to point out that there is no standard sizing system in the tile industry and that most imported tiles will be sized in centimeters rather than inches. What is called an 8-in. square tile by various tile manufacturers may actually turn out to be anything from $7\frac{1}{2}$ in. square to $8\frac{1}{2}$ in. square, and similarly a tile specified by a foreign manufacturer as a 20cm-square tile may be a centimeter or two more or less along each edge. Sometimes a manufacturer's specifications are meant to allow room for a specific grout-joint width, but often this is not made clear. Because of the wide discrepancy in sizing, never begin planning a layout or ordering tile until you have actually measured a sample tile or have been assured by the retailer that a tile's stated dimension is correct.

Color

Since tile is available in such a wide array of colors, selecting among them can be difficult. Generally speaking, a dark color used extensively in a room tends to make the room look smaller, whereas a light color opens up the space. Some designers I've worked with like to use thin stripes of boldly colored tile to accent the perimeter of a floor or to highlight an otherwise subdued decor. I'd be wary of such a treatment, however, or of using bold colors in general, unless you're a seasoned designer or decorator. And even then, I would suggest trying out your ideas first in a watercolor drawing.

If you're planning a very complex installation, you might consider an even more direct approach: painting the full-scale design on the wall or floor. For a floor like one I tiled with an intricate 12-color pattern, there really was no way to work out the bugs in the design other than to paint—and repaint—it directly on the floor. Experimentation of this sort is far preferable to installing tile and finding out too late that you don't like it.

Precisely because tile is so permanent and expensive to replace, I suggest choosing a color that's easy to live with and reserving the accent colors for the accessories in the room rather than the tile. On a very practical level, remember, too, when selecting floor or countertop tile that the lighter the tile, the more work it will take to keep it clean.

Style

Tile comes not only in a range of colors but also in a large variety of styles. Perhaps the most prevalent style is square or rectangular tile with square corners and square edges. Other tile combines these same shapes with soft, rounded corners and traditional, square edges, or with edges that are "cushioned" (rounded over) and which may be straight or gently serpentine. Still other tile departs from the traditional square or rectangle in favor of such shapes as hexagons, diamonds and ogees.

Depending on a tile's shape, composition, glaze, and edge and corner treatment, it can produce effects that range from the simple and classic to high-tech to rustic. And combining several types of tile in a single installation may yield anything from a streamlined Art Deco look to a Gaudí-like carnival effect. The obvious place to begin selecting a style of tile is with the installation itself. Are you tiling a formal entry foyer in your home or a utilitarian mudroom at the back of the house? A cozy kitchen or a large restaurant facility? Each installation suggests a different style of tile, and it must be a style that not only you but the other people using the installation are comfortable with.

In the end, it may be the practical needs of the installation that dictate the selection of one tile over another. But choosing tile is a funny business, and I've seen even the most practical of people throw caution to the wind and select an exquisite but thoroughly impractical tile for their installation. The tiles selected for the countertop installation in Chapter 11, for example, were sturdy vitreous tiles, quite suitable for a kitchen countertop in all but one respect. Their lovely but delicate black glaze scratched far too easily for a kitchen work surface. Yet the customer had made up his mind, and nothing but these tiles would do. So we reached a compromise: I set his black tile countertop, and he made some wooden cutting boards to place over the countertop whenever using it.

Although this might seem an example of how not to choose tile, it points up a consideration as powerful as any: how you feel about the tile. In the end, almost every choice of tile will involve some compromise. But, provided that choice doesn't invite disaster (as would, for example, nonvitreous tile used outdoors in a freezing climate), I would urge you to compromise last of all on the look of a tile you really like.

Trim Tile

In use, all tile is either field tile or trim tile. Field tile is that set in the main field of an installation, which, if glazed, is glazed on the top surface only. Trim tile is glazed on one or more edges and is specially shaped to border and complete the main field of most installations. (No trim tile is used for floors tiled right to the walls, unless there are baseboard tiles around the perimeter.) Trim tile comes in a variety of shapes, sizes and colors to match many, though not all, lines of field tile. In general, this trim tile falls into two broad categories: surface trim and radius trim.

Surface trim

Surface trim, also called surface bullnose, is essentially flat tile with one edge rounded over. In general, this tile is used at the margins of an installation whose setting bed is flush with the surrounding surface—for example, at the front edge of many countertops, around door jambs, on windowsills and on the top row of back-

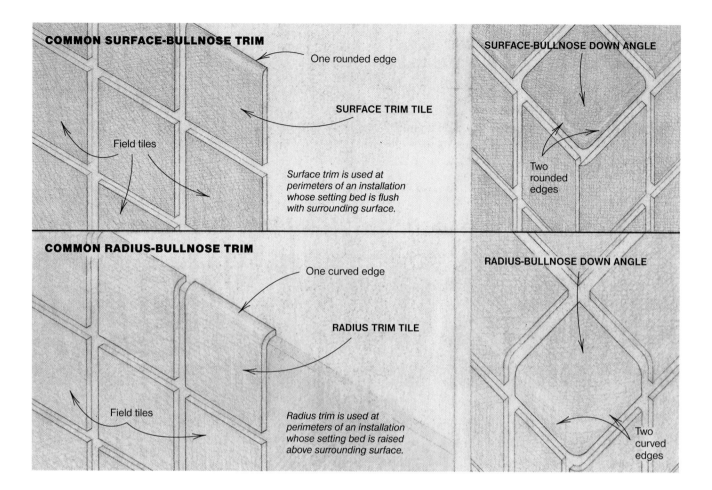

COMMON SURFACE-BULLNOSE TRIM

One rounded edge

SURFACE TRIM TILE

Field tiles

Surface trim is used at perimeters of an installation whose setting bed is flush with surrounding surface.

SURFACE-BULLNOSE DOWN ANGLE

Two rounded edges

COMMON RADIUS-BULLNOSE TRIM

One curved edge

RADIUS TRIM TILE

Field tiles

Radius trim is used at perimeters of an installation whose setting bed is raised above surrounding surface.

RADIUS-BULLNOSE DOWN ANGLE

Two curved edges

splashes or tile wainscoting. Sometimes a second rounded edge is added to surface bullnose to make a trim piece called a down angle, which serves to finish off an outside corner (see the drawing above). If only a single corner on the tile has been rounded or curved, the trim piece is called an up angle and is used to finish off an inside corner. If a line of bullnose trim does not include a down angle or a sink corner, regular surface bullnose can be mitered to form this configuration.

Radius trim

Radius trim, also called radius bullnose, is curved trim tile that can be used to complete the same installations as those mentioned for surface bullnose, except that it is designed for installations whose

setting bed sits above the surrounding surface (usually a traditional mortar setting bed, or backer board mounted over existing drywall). Like surface bullnose, radius trim is usually available in a variety of shapes, including down and up angles as well as quarter-round pieces called beaks, which finish off quarter-round trim. In addition to surface and radius bullnose, complementary pieces like speed cap and V-cap for countertops (see p. 192) and cove trim are also often available, enabling a setter to finish off almost any imaginable installation.

If a line of tile lacks a coordinated array of trim, some manufacturers produce pieces of field tile with one or two glazed edges, which can serve as finishing trim.

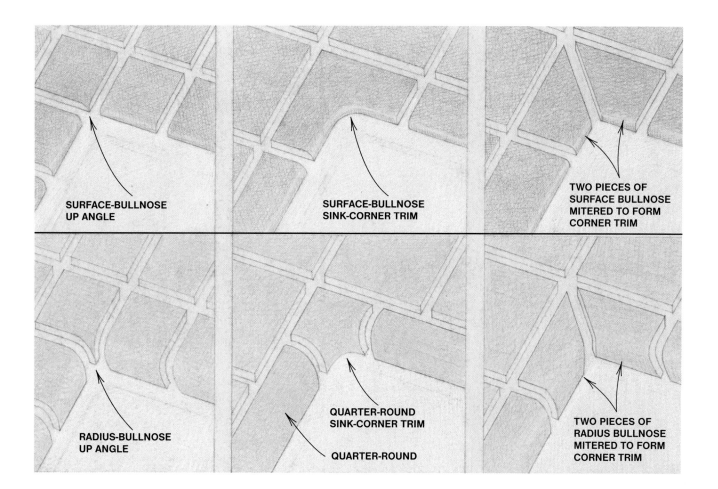

SURFACE-BULLNOSE
UP ANGLE

SURFACE-BULLNOSE
SINK-CORNER TRIM

TWO PIECES OF
SURFACE BULLNOSE
MITERED TO FORM
CORNER TRIM

RADIUS-BULLNOSE
UP ANGLE

QUARTER-ROUND
SINK-CORNER TRIM

QUARTER-ROUND

TWO PIECES OF
RADIUS BULLNOSE
MITERED TO FORM
CORNER TRIM

If no trim at all is available for the tile you select, look at that produced for another line of tile. Sometimes a very similar trim can be found, or a contrasting color may look good. If the trim pieces are larger than the tile you're working with, they can be cut to size.

In the case of unglazed, soft-bodied tiles like Mexican pavers, for which there is usually no trim tile, a substitute can be made by rounding the edge of a flat tile with a masonry rubbing stone or a small hand grinder. Rounding two of the tile's edges produces a down angle, while rounding one of its corners creates an up angle. If the trim is needed for outside angles, for example on a staircase, it may speed up the process and make for a neater finished appearance if the tiles are rounded after being set (as shown in the photo at right). The sealer used for the surface of this tile will, of course, need to be reapplied to the newly rounded edges.

Finally, an alternative to trim tile that's gaining popularity for finishing the edges of countertops is wood trim. Although this trim may be much less expensive than ceramic trim, combining these two materials in a wet installation raises problems. The wood expands when it gets wet, while the tile does not. For this reason, the joint between the tile and trim must be caulked to prevent the inevitable cracking that would befall a grouted joint there. (For a full discussion of using wood trim with tile, see pp. 204-205.)

Sloan Howard

The edges of soft-bodied tiles like Mexican pavers are easily rounded with hand tools.

Chapter Two

Natural Stone Tile

More and more, various kinds of stones are being cut for use as floor, wall and countertop tiles, among them marble, granite, slate, flagstone and onyx. Whereas ceramic tiles are manufactured under tight controls and produced with durable wearing surfaces, stone tiles are products of nature and may be subject to soft spots, uneven wear, cracks, fissures, spalling and warping. As such, a stone-tile installation requires considerably more care and maintenance than a ceramic-tile installation, although the actual setting techniques for both materials are basically the same.

In this chapter, I'll offer some advice on selecting the right kind of stone tile, demonstrate how stone tiles can be worked with tools and explain how they can be repaired, restored and maintained. But first, let's look briefly at how stone tiles are made.

Stone-Tile Production

Stone tiles are made either from processed stone or agglomerated stone. Processed tiles are sawn ("gauged") or split ("cleft") from larger blocks, cut into precise shapes and polished. Agglomerated (or "recycled") tiles are made from stone dust and chips mixed with cement or synthetic binders.

Processed stone tiles

Once a block is freed from the quarry, it is sliced into slabs, either with a gang of reciprocating blades or very large diameter carbide or diamond sawblades. The individual slabs are then gang-sawed into strips, which, in turn, are trimmed to a specific length, width and thickness. Next, the face of the strips are polished, the strips are cut into tiles and the edges are chamfered and polished to match the surface finish.

Not all stone tiles are polished to a mirror finish, however. Some are honed to a matte finish, some are treated with rotating wire brushes, and some are even subjected to flame finishing, which imparts a distinctive coarse texture to the face of the stone. A few stones that are made by simply splitting small blocks (such as slate) are given no finish treatment.

Agglomerated stone tiles

Agglomerated stone tiles are manufactured from a combination of stone dust and fine particles left over from milling operations, and either cement or resin binders (epoxy, for example) to hold the mixture together. The plastic mix is extruded, molded or pressed into tile form, and allowed to cure and harden (sometimes this process is speeded up with the help of a low-temperature kiln or dryer). After curing and hardening off, the tiles may be further processed by milling to exact size and then, as a final step, given either a honed or polished finish.

Agglomerated stone tiles are a serious attempt to do something positive with the waste products of stone making, but they are typically not as strong or as desirable as processed stone tiles. Although some brands of agglomerated tiles may have special installation requirements, most can be installed like regular ceramic or natural stone tiles.

Choosing Stone Tiles

Stone tiles are available in marble, granite, limestone, sandstone, slate, travertine, onyx and other stones both rare and ordinary. The per-square-foot cost should never be used as a yardstick for a particular stone's field performance, however. As with so many other natural things, the rare is often the most fragile.

Popular stone tiles for floor, wall and countertop installations include (from top, clockwise) green aosta marble, red alicante marble, French grey marble, green destours marble, granite and slate.

Grading systems

Some stone tiles are more suited than others for particular applications. To help builders, designers and owners choose appropriate stone materials, the Marble Institute of America has classified marble and stone into four groups, based on characteristics encountered in typical production and fabrication:

GROUP A   Sound marbles and stones with uniform and very favorable working qualities (materials that can reliably be worked without special tools, and without too much fear of breakage).

GROUP B   The stones in this group are similar to those in Group A but with somewhat diminished working qualities. Some breakage during production or fabrication can be expected and can be repaired with relative ease. Slight surface imperfections may have to be filled or waxed.

GROUP C   Marbles and stones with some variation in working qualities caused by geologic flaws, voids, veins or lines of separation. Breakage and surface imperfections should be expected during production or fabrication. Lining (backing with a sound stone veneer) or rodding (reinforcing with embedded steel rods) may be required.

GROUP D   The stones in this group are often the most beautiful, but during production or fabrication they are the most problematic and require extensive repairing, filling and reinforcing.

It is helpful if your dealer can direct you to local installations that feature a stone tile you want to use (but keep in mind that variations in color and surface texture are an inherent part of most stone tiles). If not, there are other ways to determine a tile's track record. Contact the manufacturer and ask for a list of suitable applications. If you cannot get a reasonable assurance of the stone's durability, send a sample of the stone to an independent testing lab (check the Resource Guide at the back of the book), take a risk or choose another stone. Also be sure to ask your dealer if the stone you have selected has a history of warping (see the sidebar at right).

As in the installation of any finished product, it is a good idea to order extra material. If the stone tiles you have selected are from the Group A category and your installation requires no elaborate cutting or fabrication, only a reasonable amount of extra tile (to account for normal breakage and repairs) should be ordered—say, 5% extra. If the tiles are from Group D or there is extensive cutting and fabrication, even more extras may be required. (On a recent installation that was quite complicated, I arranged for twice the amount required to ensure that the architect's design could be realized.) Always make certain that you order enough stone tiles, for unlike their ceramic cousins that can be duplicated, stone tiles cannot be replaced from an exhausted quarry.

Installing Stone Tiles

Given the benefit of an appropriate selection, most stone tiles can be installed wherever a ceramic tile can be used. In that sense, they require the same setting beds and support (see Chapter 3) and the same thinbed skills (see Chapter 8) used for ceramic tiles, but there are some differences in installation.

Extra care must go into selecting compatible thinbed adhesives and grouts that do not react negatively with the stone. Because the performance of a natural product can often vary quite sharply, it is a good idea to use premium installation materials. Use white thinset adhesives under white, light or translucent stones, rather than grey, which could possibly show through. A number of stones, especially lighter colors, can be stained by the pigments in colored grouts. Stones, even dark ones, can be stained by the solvents found in some related installation materials. A good example is plumber's putty commonly used to seal around faucets and valves; it can leave a stain that is difficult to remove on any kind of marble.

If there is any doubt regarding the compatibility of the stone you are using and any installation material purchased for the work, make a sample cross section of the installation with a minimum of four tiles. Construct the sample over a section of cement backer board (see p. 35) and use the same adhesive, grout, caulk and sealers specified for the actual installation. Give all materials ample time to cure and let the mockup age as long as possible to see if the stone will be affected (some stains may take days or even weeks to appear).

Processing may leave a very thin layer of dust on the back of the tile that must be removed prior to installation for the adhesive to effect its maximum grip on the tile. Wipe your finger over the back, and if any residue appears, clean each tile with a sponge and fresh water, and allow to

WARPED STONE TILES

Strange as it may sound, some natural stone tiles have a tendency to warp when in prolonged contact with water. If your installation calls for stone tiles, check with the supplier to see if there have been any reported problems with your selection. So far, this trait has been limited to a small group of marbles, including Rosso Levanto, Verde Issori, Negro Marquina and Verde Green.

If there is any doubt, perform a saturation test with at least two tiles. Support the tiles so that one face and one back are submerged for at least 24 hours—longer if possible. Check the sample tiles with a straightedge before submersion and again every 24 hours.

If there is any warpage, your dealer should be able to recommend a 100% solids epoxy adhesive and grout (see pp. 41-42) for installation of the tiles. Unlike regular or polymer-modified thinset adhesive, 100% solids epoxy contains no water and can help to minimize the problem of warping.

Stone tiles are commonly available as 12-in. by 12-in. squares, but the tiles can be cut and profiled for endless design possibilities. Shown here are a red-marble fireplace (with Mexican pavers on the hearth), a green-marble shower floor and a bathroom detail with three types of stone tile.

Carolyn L. Bates

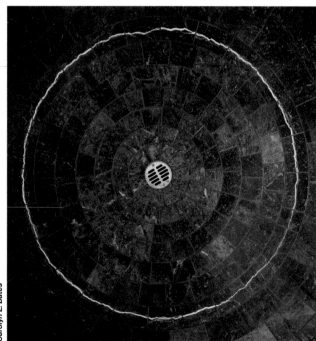

Carolyn L. Bates

Carolyn L. Bates

dry before bedding in adhesive. When spreading the adhesive for tiles 12 in. square or larger, make sure to comb out the ridges in one direction only (as explained in the sidebar on p. 145).

Back-buttering vs. grinding

Like most other products manufactured from natural materials, stone tiles are not always uniform in size. For thinbed work, inconsistencies in the length and width of a tile are easily compensated for during layout. However, variations in thickness can cause considerable increases in labor. There are two approaches to overcome this kind of variation. In the United States, most professional installers spend a lot of time ensuring that their stone floors are finished in a smooth, even plane by "back-buttering" (spreading adhesive on the back of a tile) and testing to be sure that each stone is flush with its neighbors and completely bedded in adhesive. On most residential work, because of limited space, the time spent back-buttering is not a problem. In the larger, open spaces of some commercial installations, however, hours spent back-buttering tiles add up fast.

In Europe, the approach is radically different: Installers concentrate on alignment of the x and y axis and bedding each tile in a uniformly thick layer of adhesive—without regard to differences in height. After the tiles have been grouted and the installation materials have cured, portable grinders are used to correct differences in height and shape the surface into a smooth plane. In my opinion, this method gives better results because the adhesive layer is as uniform as the top, which can be important in the long run. Although this is primarily a European technique, an increasing number of U.S. contract installers are turning to grinding, polishing and restoration tools to provide the finishing touch on stone-tile floors (see the Resource Guide).

Basic Fabrication Techniques

Some lines of stone tile offer bullnose trim pieces, and many suppliers offer edge-profiling services, but because stone tiles can be cut and shaped (with a beveled or bullnose edge, or some other profile) on the job site, factory trim pieces, like those used to complement ceramic tile, are not always required.

Cutting

Stone tiles are best cut on a wet saw fitted with a diamond blade engineered for the purpose (see pp. 59-60). Multi-purpose blades are available, but a well-equipped installer should have a variety of blades to handle a range of stones: for example, soft blades for white marble, hard blades for granite. Saw-rental companies often base their charges on the amount of blade a customer uses up, so make sure the blade supplied with the machine matches the stone you need to cut. Beyond that, wet-saw cutting proceeds the same as for ceramic tiles: a slow approach to the blade until contact is made, more pressure and cutting speed through the body of the tile, and then a slow exit at the end of the cut. (See Chapter 4 for more on wet-saw operation and safety.)

For cutouts in individual tiles, it's much easier to use a dry-cutting diamond-blade saw. The small blade allows you to get right into the corners for a very clean finish (see the photos at right).

Edge treatments

Edge profiling is a basic installation skill for stone-tile work. The corner edge of most stone tiles is finished with a narrow bevel. If the corner edge of a tile you are trimming with the saw is exposed after it has been set, the corner will have a much neater appearance if its edge profile matches the factory edge. A small profile like this can easily be done by hand using a rubbing stone or a piece of sandpaper wrapped

Sloan Howard

A dry-cutting diamond-blade saw is the best tool to use for cutouts in stone tiles (such as the receptacle opening shown here). After all the cuts have been made, the cutout can be tapped out and the corners trimmed with biters.

The corner edge of cut stone tiles can be rounded by hand or on a belt sander.

around a block of wood. If you have a lot of tiles to profile, it's more efficient to use a belt sander.

If only the corner is revealed, it's usually not essential to polish the new bevel. But if the entire edge of the tile is revealed—as it would for site-fabricated bullnose—the new surface, whether it be a rounded bullnose or another profile, should be given a polish to match that of the tile's factory surface finish. With a small number of simple bullnose edges, it is possible to achieve a mirror polish using mostly hand labor and basic equipment, but for making a large number of edges, most professionals rely on power tools fitted with diamond and other abrasives. Either way, the process is essentially the same: Rough the shape of the edge with a saw or wet or dry grinder, and then use progressively finer grades of abrasive paper or pads to remove scratches and bring the surface to a honed or polished finish.

This aspect of using stone tiles is particularly exciting because it allows the installer to fabricate beautiful shapes not possible with regular ceramic tile. Although you can use segments of factory-made

For the smoothest transition between profiled tiles, round the edges after the tiles have been set.

ceramic-tile trim to finish off a curve, the results are not as delicate as with stone tile. To produce a detail like the curved stone shower threshold shown in the bottom photo on the facing page, I begin by cutting the individual stones to the desired width and shape on the wet saw, and then set them in place with thinset mortar. When the adhesive has cured (after about 48 hours, depending on what I'm using), I round over the edge with a tile rubbing stone (practically any kind of abrasive stone will work at this stage, even coarse carbide paper).

Next I use 120-, 200-, 320-, 400- and 600-grit wet carbide paper, with enough time on each successive grit to erase the scratches made by the previous grit. Then, while the stones are still wet, I use a finishing polish to raise the degree of shine I want to obtain. Most stone-polishing compounds are concentrated and powerful. Follow manufacturer's instructions to avoid accidentally damaging the surrounding stones; masking unaffected areas may be required. Both sides of the threshold

(about 6 lin. ft.) in the photo took approximately one hour to finish by hand. Although I could have finished all the edges before the tiles were installed, it is unlikely that the transition between neighboring tiles would have been as smooth as that achieved by rounding the edges after the tiles are set.

Lipping

Lipping, or lippage, is a condition where two adjoining tile edges do not align. Sometimes the result of an installation error, though more often the result of a tile that has warped or twisted from processing, some lipping is moderated by virtue of the width of the grout joint between the unequal edges. Narrow joints (less than ⅛ in.) accentuate lipping, while wider joints tend to mask the condition.

On installations where lippage is a problem in only one or two tiles, the same basic techniques used for edge profiling can be employed: using a rough stone to remove excess material quickly, and then

Sloan Howard

On floors where a few adjoining tiles are out of alignment, as on this floor combining Mexican pavers with natural-stone spots, use hand stones to grind off the excess lippage.

finer grits to raise the shine. Excessive or objectionable lipping can be repaired by removal and replacement of a tile (see Chapter 13) or by grinding and polishing. Grinding lippage requires considerably more energy than does edge profiling. On installations where lipping is pronounced or severe, I recommend that you contact a stone-refinishing service to do the work. Suppliers of stone fabrication tools and supplies may be found in the Resource Guide at the back of the book.

Fabrication Repairs

When installing stone tiles from Group A or Group B (see pp. 24-25), breakage is rarely a problem. The cross section of stone in the path of a cut or profile treatment is fairly consistent, with no open veining that could weaken the tile. Nevertheless, accidents can happen, and you can save considerable time during an installation by being prepared with polishing materials, some glue and bit of filler.

When fabricating a large amount of stone tiles, I might use a manufactured filler, but for most residential installations, I use a clear, waterproof, fast-setting epoxy for repairing breaks, or mix it with some dry stone dust (ground from some scrap pieces) for filling minor gaps or chips. Once the epoxy has hardened, I use a knife blade to trim away any excess that has oozed from the break, and use my regular polishing techniques to flatten any fills. Generally speaking, I don't waste time gluing every tile I break. In fact, I usually toss the broken tile into the waste bucket. But if the stone was chosen for a particular veining or color or other feature, simple repairs can save both time and energy, and minimize frustration.

Maintaining Stone-Tile Installations

A large part of designing with stone tiles is matching the right materials to the traffic or use an installation will get over its lifetime. Choosing the right stone can substantially reduce the amount of maintenance required. Mirror finishes look fantastic when bright and new, but they

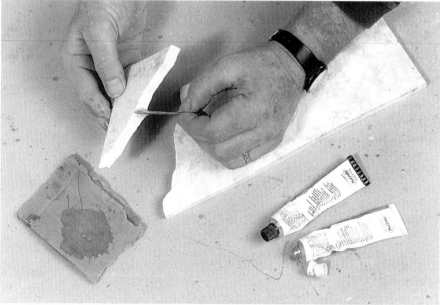

Breaks in stone tiles can be repaired with a clear, fast-setting waterproof epoxy.

can also require constant maintenance and polishing to keep them that way. A matte finish can mask normal wear and tear much better than tiles with a very high polish.

To get the most life from your stone tiles, I recommend that you apply an impregnator to the tiles once all the installation materials have cured. Unlike conventional sealers or top coatings, impregnators are absorbed into the stone and leave neither a coating nor a residue when properly installed. Impregnators were designed specifically to aid in the removal of spray-paint graffiti from stone and masonry surfaces. They are more expensive initially than conventional sealers, but they do not discolor with time, last longer and protect better.

Cleaning stone tiles

A clean mop, some lukewarm water and a small amount of laundry detergent are all that's required for routine cleaning of stone tiles. Avoid using solvents or harsh chemicals.

For stubborn stains, don't use abrasive pads or powders; instead, use a poultice made specifically for stone products (or ask your dealer for a specific recommendation). Poultices come in two forms: wet and dry. Wet poultices are applied directly to the stone; dry poultices need to be mixed into a paste with water first. In a pinch, you can make a poultice from any laundry detergent that does not contain bleach. Slowly mix together detergent and water until there is enough paste to cover an area several inches larger than the stain. Apply the poultice about $\frac{1}{4}$ in. thick and then cover with a layer of food wrap (to keep the poultice wet as it draws out the stain).

Sometimes the only way to remove a stain or blemish from a stone tile is to polish it away (see below).

Restoring stone tiles

Even with the best of care, most stone floors and countertops eventually may need to be partially or completely refinished. Professional restorers use a variety of diamond, carbide and other abrasive pads, stones and polishes to bring stone back to life. For an entire installation, powerful floor machines can grind down stone tiles in much the same way that a wooden floor can be refinished. For more localized repairs, a hand-held grinder with the appropriate discs and pads can be used. For individual scratches and nicks, hand pads may be used. Regardless of the method or tools used, the strategy is the same: Remove only as much material as is needed to get below the blemish, get to the bottom of defects with coarser grits, gradually advance to finer grits and feather the grind into the surrounding material to help mask the repair.

Unlike stone-tile installation, which is relatively simple work, stone restoration demands qualified experience, specialized tooling and knowledge of some rather potent chemicals. I don't mind taking care of a small stain or blemish on a familiar stone tile, but for anything larger or unfamiliar, I call in a stone-restoration expert. Your local stone supplier should be able to refer you to qualified restorers.

The Resource Guide at the end of this book can direct you to a source for stone-maintenance products, including impregnators, poultices, polishes and waxes, that I feel comfortable using. There are also a number of proprietary treatments that claim to harden the wear surface of stone tile. This process (sometimes referred to as "crystallization") involves cleaning the tiles with a special cleaner, then following up with one or more applications of liquid compounds. Some methods may also require the application of a neutralizer to the surface. My experience with these treatments is too mixed for me to make a recommendation. If you are contemplating such a treatment, get a performance guarantee in writing from the manufacturer first.

Chapter Three

Setting Materials

While the surface of the tile is the most visible part of any installation, what lies unseen beneath is perhaps the most important element of all. For tilework to be effective and durable, the choice of tile must be backed up with equally thoughtful decisions about setting materials. Regardless of their type, size or cost, all ceramic or stone tile installations require a setting bed for support, an adhesive to affix the tiles, a matrix of grout to protect each tile, and caulk or sealant to isolate the field of tiles from surrounding materials.

Because many new installation materials are developed yearly, the range of choices has become enormous, and making the right selections can sometimes be perplexing even for an experienced tile installer. Although many products on the market are excellent and consistently reliable, there are also many that are markedly inferior. For this reason, it's a good idea to select name-brand materials

made specifically for tile installation, and particularly those with the seal or hallmark of a major tile organization printed on the label (see the list of tile organizations in the Resource Guide). The presence of such a seal means that the product has been thoroughly tested and proven to have certain performance characteristics.

If a material you plan to use does not carry such a seal or recommendation, try to get a written approval or warranty from the manufacturer. In any case, make certain that the materials you purchase for the installation have been stored properly and that the container or packaging is intact and unopened. All installation materials (including tile) need protection from environmental extremes (heat, cold and moisture) that can render them ineffective or useless and careful handling during transportation to the job site. On arrival, they need continued protection from the usual job-site hazards and

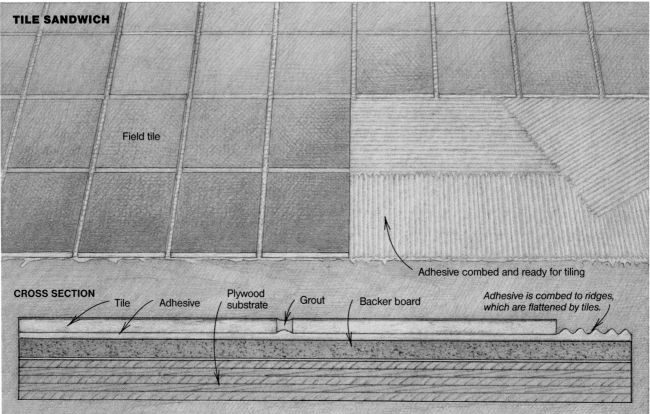

TILE SANDWICH

Field tile

Adhesive combed and ready for tiling

CROSS SECTION — Tile — Adhesive — Plywood substrate — Grout — Backer board — *Adhesive is combed to ridges, which are flattened by tiles.*

Vincent Babak

conditions, and time to acclimate to normal room temperatures. If the materials are being delivered to the site, make sure you are present for the unloading and able to inspect the packaging for rips, tears, water stains or other obvious signs of damage. Installation materials are heavy, and a small amount of damage is to be expected. Most suppliers will provide replacement materials if damage was not evident at the time of purchase, but buyers should be prompt about any claims.

Making the right material selection depends on budget, the level of performance required of the material, the skill level of the person installing the tile and a comparative understanding of the available options. The selection process begins with the setting bed.

Setting Beds

Tile can be set on a wide variety of setting surfaces, including backer board, drywall, concrete slabs, plywood, floated mortar beds and even old tilework. This chapter considers materials that can be used as setting beds for new construction, some of which are manufactured specifically for tilesetting whereas others have applications beyond tilework. Existing materials that can be used as a setting bed for hard tiles, including masonry or plaster walls and existing fields of ceramic tile, usually require conditioning and are discussed in Chapter 5.

Backer board

Backer boards, referred to in the trade as cementitious backer units or CBUs, are made specifically as a ready-to-use substrate for tile. They are more expensive than plywood and other sheet goods, but because of their superior strength and durability they are the ideal surface for tiling. CBUs can be used as setting beds for wall, floor and countertop tiles in both wet and dry areas. The boards themselves are unaffected by moisture, but when used in wet areas, they must be installed with a waterproofing membrane to protect the supporting structure or framing from water seepage at the joints between boards (see Chapter 6).

There are two different types of CBUs (see the photo below). The type most commonly available in the United States has a core of sand and portland cement, and an outer reinforcing skin of fiberglass mesh. This type is available in ¼-in., ⁵⁄₁₆-in., ⁷⁄₁₆-in., ½-in. and ⁵⁄₈-in. thicknesses, with individual sheets ranging from 32 in. to 48 in. wide by 3 ft. to 10 ft. long. I prefer to use the thickest board possible (and nothing thinner than ⁷⁄₁₆ in. over bare studs), though I do sometimes use ¼-in. board over drywall. Mesh-reinforced boards can be cut with a special hand

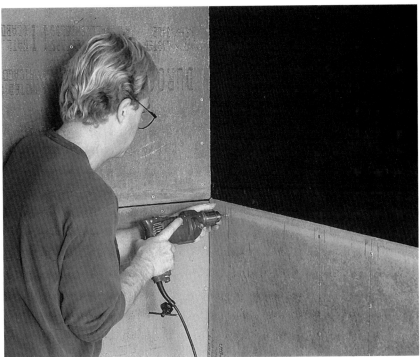

Kevin Ireton

Backer boards are manufactured specifically as a substrate for tile. In the tub-enclosure installation shown here, the boards are being secured over a waterproofing membrane.

scriber or with power tools equipped with masonry blades (for more on cutting backer board, see pp. 74-76).

The other type of CBU is a ¼-in. thick board, made from a mixture of sand, cement and mineral fibers. This board has integral fibers rather than an outer skin as the reinforcing element. The fiber-reinforced boards are dense, take fasteners well, provide the same general performance as the skin-reinforced type and can be cut with the same hand or power tools.

There are numerous CBUs on the market (the Resource Guide at the end of this book lists a few of my favorites). Some are designed for interior use only, while others are suitable for both interior and exterior applications. Some boards carry a warranty, others do not. Whichever CBU you select, read the manufacturer's instructions to ensure that you have prepared the sub-structure properly and are using the right installation materials (screws, nails, mesh, etc.). For a detailed discussion of installing CBUs, see pp. 77-79.

Sloan Howard

Cementitious backer units are available as fiber-reinforced boards (top) and mesh-reinforced boards (bottom).

Glass-mat gypsum backer board

Not to be confused with regular or moisture-resistant gypsum drywall (see below), glass-mat water-resistant gypsum board is another material made specifically as a backing for ceramic tile. Although not as strong or durable as cement backer board, gypsum backer board can be used for most light-duty applications, including wet areas like a tub surround. Generally, these boards feature a water-resistant coating and a core treated to repel moisture. The panels are reinforced with embedded fiberglass mats. Although the boards themselves are water-resistant, the joints between boards should be sealed with silicone caulk.

Available in 4x8 sheets, the boards are relatively easy to handle, cut and install, and although they are not as strong as CBUs, some carry extended performance warranties. Glass-mat gypsum boards are cut using score and snap methods (see pp. 74-75) and are fastened to studs with moisture-resistant screws. However, since application specifications can vary from manufacturer to manufacturer, consult the printed instructions for specific details.

Moisture-resistant gypsum drywall

Moisture-resistant gypsum drywall, commonly referred to as greenboard or blueboard, is for use as a base for paint, wallpaper or wood paneling in damp areas such as bathrooms. This board cannot tolerate repeated wettings and is a very poor setting bed for ceramic tiles in any area routinely subject to water. It should be used as a setting bed for tiles in wet areas only if CBUs or glass-mat gypsum boards are unavailable, and even then only after the surface of the gypsum board has been treated with a waterproofing membrane (see Chapter 6).

Regular gypsum drywall

Regular gypsum drywall makes a suitable setting bed for tiles in a dry area. Like the moisture-resistant variety, regular gypsum drywall can be pressed into wet-area service provided its surface is covered with a waterproofing membrane.

A tile installation gets much of its strength from the backing on which it is applied. A layer of $\frac{1}{2}$-in. or $\frac{5}{8}$-in. drywall is a bit flimsy. If this is the material you must use, consider adding another layer of $\frac{1}{2}$-in. drywall to strengthen the installation. For more about drywall installations, see p. 80.

Plywood

Before the introduction of cement backer boards in the late 1970s, installers had few choices but to install most floor tiles directly to plywood. Millions of square feet of ceramic and stone tiles have been installed on plywood setting beds with no apparent problems. Mortar manufacturers continue to produce and research thinbed adhesives that bond extremely well to plywood, and one manufacturer even offers a lifetime limited warranty on its plywood installation system. As a consultant, however, I have inspected hundreds of failed plywood installations and consider them to be problematic.

Plywood installed as a setting bed in dry, moderate climates should remain relatively stable, but in damp or wet areas, and in locations subject to seasonal changes, plywood is a less than ideal choice for tile. Unless it has been protected with a waterproofing membrane made specifically for use with ceramic tile, plywood should never be used as a setting bed in a wet or damp installation. Wet or dry, your installation will be more durable if you select a backer board made especially for tile. Choose plywood only if CBUs (or other products made specifically for tile installations) are unavailable.

If you do opt to use plywood, select APA-rated exterior boards CC (plugged) or better—for example, marine-grade, which is quite expensive, or AC exterior plywood, which is the most commonly available construction grade. When buying plywood, select only stamped and graded material and carefully examine each sheet, whatever its grade. Reject sheets that are warped or that have visible voids or separations between the plies. Also be sure to avoid any sheets with beads of wood resin on the surface (usually seen on pine plywoods), because the resin will prevent some thinset mortars from bonding properly.

Unlike the grades of exterior plywood mentioned above, interior-grade plywood, particleboard, flakeboard and oriented-strand board (OSB) are unsuitable setting surfaces for floors and countertops. Interior-grade plywood uses glues that are not waterproof and that can be dissolved or softened by the moisture present in some thinset mortars. Particleboard, on the other hand, expands when wet and fails to contract fully when dry. Interior-grade plywood can be used as a setting surface for wall installations that won't get wet. However, the material must be at least $\frac{5}{8}$ in. thick and adequately secured to the studs. (For specific information on installing plywood as a setting bed for tile, see pp. 80-82.)

Concrete slabs

Concrete slabs make excellent setting beds for ceramic or stone tiles, but they must be produced specifically for tile and be flat and level to within $\frac{1}{8}$ in. in 10 ft. (see the sidebar on standards on p. 72). Concrete setting beds must not be produced with liquid curing compounds or other coatings that may prevent a sufficient bond between the tiles and concrete. A fine broom finish is preferred over steel troweling.

It is not the goal of this book to provide instruction in the art and science of concrete and its placement, but the Resource Guide has sources of information on this subject. Most concrete surfaces need some kind of waterproofing, leveling or other preparation before they can receive tiles. In addition to explaining various surface-preparation options, Chapter 5 also explains how to specify this material for ceramic tile (see pp. 82-84).

Mortar beds

For thousands of years, installing tiles over a thick bed of mortar has been considered the most appropriate, accurate and durable method of installation. Mortar can be floated over any type of surface and can bear considerable weight. In my own work, a mortar bed is consistently my first choice of setting bed, unless factors on a particular job dictate otherwise. I enjoy the flexibility that mortar work allows: I need only frame a rough shape, allow for a certain minimum thickness for the mortar bed (floor or wall), and then produce accurate planes of any shape or size with mortar. (For information on floating a mortar bed, see pp. 88-89.)

A bed of mortar makes an excellent surface for setting tile but requires considerable skill to apply.

However, the skills (and strength) required to float a mortar bed are considerable, and I wouldn't recommend this setting surface for an inexperienced tilesetter. Although on certain jobs mortar is the only substrate I would consider using (for example, when creating a sloped floor in a shower stall—see Chapter 12), for most residential installations there are alternative substrates that are as effective as mortar (see the sidebar at left). If you feel that a mortar bed is the only substrate that will work for your particular installation and you don't feel qualified to undertake the job, call in a professional tilesetter or mason to float the bed properly. Then lay the tile and complete the job yourself.

Self-leveling compounds

There will always be a place for mortar beds in the tile trade, but they can be expensive to produce on a large scale. For that reason, manufacturers have responded with numerous self-leveling compounds that give the benefits of mortar without its accompanying need for highly skilled labor. Such compounds need only light mixing and are then simply poured onto the substrate. Within minutes, the material is level, and within hours (with some) they can be covered with tile. Self-leveling compounds have been proven to stand up to heavy-duty use, but not all are suitable for use on ceramic or stone tile applications. Make sure that the leveling compound you choose is made specifically for use with tile. (For more information on self-leveling compounds, see p. 89.)

Adhesives

There are two basic types of tile adhesives on the market: organic mastics, which are ready-to-use, petroleum- or latex-based products; and thinset adhesives, which are powdered products that must be mixed with liquid before use. (At this writing, a few ready-to-use thinsets have recently been introduced to the market, and there will doubtless be many more available in years to come. Since the vast majority of thinsets still require mixing, however, the discussion of thinsets here will be limited to this category.)

Whatever the setting bed, one of these two types of adhesives will be used. If that bed is a floated bed of mortar, the installation will be termed a thick-bed installation. If another type of setting bed is used, the installation will be called a thinbed, or thinset (whichever adhesive is actually used), installation. Thinset mortar serves as a generic name for the adhesives that hold tiles to a substrate. Since the terminology can get a bit confusing for those new to tilesetting, I've reserved the term *mortar* for the sand-and-cement mixture used for floating mortar beds and referred to adhesives by their specific names (see the sidebar on the facing page).

Organic mastics

The term sounds like something you buy in a health-food store. Actually, organic mastics are made of either latex or petrochemical materials and have two major components: a bonding agent (the actual adhesive) and a carrier. The carrier imparts working qualities to the adhesive and then evaporates as the adhesive begins to dry and cure. In the case of petroleum-based mastics, the carrier is a solvent, and in latex-based mastics, it's water.

Of all the adhesives, mastics are the least expensive per square foot of coverage, though only by a couple of pennies. Because mastics need no preparation or mixing, they're also considerably easier and less time-consuming to use than thinset adhesives (see the sidebar on p. 138 for information on working with mastics). And since they begin gripping firmly even before they're fully cured, they're good for setting wall tiles—there isn't as much tile slippage to deal with as with some other adhesives. For these reasons, organic mastics are probably the most commonly used adhesives, but they're nonetheless generally inferior to other adhesives. For the most part, they don't have the bond

Mortar refers to a wide range of materials made primarily, but not exclusively, of portland cement and sand. Among the more common mortars are:

BRICK AND BLOCK MORTAR

Made of fine, medium and coarse sand, lime and portland cement, and mixed to a stiff consistency. Usually site-mixed using bulk or bagged sand. Although often used as a setting bed for tile, not as suitable as mortar mixes made specifically for tile.

SETTING-BED MORTAR

Made of fine and medium sand, portland cement and other ingredients (lime, retarders, accelerators, etc.). Available pre-mixed and in bags for both floor or wall use. Needs only site mixing with water or liquid polymer. Not to be used as a tile adhesive.

THINSET MORTAR

Made of fine sand, portland cement and other ingredients to produce a pasty adhesive for sticking ceramic or natural stone tiles to a variety of substrates. Achieves maximum strength in thin cross sections ($\frac{3}{32}$ in. is ideal). "Thinset mortar" is a generic term that includes some adhesives that contain an epoxy resin rather than portland cement. Four common types are:

REGULAR THINSET MORTAR—no added polymers (water mix only)

POLYMER-MODIFIED THINSET MORTAR—made with dry polymer or site-mixed with liquid latex or acrylic

MEDIUM-BED THINSET MORTAR—formulated to work in thicker cross sections to facilitate installation of irregular tiles (such as Mexican pavers)

100% SOLIDS EPOXY MORTAR—dry ingredient (dyed silica) sometimes factory-mixed with one of liquid components (resin or hardener) to control dust; mixing resin and hardener begins cure; used as an adhesive or grout

GROUT MORTAR

For tiling narrow joints, made from plain (white, grey, colored) portland cement and water. Latex or acrylic additive can be used in place of water for strength. Factory-prepared grout powders may also contain dry polymers (latex or acrylic), texturizers or other ingredients to improve workability and performance. For joints wider than $\frac{1}{16}$ in., sand must be added to reduce shrinkage and cracking.

LEVELING MORTAR

Made of fine sand, portland cement and the usual secret additives. Used primarily in thin cross section (less than 1 in.) to level floors. May be self-leveling or require screeding.

---

strength or compressive strength of thinset adhesives, nor are they as flexible when cured as some of the thinsets (latex thinsets in particular).

Whether solvent- or water-based, mastics are used primarily for setting tile over drywall and plywood, although some brands can also be used on concrete slabs, mortar beds and other surfaces. If your installation is going to be around water, use only those mastics made specifically for wet areas. Mastics should be avoided in areas that will be exposed to heat—a fireplace hearth, for example. Packaging labels on the mastics themselves will provide information on the appropriate uses for a given product.

While discussing surfaces on which mastics can be used, I should mention that the setting bed for a mastic should be completely flat (flatness is not as critical with thinset adhesives). Low spots on the setting bed should never be filled with mastic. When this is done, the thicker cross section of mastic may remain soft and never cure, causing a weak spot where tiles can literally punch through and crack. If the bed has any low spots, use an approved filler.

Thinset adhesives

Thinset adhesives are powdered products that must be mixed before use, with either water, liquid latex or acrylic additives, or epoxy resin. Some thinset powders, known as polymer-modified thinsets, have the latex or acrylic additive factory-proportioned. All thinset adhesives have much greater bond strength and compressive strength than organic mastics, and, because they can support considerable weight, are especially recommended for floor installations. They generally set up more quickly than mastics and when manufactured or site-mixed with a polymer (latex or acrylic) tend to be more flexible. Most thinset mortars can be used both for wet installations when paired with the right setting bed, and in areas where heat is a factor.

For information on mixing, spreading and cleaning up thinset adhesives, see Chapter 8.

WATER-MIXED THINSETS   Water-mixed thinset powders are made from sand, cement, texturizers and retarder additives (which slow down the curing process), and are site-mixed with clean water to produce an adhesive with both high bond and high compressive strength. After they've cured, these thinsets are unaffected by water and can therefore be used for dry and wet installations alike. They're generally used over mortar setting beds or concrete slabs, although some can be used over tile backer boards and plywood (product labels will provide information on use). Packaged in 5-, 10-, 25- and 50-lb. sacks, water-mixed thinsets cost slightly more than organic mastics per square foot of coverage.

POLYMER-MODIFIED THINSETS   At one time, the best way for a tile installer to increase the flexible strength of regular thinset mortar was to use a liquid latex or acrylic additive instead of water. These additives are still very much in use today, but many manufacturers have made the process of mixing thinset mortar easier by adding these polymers to thinset powders in dry form at the factory. Thus, an installer need only add water, which means there are no heavy buckets to haul around. Although I still use a liquid additive for much of the work I do, whenever possible I try to specify an adhesive containing dry polymers.

Compared to regular thinset mortars, latex and acrylic thinsets (either dry polymers or liquid admixtures) have both higher bond strength and higher compressive strength. And because their sand and cement particles are bound up in a pliable matrix, these adhesives are also more flexible than regular thinsets.

Generally speaking, polymer-modified thinsets can be used over any substrate, though some may not be recommended for tiling over plywood (check the product label). While these thinsets are not strictly waterproof, their plastic matrix makes them more moisture-resistant than regular

Kevin Ireton

Tiles can be bedded in mastic, but a thinset adhesive (shown here) generally produces better results.

The thinbed method works best when the tiles are as flat as the substrate. Fortunately, most machine-made tiles are reliably flat, but many handmade tiles are anything but flat. If the tiles you are planning to install have irregular backs or require a thick layer of adhesive, use medium-bed thinset mortar instead of regular thinset. With regular thinset mortar, bond, compressive and shear strengths all plunge when the adhesive layer gets thicker than $\frac{1}{4}$ in. ($\frac{3}{32}$ in. is the ideal). Medium-bed thinset mortar is designed to achieve its maximum strength in thicker cross sections.

Sloan Howard

thinsets, and, when combined with a properly waterproofed underlayment, they make excellent adhesives for wet as well as dry installations.

Liquid additives for these thinsets are packaged in quart, half-gallon and gallon jars, 5-gallon buckets, and 55-gallon drums and, for best results, should be mixed with a companion powder made by the same manufacturer. (That is the ideal combination. Most liquid additives can be used with other brands of thinset powder; to be sure, check with the manufacturer.) The dry ingredients mixed with these additives are usually purchased separately. Per square foot of coverage, these thinsets cost only a few cents more than organic mastics and regular thinsets. While easy to mix and use (see Chapter 8), these thinsets must be cleaned up rapidly because once dry they're extremely difficult to remove from tiles, tools and hands. So when working with polymer-modified thinsets, wear rubber gloves and clean up quickly, using water, a sponge and a light touch to prevent disturbing tiles that have begun to set up. Despite the extra care required in cleanup and their slightly higher cost, I recommend these adhesives over regular thinsets because of their resilience and bond strength.

Years ago, I used to experiment with different combinations of thinset powders and liquids to get a variety of mixes useful for quick repairs or slow setting. I would always check with technical reps to make sure I was not creating a monster, but, nevertheless, some of my creations flopped. Fortunately, thinset-mortar manufacturers have responded with a broad range of mixes suitable for a variety of situations, so when an installation calls for a special adhesive (quick-setting, slow-acting, etc.), I purchase a factory-made product. If I were a chemist, I might still experiment, but as a tile installer I need products I can rely on.

EPOXY THINSETS Most epoxy tile adhesives are composed of three parts: a liquid resin, a liquid hardener and a filler powder. Two kinds of epoxy adhesive are available. One kind (regular epoxy adhesive) uses a base powder of sand and portland cement; the other, called 100% solids epoxy, uses a base of silica sand and dye. Regular epoxy adhesives are used primarily for setting tiles, whereas the 100% solids types, available in a variety of colors, can be used as adhesive or grout.

The powder of some 100% solids epoxies is combined at the factory with one of the two liquid components. For the tile installer, this cuts down on the problem of exposure to harmful dust and simplifies mixing. Like latex and acrylic thinsets, epoxy thinsets are quite flexible and have high compressive strength and high bond strength. They develop their bond strength quickly, and, in fact, many setters use epoxies on commercial jobs when an installation must be returned to service in a hurry.

Unlike other thinsets, epoxy thinsets can be used on any setting surface, including metal, but they're particularly effective when combined with a plywood substrate. Although these adhesives are not water-proof, hardened epoxy can be considered water-resistant. Thus, with proper water-proofing, epoxy thinsets can be used for wet as well as dry installations.

Epoxy liquids are packaged in a variety of sizes, from pints, quarts, half-gallon and gallon jars to 55-gallon drums. The dry ingredients are usually packaged in factory-proportioned sacks and are included with the liquids as a complete package. Per square foot of coverage, epoxies are considerably more expensive than other thinsets, but because they have very high bond strength and flexibility, and are unaffected by water, these are the thinsets to use when tiling over a substrate that's incompatible with other adhesives. Consequently, if you have any doubt about whether an adhesive recommended in this book for a particular setting surface will work on your given installation, use epoxy. (Note that, while the all-purpose epoxy adhesives used for small household repairs would certainly adhere tile to a substrate, they would be exorbitantly expensive in the quantities needed for most installations. What you want is an epoxy tile adhesive.)

Choosing the Right Materials

Deciding which type of adhesive to use for a particular job depends on a number of factors, most important, the kind of substrate on which the tiles will be set and whether the installation will be exposed to water or remain dry. Other things that will influence your decision include the cost of the adhesive, its availability and its ease of use. There are a few prepared adhesives on the market that claim to be suitable for any type of installation, but while these adhesives will doubtless adhere the tiles to the setting bed, the results are liable to be mediocre and short-lived. If you want the job to last and be of high quality, begin by choosing the setting bed best suited to the wear the installation will receive and then select an adhesive that's specifically matched to this type of bed.

If I'm planning tilework for new construction, I have the luxury of picking the ideal setting bed and adhesive for the given job. If, however, I'm setting tile on existing floors or walls, I'll probably be limited in my choice, since the ideal setting bed for the job may be out of the question due to the extensive surface preparation needed and hence the added expense.

Wet or dry installation?

Whatever the limiting factors on a given job, I always try to produce the most durable installation possible. To determine which setting bed and adhesive will give the best results, I begin by asking the customer whether the area being tiled will frequently get wet, occasionally get wet or essentially remain dry. A floor in a bathroom that gets used daily, for example, is likely to be wet more consistently than the floor in a guest bathroom or a half-bath. For this reason, tile set in the main bath should be considered a wet installation and should be fully waterproofed, while the tilework in the second bathroom and half-bath could be considered an installation that occasionally gets wet and which would thus require less waterproofing. If, however, the customer wants to provide for the possibility that the second bathroom may someday be used as much as the first, it, too, should be treated as a wet installation and be fully waterproofed.

Heavy duty or light duty?

Not only do you need to establish whether the installation will be wet or dry, you must also determine the kind and degree of use it will get. A tiled countertop in a large restaurant kitchen, for example, will get considerably heavier wear than would the same countertop in most home kitchens. Therefore, the tilework in the former should be considered a heavy-duty wet installation, while that in the latter could be treated as a medium-duty wet installation. This means that the home installation, while needing waterproofing, could use both a lighter-duty substrate than that in the restaurant and, in turn, also a lighter-duty waterproofing membrane, adhesive and grout. (For detailed information on waterproofing, which is needed for all the wet installations mentioned below, see Chapter 6.)

Setting bed/adhesive compatibility

Once the requirements of the installation have been determined and the substrate chosen, the next step is to select an adhesive that is compatible with both the substrate and the needs of the installation. If backer boards are to be used as the setting surface, match them with either a latex thinset (the best choice) or a water-mixed thinset for both wet and dry installations. On dry jobs with backer board, a compatible organic mastic can also be used, although this is less effective than the thinsets. If the setting surface is to be a mortar bed, it's best paired, for both wet and dry installations, with a latex thinset adhesive or, as a second choice, with a water-mixed thinset.

For a wet or dry installation using plywood as the setting bed, select a latex thinset designed for use over plywood, or, if cost is not an issue, an epoxy thinset. You should also include a waterproofing membrane if the plywood is part of a wet installation. Adhesives for dry installations on drywall are, in order of preference, a latex thinset, water-mixed thinset and organic mastic. On a concrete slab, the best adhesive for wet or dry installations is a latex thinset; for dry jobs, the second choice would be a water-mixed thinset and the third choice an organic mastic. For dry installations over linoleum or synthetic sheet flooring (see p. 85), use an epoxy thinset or, as second choice, a compatible latex thinset. And when old tilework is the setting bed, the best adhesive for both wet and dry installations is an epoxy thinset, with the next best alternative a compatible latex thinset.

The setting surfaces listed above are those most commonly used for tiling. If the surface you're interested in doesn't appear in this list, or you're uncertain of which surface to select, talk with your local supplier to see if appropriate materials can be provided. If your supplier is in doubt, ask for the technical service number for the materials that are available and then speak directly with the manufacturer for suggestions.

Grout

Tile grout, with a few exceptions, is another form of mortar that is generally packaged as a powder and mixed with a liquid to form a stiff paste that's used to fill the joints between the tiles, protecting, supporting and framing their edges. Because good grouting practices call for the grout to be forced into the tile joints, grout also helps retard water penetration into the joint. No grout, however (at least those on the market today), can ever be considered completely waterproof; that is, able to stop water or moisture from entering the substrate.

Kevin Ireton

Grout is usually packaged as a powder and mixed with a liquid to form a stiff paste.

GROUT COVERAGE TABLE

TILE SIZE	JOINT WIDTH			
	1/8	1/4	3/8	1/2
1 x 1 x 3/16	30			
2 x 2 x 3/16	17	34		
4 x 4 x 1/4	15	30	45	60
6 x 6 x 1/2	25	50	75	100
8 x 8 x 3/8	13	25	38	50

Note: *The amount of grout needed to cover a given area depends on the size of the tile and the width and depth of the grout joint (which are given here in inches). The table above shows the approximate number of pounds of grout powder needed to cover 100 sq. ft.*

The portland-cement-based grouts I use come in two forms: plain and sanded. Plain grout is essentially cement mixed with additives to give it certain performance characteristics—easy spreadability or a slow curing time, for example. Plain grout is used for joints less than 1/16 in. wide. Sanded grout—simply plain grout to which sand has been added for strength—is preferable for joints larger than 1/16 in. and may come in different grades (different-size sand particles) to accommodate a range of joint widths (the wider the joint, the larger the particle size). Some brands of these two grouts can be used with both vitreous and nonvitreous tile. Others are designed specifically for one kind of tile.

If the grout specified for an installation is not manufactured with a dry polymer in the bag, I use a liquid latex additive instead of water when mixing the grout. (For a full discussion of mixing and applying grout, see pp. 147-149.) Hardened polymer-modified grouts are more flexible than regular grouts, they retain their color longer and they are more resistant to water penetration.

If you want to make your own natural cement-colored grout, you can do so economically. If the joint is to be less than 1/16 in. wide, use straight portland cement mixed with an additive. If the joint is to be wider than 1/16 in., you'll need a mixture of one part portland cement to one part sand. For joints 1/8 in. to 1/2 in. wide, get 30-mesh sand. For joints 3/8 in. to 1 in. wide, all-purpose sand is the best choice. If a grout additive is to be used, follow the additive manufacturer's recommendations on proportions. Because of the many variables involved with applying tile grout, no single coverage table is good for all brands of grout. For some guidelines on the amount of grout needed to cover a given area, however, see the grout coverage table at left. For actual coverage, refer to the manufacturer's guidelines.

Colored grout

At one time I used to mixed my own colored grouts from raw ingredients (cement, sand and dye), but the results were often flat and uninteresting and the grout rarely retained a consistent color. Today, I simply choose the exact color I want from any one of hundreds of premixed colors. Commercial premixed grouts are uniform in color and are far superior to anything that you can mix by hand.

Choosing a grout color is largely a matter of personal taste, but keep in mind that the color and shade of grout used with tile can greatly affect the look of the installation. Generally, a combination of dark-colored grout with light tiles—or light grout with dark tiles—emphasizes the geometry of the installation, while grout similar in color to the tiles de-emphasizes the geometry.

Sloan Howard

The green grout used on this inlay was chosen to highlight the effect of the Celtic-knot border.

Like all other kinds of building materials and methods, ceramic-tile installations benefit from a systems approach. A thousand years ago when buildings were massive and inflexible, they were adorned with tiles installed over equally inflexible beds of mortar. That was the system that worked then.

The tile installation of today is typically located within a building whose walls and floors allow for considerable movement. The best way to isolate and protect tiles from this movement is to attach and surround them with flexible materials. For this reason, I specify latex or acrylic additives (polymers) in place of water, or use a thinset mortar or grout powder with a factory-added polymer in dry form.

In addition to the adhesive and the grout, the third component in a modern thinbed system is a grid of expansion joints filled with an elastomeric caulk or sealant. The key word here is elastomeric, which is the tile industry's way of saying that the material will remain flexible. This flexibility allows normal and expected building movement to occur without causing damage to either the structure or the tiles. Many mortar manufacturers now fill out their product line with flexible caulks and sealants to match their grout colors.

If you want a color other than white but are unsure of what to select, cement-colored grout is a good neutral choice. Cement-colored grout, or "natural" as it is sometimes called, is my choice for irregular tiles like Mexican pavers. If you use grout that starkly contrasts with the color of such tiles, the viewer's eye will tend to be seized by the irregular grout lines.

Whatever tile you're setting, if you choose a drastically contrasting color of grout, test it on a sample tile before grouting to see if it can be grouted without being permanently stained. If it does stain, you should pick another grout or use a grout release, an installer-applied liquid used to coat the tiles just prior to grouting. For large amounts of tile on commercial installations, the release is applied to the tiles at the factory in the form of wax, which is then steamed off the tiles after the grout has cured. To test, mix a small batch of grout slightly thinner than normal and smear it on the face of the tile. If you have difficulty cleaning the surface, use a grout release or sealer (see the Resource Guide) on the installed tiles before grouting. Very porous tiles, such as handmade Mexican pavers, must be sealed prior to grouting.

Caulks and Sealants

Caulks and sealants are the flexible materials used instead of grout in expansion joints to isolate a field of ceramic or stone tiles from surrounding materials. Unlike other tile-installation materials, caulks and sealants wear out and need replacement from time to time. Generally speaking, sealants last longer than caulk but are more difficult to install.

In the past, with limited color selection and frustrating, messy application the norm, it is easy to understand why tilesetters avoided caulks and sealants and filled expansion joints with grout instead. Today, however, plain and sanded caulks and sealants are available in a limitless range of colors to match any grout, appliance or paint (see the Resource Guide). The brand of caulk I use for most residential and light commercial work installs and cleans easily with water, and because it is sanded produces a flexible joint virtually identical to the grout it is specified to match. (For information on caulking expansion joints, see pp. 102-103.)

Chapter Four

■ ■ ■

Tools and Safety

Like any other trade or craft, tile installation requires a number of special tools. Some of these can make the job easier; some are necessary for professional-looking results. Many of these tools can be found in the average home kit, while others can be readily adapted from tools you have on hand. Several highly specialized tools are needed for tiling, but unless you plan on doing extensive work, generally you can rent these at a tool rental shop or a tile store rather than invest in them.

For convenience, I've grouped the tools presented in this chapter according to function and arranged them in the general order in which they're used on the job—though, of course, some of these tools will be used at several stages of the installation. While the many tools shown here are essential for the professional tilesetter, they are not all required for every installation. The novice or occasional setter can, in fact, do many small home projects with a minimum of tools. (For a tilesetting tool kit of bare essentials, see the sidebar on p. 49.)

Keeping tools sharp and clean is always a good idea, no matter what they're being used for, but in the case of tilesetting tools, careful and prompt cleanup is crucial unless you can afford to replace them constantly! Left to harden on tools, tile adhesive, mortar and grout become downright stubborn to remove. It's also wise to test any tiling tools you're unfamiliar with on scrap material, and to get acquainted with them before starting a project. This suggestion applies especially to power and manual tools used for cutting tile.

Because some tilesetting tools can be dangerous to use, the discussion of the individual tools contains necessary warnings and suggested precautions. The chapter concludes with a look at the general health hazards involved in tilesetting and the safety measures that can be taken to avoid or minimize these hazards.

Before using any of the tools or techniques discussed in this chapter, be sure to read the safety section on pp. 66-69.

Surface-Preparation Tools

Tile can be set on a number of surfaces, and most will need some sort of preparation. The preparation of the setting bed may involve nothing more than cleaning off a little dirt and grime, or it may mean grinding a nice, flat surface on a slightly uneven concrete slab, or perhaps building a new subfloor. To ready a surface for tiling, you'll probably need either cutting tools, sanding, grinding and scraping tools, or cleaning tools. Or you may need them all!

Cutting tools

While professional union tilesetters may only set tile, leaving the surface preparation to others, independents and do-it-yourselfers are obliged to handle all aspects of tiling, which in many cases includes some basic carpentry to build or rebuild floors, countertops and walls. For such work, handsaws and power saws are obviously essential. When precision cuts are not critical, a reciprocating saw can be used for cutting out old wooden floors or walls, or doing other demolition work. When greater accuracy is required—for example, when cutting contours in plywood for floors or cutting sink holes in countertops—use a saber saw. If you want to speed up the tedious process of making numerous straight cuts, switch to a circular saw.

Although handsaws could certainly be used in place of these power saws, the job will take far more time. One task for which a handsaw is better than a power saw, however, is trimming door casings and molding around which tile is to be set. It takes far less time to trim the casing or molding to the height of the tile than to trim the tile itself. The best saw for this job is an offset dovetail saw with a reversible handle.

Surface preparation may occasionally involve ripping out old tilework set on a concrete slab or on plywood. A wide-blade masonry chisel and a hammer or hand maul are handy for this. (A grout saw is useful for small repairs or removing a single tile.) If the tile being removed is set on a

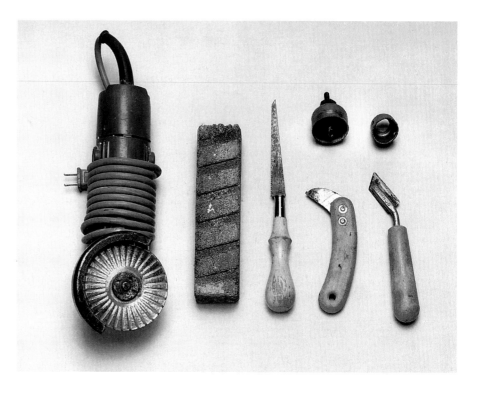

In addition to the general carpentry tools often used to prepare setting beds for tiling, there are some other tools that come in handy, including (from left) a dry-cutting diamond blade mounted in an electric grinder; a masonry rubbing stone; a keyhole saw; a backer-board scoring tool, also called a carbide scriber; a grout saw; and (above) two hole saws.

mortar bed, chip the tiles away with a hammer and chisel. To remove the bed, use a dry-cutting diamond blade mounted in either an electric grinder or a circular saw. This blade speeds up the process and also prevents damaging any neighboring drywall and the framing below. (For more information on removing old tilework, see pp. 225-228, and for a full discussion of tile-cutting tools, see pp. 55-64.)

If you need to cut backer board to prepare the new setting bed, you can use either the dry-cutting diamond blade (see the photo below) or a backer-board scoring tool, also called a carbide scriber. The latter is a hand tool, which usually has a wooden handle affixed to a slender metal shank shaped like a hawk's bill. (A plastic-handled version of the backer-board scoring tool is shown in the photo on p. 75.) The end of the shank holds a small, sharpened chunk of carbide, which will score the hard surface of backer board so that the board can be broken along the scribed line. The edges of the cut won't be as clean as those produced by the diamond blade, but they are suitable for most tilesetting projects. The scoring tool is relatively inexpensive, can be bought at a tile or building-materials supply house and is easy to use. One disadvantage is that it can be used only for straight cuts. (For more information on cutting backer board, see pp. 74-76.)

Whenever you're using power saws for preparing setting surfaces, use caution and common sense. The obvious danger in working with these tools is increased if you give in to temptation and remove the blade guard from a power saw. Don't do it! These tools can slice bone just as easily as construction materials. Make sure, too, when working with these tools that you wear goggles or safety glasses to protect your eyes from flying debris, and hearing protectors to combat the noise (see pp. 66-68 for additional safety information).

Sanding, grinding and scraping tools

Whether you're tiling new construction or doing a remodeling job, it's easy to get globs of construction adhesive, tar and taping compound on the setting surface. To remove these, you can use a stiff putty knife, paint scraper, trowel or inexpensive wide-blade wood chisel. These same tools can be used to remove old resilient tiles or foam-backed carpeting stuck to the floor. For thin, dried deposits of construction goo that resist the scraper, use a power sander or just a hand-held block sander. Remember when using the power sander to wear safety glasses and a filter mask. The mask is a good idea when hand-sanding, too.

Use a hand-held masonry rubbing stone or a hand-held power grinder with an abrasive wheel to flatten a hardened

A BASIC TILESETTING TOOL KIT

Tape measure

Straightedges

Spirit level

Square (combination or carpenter's)

Chalk line

Pencil or felt-tipped pen

Flat trowel, margin trowel, notched trowel (size depends on tile being set) and grout trowel

Snap cutter and biters (if tile needs to be cut)

Tile spacers (and possibly wedges)

Two buckets, a sponge with rounded corners, and cheesecloth

Appropriate safety equipment

Sloan Howard

A dry-cutting diamond blade mounted in an electric grinder is a handy tool for cutting backer board (shown here), ripping out old tilework and setting beds, and trimming new tiles.

mortar bed or an uneven concrete slab. (I also use the rubbing stone to grind the edges of unglazed Mexican pavers and shape them into trim pieces, as shown in the photo on p. 21.) And for a slab whose surface is slick (which means it was finished with a steel trowel rather than a wood float), rough it up with hand or power grinders so that the tilesetting adhesive will grip it properly. Again, safety glasses are essential when power-grinding.

On large concrete slabs needing extensive grinding or conditioning, hand tools are impractical. In such a situation, self-propelled abrasive wheels or shot blasters can be used to remove substantial amounts of concrete (as well as hardened mortar, old ceramic tiles and other hard surfacing). It is beyond the scope of this book to include all the various kinds of powered surface-preparation tools (and, besides, installations involving this kind of scale are beyond the abilities of most beginners). Nevertheless, the Resource Guide lists a source for power tools that can be rented for this purpose.

Cleaning tools and materials

You can clean a surface to be tiled by scraping or grinding it or by some other mechanical means. Avoid using cleaning solutions at the outset, because their residues may prevent a good bond between the tile adhesive and the setting bed. If you have trouble removing oil or grease by mechanical means, try a detergent-and-water solution. Use degreasers, wax removers and other cleaning solutions only as a last resort. To clean tilesetting tools, also begin with mechanical means (see the sidebar at left).

Another cleaning tool that's imperative on any tile job is a good vacuum cleaner. I have an industrial-strength model, which I keep on the site until I've finished an installation. For small jobs, a home vacuum cleaner will be adequate. In addition to the vacuum's obvious merits, I use it during demolition work to draw away excess dust

created by power tools. It is especially useful for drawing dust from the pores of a setting bed just before the tile is set, vacuuming up scraped-out grout joints and cleaning up tile chips, sand and chunks of mortar that might get tracked into other areas of the work site.

To help keep finished floors clean elsewhere in the house or building, I spread protective or waterproof paper over them and cover the paper with tarps. The tarps cushion and protect the flooring from scratching, and the paper prevents water, adhesives, wet mortar and grout from seeping onto and staining finished surfaces. After the job is finished, I roll up the tarps and paper together and shake out the debris at the dump. I protect finished countertops, walls and the fronts of cabinets by taping waterproof kraft paper or plastic sheeting over them with masking tape.

Measuring and Marking Tools

Accuracy is crucial when setting ceramic and stone tiles. Setting surfaces should be flat, square and plumb, and grout joints must be straight and evenly spaced. To install tile properly, you need accurate measuring tools. Some of these tools can be found in the average home shop, and many of them can be rented.

The measuring and marking tools required for the average home tile installation will largely depend on the size and complexity of the installation, but a basic kit would include a measuring tape, some straightedges, a good level, squares (combination and carpenter's), a chalk line and, of course, a marking pen or pencil. For larger jobs, the setter's tool kit obviously needs to grow. When I'm doing a very large commercial job, I may even call in a surveyor to measure and lay out the job with surveying tools.

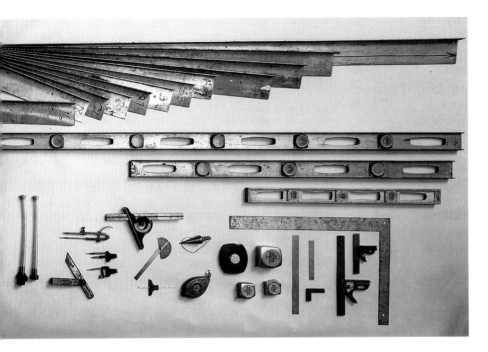

Measuring and marking tools used in tilesetting include (from top, clockwise) a set of graduated straightedges and spirit levels; a carpenter's square; combination squares; steel scales and machinist's square; measuring tapes; plumb bob and chalk line; protractors and depth gauge; compass, trammel points and sliding T-bevel; and water levels.

Tape measures

The tape measure I use on the job is a 10-ft. steel tape with a hooked end, graduated in sixteenths of an inch. When buying a new tape, I check both its inside and outside measure for accuracy against a 12-in. long flat steel scale made by L.S. Starrett (see the Resource Guide). A tape measure is easily damaged when dropped and the hook slide gets worn in the abrasive environment of tilesetting, so I recheck it from time to time. Once the hook slide is worn out, I invest in a new tape. When using the tape, I also make sure to clean off any adhesive, mortar or grout that gets on the hook before it has a chance to harden on the slide, which would give imprecise readings.

Straightedges

Straightedges serve as a guide in marking underlayment, laying out installations and adjusting rows of tile, as well as in innumerable other tilesetting tasks. A serious setter should buy a set of nesting aluminum straightedges in graduated sizes (as shown in the photo above). If you

have access to a jointer, you can make a wooden set, but it won't be as sturdy or as accurate as an aluminum one. I think a pair of 32-in. and 48-in. straightedges are essential for most installations, but if you're tiling a smaller area, you'll obviously need a shorter straightedge. A spirit level can also be substituted for a straightedge, as can a narrow strip of plywood with a true edge cut on a table saw, or a straight piece of aluminum or steel stock. In a pinch, a piece of string stretched tightly on the work surface can even take the place of a straightedge.

The important thing about a straightedge is that it be straight! Provided you have good eyesight, you can sight along the edge to make sure that it isn't bowed. Alternatively, lay the straightedge on a flat surface (such as a subfloor) and scribe a line from end to end; then flip the straightedge over to the opposite side of the line and scribe another line directly over the first (as shown in the top drawing on p. 52). If the straightedge is straight, you will have drawn a single line with no bulge in the center and no split tails on the ends. If you do a lot of setting, you should

Use a straightedge and level to mark layout lines on the setting bed.

Kevin Ireton

periodically check your straightedges for accuracy and, if need be, adjust them. Because my aluminum straightedges see lots of duty and wear down at the ends, I take them all to a machine shop periodically for truing up.

Levels

Other staples in the tilesetter's tool kit include a graduated set of spirit levels and a plumb bob, the latter for checking the accuracy of the levels. At one time, I kept a 12-in., 24-in., 32-in., 48-in. and 72-in. level handy. Now, however, I tend to rely on an 18-in. level clipped to a straightedge of appropriate length with a small spring clamp, which means fewer tools to lug around. Because regular use and the accumulation of minor, unavoidable damage can impair precise functioning, a level should be checked often (I check mine before beginning every new job) and replaced when required. In choosing a new spirit level, look for an aluminum one with adjustable vials. Although mahogany levels with brass inlay are beautiful, they're impractical for tilesetting because they frequently get wet and can warp out of shape.

To check a level for plumb, compare it to a plumb line—gravity never fails. To check it for level (see the bottom drawing at left), place the tool on a flat surface and check that the bubble is dead center in the vial. (If the surface itself is out of level, shim up the level with paper or wooden strips.) Scribe the outline of the level, then rotate the tool 180° and place it within the outline. If the leveling bubble is dead center again, the level is true. In the event that there are several leveling vials, repeat this process to check that each one is true.

On the job, make sure to clean off any fresh mortar, adhesive or grout from all surfaces of the level. And when tapping a level to make an adjustment, strike only the areas of the tool that have reinforcing webs. If you strike over the open areas on the level, you risk banging it out of shape. (Carpenters reading this will no doubt have

heart failure at the suggestion that a level might be struck with anything more than a light tap, but I know from experience that tilesetters and brick masons have a heavier hand! For the record, the correct technique is to tap the object being leveled, not the level itself. The object should then be checked with the level and tapped again if it's not yet correctly positioned.)

Plotting tools

For plotting angles to guide layout lines on setting beds and for marking out tiles to be cut, I use a combination of squares and protractors, as well as a sliding T-bevel. I measure depth with a depth gauge and, on very large jobs, a pair of water levels connected by a long tube. I use a set of trammel points for scribing a 3-4-5 triangle to check a room for square (see p. 123) and for plotting large arcs. For small arcs, a regular compass is fine. When I'm marking tiles that butt up against irregular surfaces, I use a contour gauge.

A carpenter's square is frequently used in tilesetting for checking and marking off 90° angles. Like other measuring tools, this one must be checked for accuracy from time to time. To do this, butt the square's short edge against a straightedge and scribe a line down the outside of the square's long edge (see the drawing on the facing page). Then flip the square to the opposite side of the line, align its long edge with the line and scribe a second line. If the two lines form a single, straight line, the square is accurate. If, instead, the lines begin to diverge or converge, the square needs to be adjusted or, if it's so inaccurate that it defies correction, replaced.

A square is an invaluable tool, so it's worth some effort to fix one that isn't doing its job. To adjust the square, scribe a line on the tool connecting its inside and outside corners. For a square that's reading less than 90°, use a center punch and a hammer to bang in a couple of dimples on the upper half of this diagonal line, which will ease the angle of the inside corner back toward 90°. Then check this angle by the method just described. You may need to hammer in a few more dimples if the angle still needs to be increased a bit more. For a square whose angle reads greater than 90°, hammer the dimples in the lower half of the line. Again check the angle and repeat this step if necessary.

Marking tools

For laying out lines or connecting points on a dry setting surface, I either draw a pencil line or snap chalk lines, using a reel-type chalk line. To avoid confusion on floors that may already be criss-crossed with someone else's lines or that may have a number of my own measuring lines, I keep two chalk lines—one red, one blue. I mark any initial measurements on the setting bed with one color and chalk in the final layout lines with the other. Using two colors eliminates any second-guessing. (To scribe layout lines on a wet setting surface, such as a mortar bed, I use the edge of a trowel.)

To create a neat, finished look for tiles whose cut edges will show, you need highly visible but very thin marking lines (ideally, no more than $1/64$ in. wide). For marking tile to be cut on either the snap cutter or the wet saw (see pp. 57-61), I use a waterproof, fine-point marker, which seems to work better for me than a pencil (if you do use a pencil, make sure to keep the point sharp). To make the mark clear when cutting dark tile on the wet saw, I position masking tape over the cut area first. With the water jet used to cool the blade partially obscuring the view, the contrast between the light-colored tape and the dark line helps a lot.

When cutting tile on the wet saw, my practice is to make an additional mark on the side of the tile I wish to keep. This way, whether I am marking tiles for someone else to cut or marking them to cut myself, the cutter will know where to put the kerf. To ensure accuracy, the standard I use for any cut tile (whether I am working alone or with helpers) is to have half the line remain after the cut has been made.

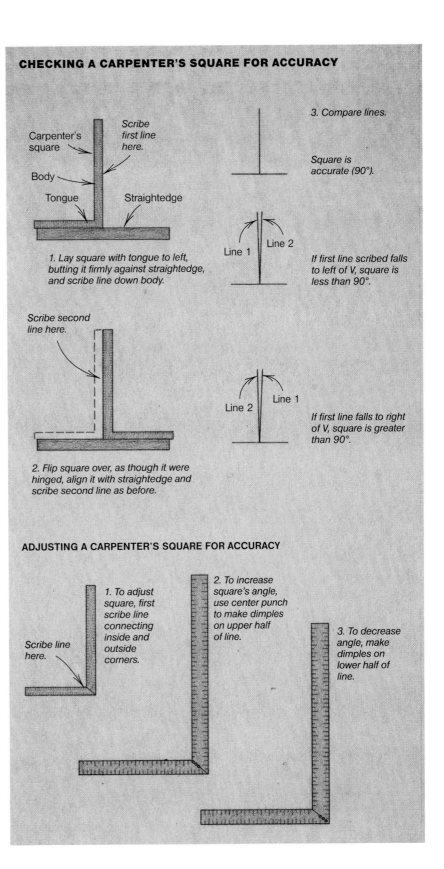

CHECKING A CARPENTER'S SQUARE FOR ACCURACY

Carpenter's square

Scribe first line here.

Body

Tongue   Straightedge

1. Lay square with tongue to left, butting it firmly against straightedge, and scribe line down body.

Scribe second line here.

2. Flip square over, as though it were hinged, align it with straightedge and scribe second line as before.

3. Compare lines.

Square is accurate (90°).

Line 1   Line 2

If first line scribed falls to left of V, square is less than 90°.

Line 2   Line 1

If first line falls to right of V, square is greater than 90°.

ADJUSTING A CARPENTER'S SQUARE FOR ACCURACY

1. To adjust square, first scribe line connecting inside and outside corners.

Scribe line here.

2. To increase square's angle, use center punch to make dimples on upper half of line.

3. To decrease angle, make dimples on lower half of line.

Mixing and Floating Tools

For preparing less than two gallons of thinset or grout, I mix the material by hand with a margin trowel. Although it's possible to do larger quantities this way, it's pretty tiring work and often produces lumpy results. Instead, I use a mixing paddle chucked in a ½-in., heavy-duty drill. (For important safety information on working with power tools around water, see p. 66.) Most home drills are light-duty drills and will burn out if used to mix 10 or 12 buckets of adhesive or grout.

If you plan to do more than a very small installation (for which you'll probably need to mix no more than a single 5-gal. bucket of each material), I suggest renting a variable-speed heavy-duty drill that can be run at around 150 rpm. It's important to use the drill with a mortar mixing paddle (which can also be rented) rather than with a paint paddle. The latter should revolve at speeds too high for mixing grout and adhesives, and can whip air bubbles into the material being mixed and weaken it.

Mixing boxes and hoes

To prepare mortar (or "mud") for floating floors, walls and countertops, I mix the ingredients by hand in a mixing box with a mason's hoe. Mixing boxes come in a wide variety of sizes and materials, from 1-cu.-ft. plastic trays to 1-cu.-yd. sheet-metal barges. For installing tile on practically all residential work, I rely on a ⅓-cu.-yd. box. For larger jobs, I use a bigger box (and employ a helper, since mixing the mud can be a full-time job).

A mason's hoe has a broad blade pierced with a couple of holes to aid in mixing. I prefer it to a rotary mixer because I can get exactly the consistency of mortar I want. Hoes are sold in several sizes, and I generally use one with a 9-in. blade. If you don't want to invest in a mason's hoe, a regular garden hoe can be used, or even a shovel or a large trowel.

Floating tools

The minimum tools needed to float a mortar bed are a flat trowel, a margin trowel, a hawk (when floating walls), a wood float, a pair of wooden float strips (their size depends on the depth and dimension of the mortar bed) and a straightedge.

Flat trowels are rectangular trowels used to apply and level a mortar bed. Available in a variety of lengths and widths, the flat trowel most commonly used for tiling is about 12 in. by 4 in. (see the photo at left). A swimming-pool trowel is an

Mixing and floating tools include, at left and center, a mason's hoe and mortar mixing paddle chucked in a hand drill. At right (from top to bottom) are a flat trowel, swimming-pool trowel and hawk; edging trowel, margin trowels and pointers; and wood floats.

oblong trowel with rounded corners, which is used for spreading mortar in pools and other curved areas.

Margin trowels are long, thin, rectangular-shaped tools that look a bit like flapjack turners. These trowels are used for a number of tiling jobs, including mixing small batches of mortar, thinset or grout, applying or leveling mortar in places too small for flat trowels, back-buttering tiles with adhesive, finishing grouted surfaces, repointing or packing joints, and cleaning other trowels. Margin trowels usually have 4-in. to 6-in. long blades that range in width from $\frac{1}{8}$ in. to 2 in. or 3 in.

Pointers are trowels whose blade, as their name suggests, is pointed. Most often seen in brick mason's kits, these tools aren't essential in a basic tilesetter's kit, but are favored by some setters for back-buttering tiles with adhesive and for spreading or leveling mortar in tight corners.

Wood floats are rectangular wooden trowels used to finish the surface of a mortar bed. They produce a coarse, open-grained surface on the bed rather than the slick surface created by the steel trowel. Because the coarser surface is more easily gripped by the adhesive, a wood-troweled mortar bed is better for tiling than a steel-troweled bed. In addition to finishing mortar beds, wood floats are also used in shaping sloped mortar floors (see Chapter 12). These tools are preferable for this purpose to a steel trowel, whose sharp biting edge can easily cut into the mortar. (For information on floating a mortar bed, see pp. 88-89.)

A hawk is a small square of aluminum with a protruding handle, which is used when floating a wall. While the mortar for a floated floor or countertop is dumped directly on the substrate, that for a floated wall must be applied in thin layers. The hawk serves to carry small amounts of mortar from the mud board (the plywood square holding the mortar brought into the room from the mixing box) to the wall.

The setter then loads up the flat trowel with mortar from the hawk. A substitute for this tool can readily be made from a scrap of plywood and a dowel.

Setting and Cutting Tools

Tiles must be set with precision if the installation is to be handsome and long-lasting. The adhesive should be applied uniformly and the tiles trimmed and placed accurately. To achieve precise results—and to do so during the critical period before the freshly spread adhesive "skins" over—the setter needs special tools for applying the adhesive and for cutting tiles. The minimum setting tools required are a notched trowel, whose size depends on the type and dimensions of tile being set; a margin trowel; a snap cutter and biters for trimming tile; a level; a straightedge; and a bucket and sponge.

A snap cutter and biters are the basic cutting tools needed (more on these in a moment), since very few tile installations can be completed without some tiles having to be cut or shaped. I use a snap cutter for most straight cuts and the biters for simple, curved cuts. For very small jobs, you may be able to get by with just these cutting tools, but for jobs where more complex, curved or angled cuts need to be made, you'll probably need to use the biters in combination with a wet saw or a dry-cutting diamond-blade saw. All of these cutting tools can usually be rented from a tile retailer or a tool rental shop for a nominal charge.

Notched trowels

Notched trowels look like flat trowels, except that they have at least two sides cut or ground with V-, U- or square-shaped notches. The trowel's unnotched sides are used to spread the adhesive on the setting bed. Then the adhesive is "combed" with the trowel's notched sides to produce a

Tools needed for spreading adhesive and setting tile include (clockwise, from top right) notched trowels, margin trowels, pointer, snap cutter, biters, brick hammer and chisel (used for cleaving stone tile), tile grindstones, and tile spacers and wedges. At center are a beating block and a rubber mallet.

Sloan Howard

This rather strange looking notched trowel with deep U-notches is made specifically for applying medium-bed thinset adhesive.

series of uniform ridges. (For a full description of applying adhesive, see Chapter 8.)

In the process of combing the adhesive, the trowel's notches are kept in contact with the setting bed and thus gauge the thickness of the layer of adhesive. The depth of the notch—and that of the adhesive—should equal about two-thirds the thickness of the tile being set. To determine if the trowel used is the right size, first spread and comb a small area of adhesive, making sure there's enough material to produce fully formed ridges. Next firmly press a tile into the adhesive and then remove it. If the tile back is not completely covered with adhesive, the layer of adhesive is still not deep enough and a trowel with a larger-size notch is needed (see the photos on p. 143). Conversely, if the adhesive oozes up around the sides of the tile when you press it down, the layer of adhesive is too deep and a trowel with a smaller-size notch should be used.

If you are using irregular-backed tiles, sheet-mounted tiles, stone tiles or tiles like Mexican pavers that are not completely flat, you may need both to comb adhesive on the setting bed and back-butter the tiles in order to ensure a strong bond of the adhesive.

If you're a novice setter and don't want to invest in a lot of tools, you may be interested in the disposable notched trowel, which is available at tile supply stores. This trowel—simply a piece of stamped metal or molded plastic with notches on one side—is inexpensive and can be thrown away at the end of the job, eliminating cleanup. Though this tool may not be as sturdy as a regular notched trowel, and can be expected to last just about one installation, it should be used in exactly the same fashion.

Biters

Biters, or nippers, are the least sophisticated of the cutting tools and are generally used to cut irregular shapes of tile to fit around faucet valves, toilet flanges, door casings and any other obstruction. Because biters tend to produce cuts with sharp, jagged edges, this tool is not used to make straight cuts. In a pinch, a pair of pliers could be substituted for biters, but the cut produced by pliers is even more ragged than that of the biters.

Biters come in several sizes with different jaw configurations. The pair I prefer to use has two carbide-tipped jaws—the upper jaw ground straight across to contact the glazed face of the tile and the lower jaw curved to grip the rougher texture of the bisque.

Biters work by nibbling small bits of tile, and biting hard, vitreous tiles takes more patience than cutting soft-bodied tiles. The tricks to biting both types of tile are finding and maintaining the correct jaw position, and knowing how much tile to bite off (see the sidebar below).

Snap cutter

For repetitive, relatively straight cuts, the snap cutter does the quickest, most efficient job. Some tile stores will lend out these cutters with the purchase of tile. There are several different types of snap

MAKING CURVED CUTS

When using biters to make a curved cut, I start each bite by marking the cut on the face of the tile with a fine-point marker or pencil. The position the jaws take when in contact with the tile determines where the glaze will be fractured and how each bite will be shaped. I try to keep the jaws parallel to the mark, and, to keep control of the cut, I also position the biters so that only part of the full spread of the jaws contacts the mark. I find that if the jaws fully contact the tile, the bite sometimes goes wild, fracturing the tile beyond the actual grasp of the jaws. The idea is not to try to make the cut in one bite, but to nibble away the unwanted area gradually, working from the sides of the cut toward the center. It may take a little practice to get the hang of using this tool.

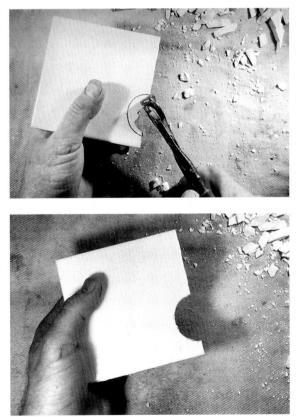

The biters are used to nibble away a waste area of tile, working from the outside (left) toward the center of the cut (top and above). To produce a clean break, use a prying motion rather than attempting to cut entirely through the tile with each bite.

cutters, but all incorporate the same basic features: a frame for holding the tile, and a housing mounted on a guide bar that's comprised of a handle, a tiny wheel for scoring the face of the tile and a device (often "wings" at the base of the handle) for snapping the tile apart at the scored line.

Before using the snap cutter, put a few drops of oil on the guide bar and the scoring wheel. Check to make sure that the wheel is secured properly (it's usually held in place by a small bolt) and that it doesn't meander from side to side, which would score the tile crookedly. Also check to see if

MAKING STRAIGHT CUTS

To make a straight cut on the snap cutter, begin by marking a cutting line on the tile with a fine-point, felt-tipped pen. Position the tile against the snap cutter's bottom edge, aligning the cutting line with the scoring wheel. (If you're making multiple cuts of a given size, screw the cutting fence in place to act as a stop.) Hold the tile in place with one hand and the wheel's handle in the other. Lift the handle so that the wheel is pressed against the top edge of the tile's surface and pull the handle toward you. Use only enough pressure to score the tile lightly and evenly in one pass. Making several passes usually produces a bad break, but remember that a mis-scored tile can be used for a smaller cut.

To snap the scored tile apart, position the wings at the base of the handle along the lower third of the tile. I hold the tile in position by putting light pressure on the handle with my left thumb, then I lightly strike the handle with the heel of my right hand. If the tile doesn't break, I hit the handle harder. If the tile still refuses to break, it means the scoring line was too light or not continuous, so I begin again with a new tile.

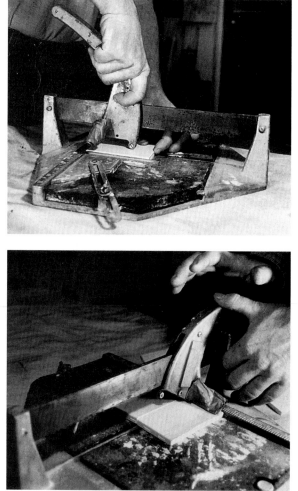

With the tile positioned in the snap cutter (left), raise the handle and draw the scoring wheel lightly across the tile's surface (top). To break the scored tile, hold it in place with the wings at the base of the handle and strike the handle with the heel of your hand (above). (Note that wrapping the wings with duct tape prevents them from marking the tile.)

the scoring wheel is worn, and, if need be, get a replacement wheel, which is readily available at a tile store.

Depending on the composition of the tile you're working with, you can use the snap cutter to produce cut tile as narrow as ½ in. Usually the denser the tile, the easier it is to cut on the snap cutter and hence the likelier it is that close cuts can be made. Since this isn't always the case, however, experiment before making the actual cuts. If you're unable to use the snap cutter to make narrow cuts, either use the wet saw or score the tile with the snap cutter and pry off the thin waste with the biters.

In a pinch, a glass cutter and a 16d nail could be pressed into service in place of a snap cutter. Score the tile with the glass cutter and then place it over the nail, aligning the nail with the scored line and pressing down on both sides of the tile with your thumbs. You might also cut tile with a carbide-grit rod handsaw, but the procedure will take five to ten minutes, compared to five to ten seconds on the snap cutter. Neither of these alternatives gives as clean a cut as a snap cutter.

If the cut edge will be exposed after the tile has been set, you may want to round over the sharp corner with a tile rubbing stone or abrasive paper (see the photo above). I keep several stones in various grades for soft and hard tiles. If the cut edge will be buried behind another tile, at an inside corner, for example, softening the edge is not required.

Wet saw

A properly maintained diamond-blade wet saw makes a perfectly straight cut, which, unlike the sharp edges produced by either the snap cutter or the biters, is smooth and slightly rounded over. I make particular use of the wet saw to make cuts whose edges will be prominently exposed when set, and when I need cut pieces that are less than ½ in. wide. I also combine the wet saw with the biters to simplify complicated cuts (see the sidebar on p. 61).

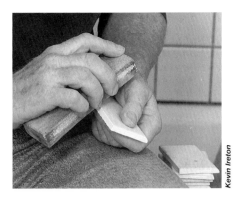

Kevin Ireton

Because cut tile often has sharp edges, especially when cut on a snap cutter, hand-held tile rubbing stones are needed to smooth these edges and round off corners (a job that could also be done with carbide sandpaper).

Both soft- and hard-bodied tiles and even stone tiles can be cut on the wet saw. General-purpose blades are available, but a well-stocked tile installer should carry several blades to suit the material being cut. The one tile that should never be cut on this saw is quarry tile with carbide chips on its face for a nonskid surface. These chips will quickly chew up the sawblade. Quarry tile should be cut instead on the snap cutter, and any rough edges smoothed down with a tile grindstone if the cut edge will be visible. (The carbide chips will also

Sloan Howard

The wet saw is the best tool to use for making clean, straight cuts and for cutting pieces of tile less than ½ in. wide.

eventually damage the cutting wheel on a snap cutter, but replacement is but a fraction of the cost of a diamond wheel.)

Most wet saws run on regular household current, and most are constructed with a stationary cutting blade and a sliding table. The wet saw gets its name because it must be used with water. With some wet saws, the blade runs partially submerged in water, but most rely on water jets aimed just above the point where the blade cuts through the tile. Commercial saws generally use a recirculating pump to deliver water to the blade and a drip pan to catch the spray and also act as the reservoir for the pump. Because these saws don't have a filter to separate the abrasive tile and glaze particles from the water that cools the sawblade, however, the blade is actually cooled by abrasive water, which shortens its life. For this reason, the water should be changed frequently. (On my own saw, I bypass the pump altogether by hooking the saw directly to a water supply with a regular garden hose. Thus the blade is cooled with fresh water only, which I think will extend its life two or three times.) The wet saw is messy to use, so for cutting indoors I rig up a hood from sheet plastic to contain the spray. Alternatively, you can set up the saw outside or in a garage.

CUTTING TECHNIQUE   Whatever the wet saw's construction, its cutting action is the same. The amount of pressure needed when holding the tile against the blade depends in part on the blade's condition and the density of the tile. Nonetheless, generally speaking, this pressure should be light when the tile first contacts the blade, increase as the blade cuts through the tile and decrease as the end of the cut nears.

Throughout the cutting procedure, the tile should be kept in contact with the table to prevent vibration and to keep the blade from sticking in the middle of a cut. (For some complex cuts, however, it's necessary to hold the tile off the table, as explained in the sidebar on the facing page.) It's a good idea to hold down both sides of the tile being cut: If the tile cocks to one side, the blade can knock off tile chips and send them flying, or it can grab the entire tile from your hands and fling it away. Also, if the blade gets jammed in the kerf, chunks of the cutting rim can fly off the body of the blade—a very dangerous situation. Since this tool routinely throws off tile chips whatever cutting method you choose, I strongly recommend wearing safety glasses whenever working with it. Because of the noise of the saw, I also suggest wearing hearing protectors.

A wet-saw blade generally lasts for thousands of cuts. Occasionally the blade will clog up with ceramic material and need cleaning. One way of doing this is to cut through an old sand-mold brick or to make several cuts in a tile grindstone. Another method is to remove the blade, flip it over and let it rotate in the opposite direction (do not do this if the blade is stamped with a directional arrow). Replacement blades are available when the blade becomes too worn.

Unlike the dry-cutting diamond blade discussed next and most power saws used for woodworking, the wet saw's untoothed blade cuts only very hard materials easily. This means that the wet saw will not readily cut through skin. But because this is not a complete impossibility, the wet saw should be treated with the same respect given to any other power saw. You need not, however, be afraid of the wet saw.

Dry-cutting diamond-blade saw

Another cutting tool that's helpful to have for some installations is a dry-cutting diamond blade mounted in a small electric grinder. This tool can be used both to rip out old tilework (see pp. 227-228) and to cut new tiles. One advantage it has over the wet saw is that it requires no extensive setup—just plug it into an electrical outlet. Like the wet saw, this blade can be used

Having issued the necessary precautions for working with the wet saw, I would like to explain a practice used by most tile-installation professionals that runs counter to the safety advice given in the text. I learned this method early in my career and have used it on practically every installation I have done for over 20 years. It can be dangerous and I do not recommend it for the novice, but it is an effective technique for professionals.

This method, which is especially helpful for complicated cuts, calls for the tile to be held freehand off the sliding table. The desired cut shown in the photo below cannot be made with a snap cutter and is very time-consuming when done with biters and a tile rubbing stone. I grasp the tile firmly in both hands and rest the heels of my hands on the wet saw's sliding table. I advance the tile into the blade slowly, making a series of parallel cuts. I hold the tile at an angle so that the blade cuts clear to the marking line. Then I break away the waste with my fingers and clean the cut with the biters. Sometimes, rather than use the biters, I will use the side of the wet-saw blade to trim the remaining material. I make certain that there are no obstructions that might interfere with the smooth execution of this technique, and I focus all my attention on the blade and the kerf. (These precautions have allowed me to retain both eyes and all ten fingers.)

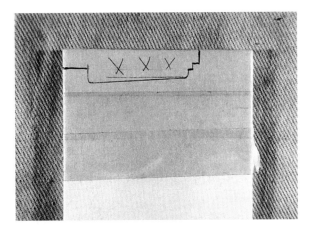

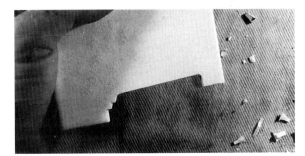

To make a complex cut on the wet saw, first put masking tape on the tile and mark the cutting line (top left). Then make a series of parallel cuts ending at the line (bottom left) and break away the waste with your fingers (top right). Complete the cut by trimming with the biters (middle right and above).

to make straight cuts and, by making a series of parallel kerfs, curved cuts. Because this tool is hand-held, however, it cuts with less accuracy than the wet saw and leaves a jagged edge. For this reason, the dry-cutting diamond-blade saw should be considered a "roughing-in" tool, though it certainly speeds up making cuts whose edges will be hidden. Another task for which this blade is very handy and quick is cutting backer board to size (see the photo on p. 49).

The only drawbacks to using this kind of diamond blade are its speed and the chips and dust it generates. Safety glasses, ear protection, a dust mask and extreme care are essential when using this tool. Unlike the wet saw, the dry saw will quickly cut through skin and bone and should be handled with the utmost caution. I always firmly hold the grinder in which the blade is mounted and make sure the work space where I'm cutting is completely clear. To combat the dust, I wear a dust mask, and where possible I get a helper to follow the cutting action with a vacuum cleaner.

Hole saws and other cutting tools

In addition to the saws already mentioned, a carbide-tipped hole saw is a very useful tilesetting tool. As its name suggests, this saw serves to cut holes (in tile, masonry, backer board, etc.), and it's indispensable for getting a finished look when tiling around faucets and supply lines and also for cutting sink corners. It cuts both soft- and hard-bodied tile, although cutting vitreous tile is pretty slow-going.

A carbide-tipped hole saw chucked in a power drill (left) is indispensable for drilling holes in tiles to be set around faucets and supply lines. This tool is also essential for renovation work, such as cutting sink corners and enlarging an existing hole for a new sink (top and above).

Chucked in a power drill, the hole saw and its ¼-in., carbide-tipped pilot drill bit are mounted on a mandrel. The saw can be used dry, but I've found that, when drilling a hole in a single, unset tile, it tends to break the tile. The reason for this is that the hole saw cuts rather slowly and heat builds up from the tile chips and dust trapped around the cutting edge. (Heat shock is not a problem with the other saws mentioned above. The wet saw is cooled by water, and the dry-cutting diamond blade not only has a toothed edge, which allows the hot dust to escape, but also cuts rapidly enough to prevent any damaging heat buildup.)

To keep a tile cool during drilling, I immerse it in a bath of water, as shown in the photos at right. Water carries off the hot dust and chips, and cools the tile being cut as well, reducing both stress and breakage; using water also increases a cutting tool's useful life.

Unfortunately, water and electricity can be a dangerous mix. Cordless tools do not present the same hazards as power tools using household current, but most lack the power and torque required for smooth, chatter-free cutting of ceramic or stone tiles. (If you choose to use a cordless drill, make sure that the battery pack is fully charged, since drilling the hole draws a lot of power.) The solution is to plug your regular power tools into a ground-fault circuit interrupter (GFCI). You can plug into an existing GFCI outlet or purchase or rent a portable unit. (For further discussion of tool safety when working around water, see p. 66.)

To support the tile while it's being cut, I build a box of scrap plywood somewhat larger than the tile and caulk the box's corners. I fill the box with enough water to cover the tile by about ¼ in. Before submerging the tile, I lightly tap a center punch to break the glaze at the center of the cut so that the pilot bit won't slip. Then I submerge the tile, position the pilot bit and turn the drill to regular speed. As the pilot cuts through the tile, the hole saw will be drawn into the tile's surface and the

When drilling single tiles with the hole saw, chuck the saw in a drill and submerge the tile in water to prevent heat shock from cracking the tile.

drill's speed should be reduced. I don't put too much pressure on the hole saw as it's cutting, because that might cause the tile to split. Instead I let the saw feed itself into the tile. Because the hole saw operates best at a slow speed of about 100 rpm to 200 rpm, it's relatively safe to use. Nonetheless, it is capable of cutting through skin and bone and should be used with care.

Beyond the basic power tools required for most ceramic or stone tile installations, other carbide- and diamond-tipped tools are available for a variety of cutting, shaping and finishing tasks. Like similar tools used for woodworking, there is a wide range of performance and quality options for tile-cutting tools. These tools are expensive, often require heavy-duty machinery and demand skilled operators. If the small job you are planning calls for special cutting, shaping or fabrication tools, I would advise turning that work over to a professional fabricator. If you are a professional looking for ways to expand your company's range, the Resource Guide will direct you to a source of production equipment.

Wedges and spacers

Wedges and spacers are molded or extruded plastic pieces that facilitate the actual placement of tile. Wedges are used like shims to hold a vertically placed tile in position until the adhesive sets up. If time permits, I like to leave wedges in place overnight, but they can be removed as soon as the adhesive has cured enough to support the tiles.

Spacers go between tiles, whether they're set horizontally or vertically, to ensure that the grout joint will be a consistent width. Spacers come in a variety

of sizes and shapes so that they can be used with square, rectangular, hexagonal or octagonal tile. Although many setters leave spacers in place and grout over them, I recommend removing them before grouting because the thinner layer of grout over the spacers will dry to a lighter shade than that of the surrounding, deeper grout (an effect known as "ghosting").

Beating block

A beating block is a block of wood that's used to seat tile firmly in its setting bed (see the photo on p. 199). The block is placed over the positioned tile and tapped with a hammer both to force the tile into the adhesive and ensure a level surface. This block can either be bought (and will then usually have a rubber face), or it can be made from a scrap piece of plywood about 6 in. by 10 in. Although you can beat in tiles measuring 8 in. or larger with just a rubber hammer, it's critical to use a beating block with the hammer for both smaller tile and sheet-mounted tile (such as 1-in. square mosaic tiles) in order to produce a successful bond and a flat surface. One type of tile on which a beating block is ineffective, however, is tile with an uneven

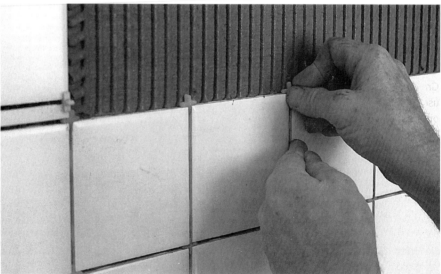

Spacers are installed between tiles to ensure consistent grout joints.

surface—Mexican pavers, for example. These tiles should instead be firmly pressed into the adhesive by hand and then tapped individually with a rubber mallet. The softer the tile's bisque, the gentler the mallet raps should be.

A beating block should never be used to "extend" an insufficient layer of adhesive, but rather to help align the surface plane of the tiles. The beating block is truly an antique tool, developed at a time when most tiles were installed over thick beds of fresh, soft mortar. Tiles were pasted onto the surface of the mortar bed with a bond coat of cement and then tapped down into the soft bed—with very little stress or shock on the tiles. Thinsetting tiles over a hard surface, however, requires a delicate touch to avoid breaking tiles. By all means use the beating block if it is effective, but first make sure there is ample adhesive beneath the tiles.

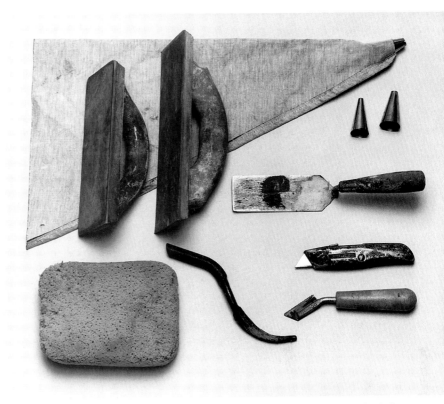

Grouting and finishing tools include (from top left, clockwise) grout trowels, grout bag and metal tips, margin trowel, knife, grout saw, striking tool and sponge.

Grouting and Finishing Tools

The minimum tools needed for grouting and completing a tile installation are a bucket for mixing and one for cleaning, a sponge with rounded corners, a margin trowel, a grout trowel, and cheesecloth or other soft cloth for removing traces of grout film from the surface of the tiles.

Grout trowels

Grout trowels are rubber-faced trowels used for spreading grout over the surface of the tiles and packing it into the joints without scratching the tile's glaze. Grout trowels with stiff rubber faces are designed for grouting sturdy floor tiles, while those with a softer rubber face, sometimes backed with foam, are intended for grouting wall tiles with more delicate glazes. After the grout is spread with the face of the trowel, the tool's edge is used to cut away excess grout from the surface of the tiles.

Cleaning tools

Once a small area of tile has been grouted with the grout trowel, cleanup can begin immediately. The key to cleaning up grout successfully is to do it before the grout hardens and to use a minimum of water. (For a full discussion of grout-cleaning techniques, see pp. 150-153.) The principal cleaning tool needed is a good sponge with rounded corners, which will not gouge out the joints. It's also useful to have white Scotch-Brite pads to remove any hardened grout that resists sponging, and stainless steel pads for really stubborn residue. To avoid marring glazed tiles, moisten the pad and test on a scrap piece of tile. (Avoid regular steel-wool pads since their splintered strands can stick in the grout joints, where they will rust and discolor the grout.)

Finally, cheesecloth can be used to remove most of the haze left on the tiles after grouting. Since this filmy residue becomes very difficult to remove once it hardens, it should be removed quickly. Many setters use acid grout cleaners to remove grout haze, but I believe that these cause more problems than they solve (see the sidebar on p. 229). I suggest staying away from these cleaners and instead cleaning up promptly with nothing stronger than water.

Grout bags

When grouting certain kinds of tile that would be particularly difficult to clean up—for example, those with a rough surface like antique brick-veneer tile—a grout bag can be used instead of a grout trowel. This bag looks like a cake-decorating bag (see the photo on p. 65) and works the same way. A metal tip, sized to the width of the grout joint, is slipped into the bag, which is then filled with grout and squeezed to lay a ribbon of grout in the joints. A striking tool is used to compact the grout into the joints, and very little grout gets on the surface of the tile, eliminating major cleaning problems. After striking, the mortar is allowed to harden a bit and a stiff brush is then used to remove any excess grout.

The disadvantage of this tool is that the grout must be mixed fairly wet to flow through the bag's tip and too much liquid mixed into the grout can weaken it. For this reason, a grout bag should be reserved for tile that cannot be grouted in the regular fashion. Also, keep in mind that you will get better results and stronger grout if you use a polymer-modified grout powder or a regular grout powder with a liquid latex or acrylic additive (see p. 44). These mixtures will flow through the narrow tip much easier than water-only mixes. (For further discussion of how to use a grout bag, see pp. 149-150.)

Setting Tile Safely

Setting tile involves contact with some tools and materials that are potentially hazardous. If you set tile only occasionally, you're not likely to have a problem. But if you set tile frequently, prolonged contact with these materials is cause for concern. Unfortunately, no industry-wide safety standards exist, and there has been no real study of the long-term health problems associated with many tilesetting materials. For these reasons, I suggest minimizing potential problems, whether you set tile daily or only once a year, by using safety equipment, common sense and care as you work. The safety equipment recommended here is available at most hardware and building supply stores, and some of the more specialized equipment can be obtained from the supplier listed in the Resource Guide.

Tool safety

Because setting tile frequently involves working around water with power tools, extra caution is needed. Even a small amount of moisture can turn what would normally be a poor electrical conductor into a very good one, and it doesn't take much electricity to cause injury or death. For this reason, use double-insulated tools whenever possible and make sure that they are all plugged into a properly grounded outlet. In addition, using a portable ground-fault circuit interrupter (GFCI) provides considerable extra protection from electrical shock. A GFCI is a fast-acting circuit breaker designed to cut the flow of electricity to a tool in the event that the user accidentally becomes part of the electrical circuit. Permanent GFCIs are now required by code in bathrooms and kitchens, so if you're tiling in one of these rooms, look to see if an outlet is equipped with a GFCI. If not, you can buy a portable GFCI, which is about the size of a standard outlet box, and simply plug it into the nearest outlet. Then plug your tools into the GFCI and start work.

When using power cutting tools, whether to rip out old walls and floors or to cut new tile to size, always wear safety glasses or goggles and a fitted dust mask—these tools readily generate not only tile chips and

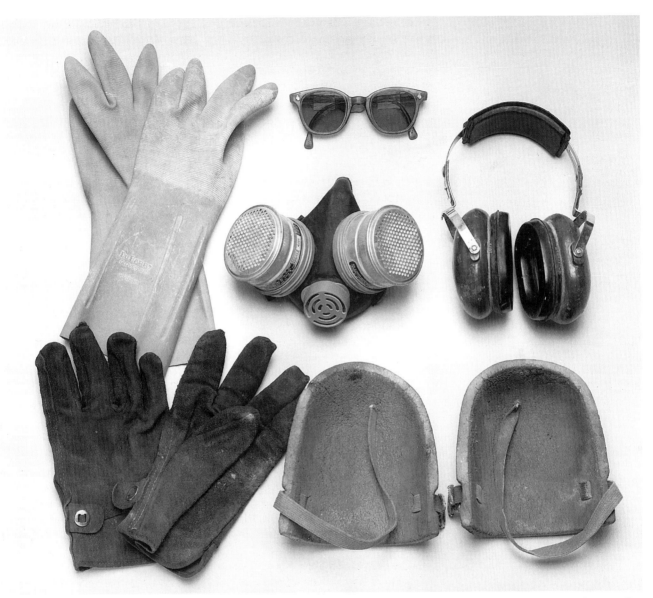

For setting tile safely, certain protective equipment is crucial, including (from left, top to bottom) both rubber and heavy leather gloves, safety glasses, charcoal-filter mask, knee pads and hearing protectors.

other debris but also considerable dust. Make sure that the dust mask you buy has a rubber faceplate that fits snugly over your nose and mouth; a flimsy paper mask with a bendable metal noseclip affords little protection. Because of the noise produced by this machinery, I also suggest wearing hearing protectors. And for obvious reasons, wear heavy shoes or boots when doing rip-out or demolition work.

It's not only power tools that throw tile chips but the snap cutter and biters as well. Therefore it's a good idea to get in the habit of wearing safety glasses whenever you're cutting tile, whatever the method. And because floating mortar beds and grouting often both kick up sand and cement particles, I always try to wear safety glasses for these tasks, too (actually, since I now need glasses for close work anyway, my safety lenses are always with me).

Since it's easy to get cut when manually ripping out walls, floors and old tilework, I recommend wearing heavy leather gloves for demolition work. As I discovered early in my tilesetting career, gloves are especially important when ripping out tiled showers. Any cut I got doing this work seemed to take forever to heal, which, my family doctor explained, was because the cuts were becoming infected by germs and bacteria harbored in some of the old tilework. Now I make it a habit to wear gloves when ripping out old tiles.

Materials safety

In addition to the mechanical hazards of tilesetting, the chemicals found in many setting materials are also cause for concern. Unfortunately, manufacturers are not required to list a product's ingredients on the label, only to indicate whether any of the ingredients are harmful or flammable. Thus you may unwittingly find yourself working, for example, with a solvent-based organic mastic that contains toluene, a petroleum by-product, or you may install a waterproofing membrane with a glue containing xylene, another problematic material. Also, you may not realize that the cement particles in all thinsets, grout and mortar are toxic when in powdered form and caustic when wet.

If you don't set tile often, you may not be bothered by any of these chemicals. Given the lack of thorough research on the long-term effects of contact with such chemicals, however, I suggest that you take precautions whenever you set tile (beginning with a check of the Material Safety Data Sheets for the setting materials you choose—see the sidebar on the facing page).

To protect against the toxic fumes given off by solvent-based setting materials, I recommend wearing a charcoal-filter mask. Unlike a dust mask, a charcoal-filter mask protects not only against dust but also against fumes and vapors. These masks are available at building supply houses and paint stores—look for one with the seal of approval of either the Occupational Safety and Health Association (OSHA) or the National Institute of Occupational Safety and Health (NIOSH). For specific information on toxic or otherwise hazardous substances, see the book *Artist Beware* (Watson-Guptill, 1979) and the three OSHA handbooks listed in the Resource Guide.

Since I have become sensitized over the years and now have severe reactions to fumes emitted by some solvent-based setting materials, I'm careful to wear a filter mask whenever working with these materials and to change the canisters the moment I smell any chemical odors within the mask. This mask is a little uncomfortable, but the protection it affords is more than worth it. Using this mask means freedom not only from worrying about the long-term health hazards of inhaling these fumes, but also from having my head spin with an unwanted industrial "high."

To protect against the toxic cement particles when mixing adhesives, mortar and grout, be certain to wear a fitted dust mask. Once these setting materials are mixed, the toxic particles are bound up in water and produce no dangerous vapors. Instead, the particles become caustic to the touch, and for this reason you'll need to wear rubber gloves when working with them. Although it's sometimes impossible to avoid handling these materials without gloves, continued exposure to them may cause skin sensitivity, severe rashes, blood poisoning and worse. I keep several pairs of rubber gloves on hand in case one breaks. At the end of the day when I've been working with setting materials, I rinse my hands and arms with an inexpensive apple-cider vinegar, which helps to neutralize these materials and condition my skin.

MATERIAL SAFETY DATA SHEETS

Government regulations are as fickle as the wind when it comes to safety, but tile installers should acquaint themselves with safety information available through the U.S. Department of Labor. Literature on a wide range of safety topics is available.

The Labor department also supplies Material Safety Data Sheet (MSDS) forms for manufacturers of all kinds of materials, including those used for tile installation. Distributors and retailers of tilesetting materials should have these forms available on request. MSDS forms list hazardous ingredients, fire and explosion information, health-hazard data and information regarding safe handling, use and disposal of materials. Although far from ideal, they are your first line of defense. If MSDS forms are not readily available from your supplier (as is required by law), make a direct request to the manufacturer.

Because solvent-based ingredients in some tilesetting materials are flammable as well as toxic, it's important to make sure that the room or area being tiled is well ventilated and that there are no sparks or open flames nearby. The latter includes pilot lights on the stove—remember to shut off the gas!

Personal safety

Finally, tilesetting is physically taxing work. Because a box of tile can weigh from 10 lb. to 50 lb. and a bucket of mortar may weigh more than 60 lb., it's very easy to pull or strain muscles. To avoid this, remember one cardinal rule: Keep your back straight when lifting. Lift with your leg and arm muscles, not your back. And always use knee pads when working on your knees—which happens often in tilesetting! I keep two pairs of knee pads handy: one for rough work and another clean pair for working on newly installed tiles (prior to grouting). For additional protection, make sure to keep the job site clean. If you don't wear knee pads, kneeling on tile chips can cause bad bruises.

Several government agencies, for example, the Department of Labor, OSHA, NIOSH and the Environmental Protection Agency (EPA), are charged with responsibility for regulating and maintaining the health and safety of the nation's workplace. In reality, however, these agencies do not protect all workers (the self-employed and, ironically, employees of federal, state and city governments are exempt, among others). Also, because of severe budget restraints and understaffing, these agencies are often slow to act on job-site problems. And they understandably have trouble keeping pace with testing and evaluating the burgeoning number of setting materials on the market, which means that some products will get widely used before being tested. In the end, the individual tilesetter must take responsibility for protecting his or her own health.

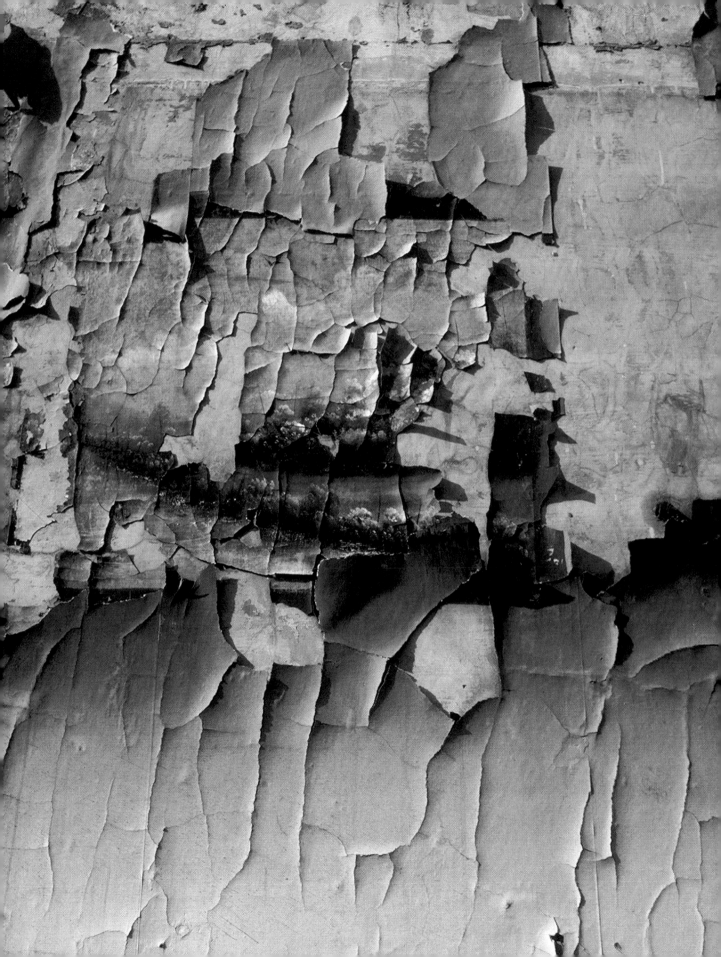

Chapter Five

▦ ▦ ▦

Surface Preparation

In Chapter 3, I described the various surfaces that can be used as setting beds for ceramic and natural stone tiles. In this chapter, I'll explain how to install these setting beds and also how to prepare existing surfaces to receive tile. Whatever setting surface you use, all share the same requirements when used for tiling: All should be clean and flat, walls should be plumb (vertically straight), and floors and counter-tops should be level (horizontally even).

You may be lucky enough, whether working with new or old construction, to find walls and floors that are perfectly constructed and need only cleaning before they are tiled. If not—and this is usually the case—you'll need to do some surface preparation, the extent of which can range from simply scraping peeling paint off a wall to rebuilding a subfloor.

Structural Requirements

If you have the luxury of working with new construction or with a complete remodeling job, make sure in advance that the general contractor or builder understands the importance of fabricating a structure that meets the minimum ANSI requirements for plumb, flat and level surfaces (see the sidebar on p. 72). Better yet, specify *ANSI A108 Standards* in the plans and contracts, or, at the very least, get a copy of the TCA *Handbook* into the contractor's hands.

Be certain that the person in charge of the construction knows which areas are to be tiled and how the walls and floors in these areas should be prepared. Make sure that the tolerances you expect, and approved methods and materials, are referenced on all plans, estimates, bids and other construction documents. Once work is under way, you may want to look at the

To make sure that installation materials perform and endure as expected, modern industries adopt methods for testing and ensuring minimum levels of performance and quality. In the United States, tile associations representing manufacturing, marketing, architectural and contractor interests provide most of the financing and research required to develop reliable standards and practices.

ANSI STANDARDS AND THE TCA HANDBOOK

The American National Standards Institute (ANSI) publishes a list of tile standards that are used by professionals in all segments of the industry. Like all standards, the ANSI tile standards (designated as *ANSI A 108 Standards*) represent a consensus view, a minimum line that cannot be crossed without a definite loss of quality. The ANSI Standards are incorporated into the *Handbook for Ceramic Tile Installation*, published and updated yearly by the Tile Council of America (TCA). The TCA *Handbook* describes all the structural details and materials required for building most tile installations from the ground up.

STRUCTURAL TOLERANCES Careful study of the ANSI *Standards* and the *Handbook* reveals two sets of tolerances: one for mortar-bed work, and one for thinbed installations. Because the thickness of a mortar bed is easily adjusted, tolerances are somewhat loose on mortar-bed work (roughly double those of the thinbed specs). Framing, subflooring and drywalling in areas to be tiled with thick mortar beds can be roughed in—the responsibility for finishing lies almost entirely with the tile mechanic and his or her deftness with mortar.

Tolerances with the thinbed method are more exacting. Here are the accepted industry specifications:

1. Subfloors must be level and flat to within $1/8$ in. in 10 ft.
2. Wall surfaces must be plumb and flat to within $1/8$ in. in 8 ft.
3. There must be no abrupt irregularities in sub or finished layers greater than $1/32$ in.
4. All functional tile installations require expansion joints.
5. All finished tiles must be installed on a smooth, even plane to within $1/8$ in. in 8 ft.

These tolerances put much of the responsibility for the outcome of the tilework on carpenters, drywallers and concrete handlers—none of the people who would normally be installing the tiles. Unlike mortar-bed work, the thinbed method provides very limited space to make corrections. But if the setting bed is within the above specifications, the tile installer's job is made considerably easier.

Because thinbed work does not require the skills of mortar-bed work, more and more people are installing tiles. Unfortunately, many installations suffer from the lack of attention, understanding or skill on the part of the installer. Add to this the obvious need for precision when preparing surfaces or installing adhesives and the potential for problems or failure increases.

The ANSI *Standards* and the TCA *Handbook* are the prime sources that knowledgeable tilesetters turn to for structural, material and other installation details. However, the material found in these two documents can be daunting, even for professionals, because it tells only how a specific installation *should* be done, not *how* to do it.

The information found in this book will explain how you can meet and exceed those minimum standards, and produce quality tilework that is up to the task for which it is specified. This can be quite different from just meeting minimum specifications. It will require that you spend more time and resources, but the results of your extra efforts will reward you with a lifetime of service.

BUILDING CODES

Finally, a word on building codes. In some parts of the country, consumers and contractors benefit from the oversight of informed local building inspectors, reasonable codes and careful permitting. The mere existence of a building code, or the fact that you or your contractor must obtain a permit, however, does not necessarily mean that your tile installation will be done correctly. Like anything else, if you want to ensure that the quality goes in, the responsibility is yours.

framing carpenter's layout before construction begins and check progress as the framing is installed. The goal is to make sure not only that the walls are plumb and square but also that hallway walls are parallel, rooms are square to one another, and the tops of the joists are installed on the same plane (otherwise, the subflooring will not be flat).

Most of the time tilesetters find themselves faced with imperfect framing, which must be "corrected" by tiling rather than by carpentry. When framing problems can't be repaired, for whatever reasons, the tilesetter must either adjust the layout of the tile (see Chapter 7) or change the installation method. In the end, however, since tiling is finish work, it can mask only so many framing and carpentry problems. This means that sometimes compromises in the installation will need to be made, for example, tiling over an out-of-level floor (see Chapter 9). And in a few extreme cases, it may be better not to tile at all and instead select another finishing material. Since there are usually several ways to approach every tile job, though, don't decide prematurely not to tile. Make sure that you've looked at all the possible options before settling for wall-to-wall carpeting or AstroTurf!

Plumb, level and square

Technically, tile will adhere to a wall out of plumb or a floor out of level as easily as it will to a plumb or level surface, but I doubt you'll like the visual effect of such an installation. For example, if you're tiling a floor and the walls are out of square, the tiles around the perimeter of the floor will need to be cut on an angle to follow the wall. Particularly if the wall is long, the grout lines will accentuate the out-of-square condition. If you're tiling an entire wall and either the floor or the ceiling isn't level, you'll have the same problem, and the grout joints will again point out the error.

CHECKING WALLS FOR PLUMB   Checking for plumb, level and square is quite simple, and few tools are needed. To determine if a wall is plumb, use a plumb bob or a long spirit level. Both allow the distance out of plumb to be measured with a tape measure, and each should be used at several points along the wall, since the wall may actually be twisted (plumb at one end and out of plumb at the other) or bowed (plumb at both ends but not in the middle).

To determine if a wall surface is flat, hold a tightly stretched string at various locations across its dimensions. A vertical surface out of plumb $\frac{1}{8}$ in. over a length of 8 ft. (the height of the average ceiling) can be tiled and the discrepancy will probably go unnoticed. If the tile is to be bordered by a boldly patterned wallpaper or by some other starkly contrasting material on an adjoining wall, however, the discrepancy may become apparent. If you're tiling two walls that meet in an outside corner, it's especially important that both be plumb, because tapering cut tiles on this projecting corner would be very unattractive. Were that corner an inside corner, though, the tolerance for out of plumb becomes a bit less exacting since the cut field tiles on one wall can be partially hidden by the field tiles on the adjoining wall.

CHECKING FLOORS FOR LEVEL   Use a spirit level also to determine if floors and countertops to be tiled are level. Check these surfaces in various directions and at a couple of different spots. In the case of floors and countertops, a surface out of level by no more than $\frac{1}{8}$ in. in 10 ft. can be tiled and will probably look fine. But if you suspect that the surface adjoining the tile will unattractively point up an out-of-level condition, the pitch of the floor or counter-top should be corrected. Likewise, the floor or countertop should be leveled when it is more than $\frac{1}{8}$ in. out of level in 10 ft., whether by using a self-leveling compound (see p. 89), floating a mortar bed (see pp. 88-89) or calling in a carpenter.

To determine if the inside and outside corners of the walls are square, check them with a carpenter's square. Unfortunately, it's possible for the corners to be square without the entire wall being square to adjoining walls. This is an important consideration and might negatively affect the layout of any floor tiles that abut such walls. To check if this is the case, set up a 3-4-5 triangle whose base and height are projected off the base of two connecting walls in the room (since you'll need to remove the baseboards before tiling, go ahead and do so before setting up the triangle). If these walls are square to each other at the floor line, a 3-ft. base and a 4-ft. height will yield a hypotenuse exactly 5 ft. long. Expanding the basic 3-4-5 module to 6-8-10, 9-12-15 or higher results in greater accuracy on large installations. (See Chapter 7 for a full discussion of 3-4-5 triangles.)

If the triangle's hypotenuse proves longer or shorter than 5 ft., the base of the walls (and the perimeter of the floor) is out of square. If the walls are off no more than $\frac{1}{8}$ in. in 10 ft., the perimeter rows of floor tile can be trimmed to fit without drawing undue attention. If the condition exceeds this tolerance, however, the resulting trimmed tiles at the perimeter might be unacceptable. If the problem is extreme, you might square up the walls either by rebuilding them or by floating a corrective mortar bed. Yet both of these solutions are costly and time-consuming, and some-times, if the condition isn't too serious and creative layout solutions work, the problem will recede visually once the room is again filled with furniture.

The decision of when to correct an out-of-square floor or wall is in part subjective and, of course, depends on the degree of the problem. Whether or not you decide to correct such a situation, however, the tile itself must be set square. Laying out floor tiles against an out-of-square wall, for example, will only lead to headaches and an unattractive job. If you decide not to correct the problem, a square set of reference lines must be established within the out-of-square area, and these should be the basis for projecting layout lines to position the tiles. (For information on adjusting a layout when a room is out of square, see pp. 124-125.)

Preparing Surfaces for Installing Tile

Below is a description of setting surfaces commonly used for dry tile installations. The listing begins with installation instructions for new setting beds (such as backer board and drywall), goes on to explain how to prepare existing beds to receive tile and concludes with a brief discussion of mortar beds and self-leveling compounds. When properly waterproofed, many of these surfaces are suitable for setting beds in wet installations (refer to Chapter 6 for detailed information on waterproofing an installation). Whenever a specific product is recommended for use in preparing a given surface, please consult the Resource Guide at the back of the book for information on the manufacturer.

Backer board

As discussed in Chapter 3, ready-to-use cement backer boards (or CBUs) are an ideal setting surface for wall, floor and countertop tiles. Installation of backer board involves the following three steps: cutting the boards to size, fastening them to the substrate and finishing the joints between them. Let's look at cutting technique first.

CUTTING BACKER BOARD   The simplest way to cut backer board (whether it's mesh-reinforced or fiber-reinforced) is with a carbide scriber using the score and snap method. Unlike soft gypsum wallboard, which needs to be scored on one side only, CBUs are hard and dense and are cut most easily by scoring on both sides.

To cut backer board with a carbide scriber, mark the board for cutting, then run the scriber's tip along the line, pressing firmly and guiding the scriber with a straightedge for an even cut.

Sloan Howard

Begin by marking both ends of the cut on both sides of the board. Lay a straight-edge between the two marks on one side, align the scoring tool with the edge and scribe a path down the face of the board (see the photo above). Working gradually, make several passes until there is a uniform, narrow V-groove about $\frac{1}{16}$ in. deep (or deep enough to cut through the fiberglass strands of mesh-reinforced CBUs). Then turn the board over and repeat the process on the other side.

When both sides are scored, the board can be snapped apart. Depending on the make of the board, the offcut can be broken away by snapping up or snapping down. I find that I get a cleaner edge when I snap the board up, but follow the manufacturer's instructions before experimenting. To snap the board up, place one hand close to the groove and press down. Then grab the edge of the offcut with your other hand and pull up (as shown in the photo at right).

The board should part easily, but the edge produced by this method can be rough. To get a smooth, clean edge, grind down the cut edge with a masonry or tile rubbing stone (see the top photo on p. 76).

To snap the scored backer board apart, press down firmly with one hand close to the score line and pull up the offcut piece with the other hand.

Sloan Howard

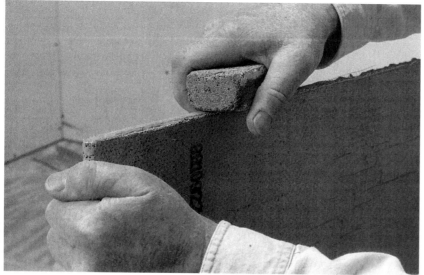

After snapping the backer board, smooth down the rough edge with a masonry or tile rubbing stone.

Backer board can also be cut with power tools, which usually results in a cut edge that requires no further smoothing or grinding. You can use a reciprocating saw fitted with a carbide-tipped blade, but for the cleanest cut I recommend a dry-cutting diamond blade (see the photo on p. 49). Cutting backer board with a saw releases potentially harmful dust. As should be standard practice with all unfamiliar materials, consult the MSDS (see p. 69) for any precautions or recommendations, such as wearing a NIOSH-approved respirator when cutting backer board.

When saw-cutting CBUs that have an outer skin of woven fiberglass mesh, I make three passes with the blade to prevent damaging the external reinforcing or tearing the mesh away from the body of the board (¼-in. fiber-reinforced boards can be cut in one pass). I begin by marking both sides of the board, then set the blade just deep enough to cut through the mesh on one side. After making the first shallow pass, I flip the board over and cut through the mesh on the second side. For the third and final pass, I set the blade to cut completely through the board. Quite often, the board will separate before the saw has done its work. When this happens, I use the side of the blade to dress the rough edge. If weather permits, saw this material

outside. If that is not practical, get a helper to follow the blade with a vacuum-cleaner hose, or use a saw equipped with a dust collector.

CUTTING PLUMBING HOLES   Clearance holes in backer board for shower-head stems, tub faucets, mixing valves and other plumbing penetrations can be made most easily with power saws and coring bits (see pp. 62-64). I use a carbide-tipped hole saw, as shown in the photo below. To make a clearance hole with hand tools, first mark the outline of the penetration on both sides of the board. Then cut through the mark with the scoring tool, making sure that its carbide tip cuts completely through the outer mesh (on fiber-reinforced boards, you need only mark and score one side). Next tip the board on edge, support the back of the intended opening with the palm of one hand, and gradually tap through the other side with a hammer until the penetration is roughed out. Dress the edge with a file or rasp.

To cut larger clearance holes in backer board, first mark the opening, and then drill a series of closely spaced holes around

Use a carbide-tipped hole saw to cut small plumbing holes in backer board.

the perimeter with a small carbide-tipped drill bit. Cut through the mesh on both sides, and then use a hammer to punch out the center. Finish off the hole with a file or rasp.

FASTENING BACKER BOARD TO WALL STUDS

CBUs can be applied to wooden or steel studs with fasteners spaced no more than 8 in. apart (6 in. is preferable). You can use galvanized roofing nails to hang the boards, but screws provide superior holding power and are less likely to split or damage the board. Avoid regular drywall screws because their heads can snap off and the screws can rust in a wet installation, such as a tub surround. Screws made specifically for CBUs come with a corrosion-resistant coating and built-in countersinks that help bury the heads flush with the panel (see the Resource Guide). Use 1 ¼-in. screws if the boards are applied directly to the face of the studs, and 2-in. screws if the boards are mounted over a layer of ½-in. drywall. The key to a durable installation is to ensure that all board edges are supported. Extra studs or blocking between studs may be required.

To speed installation, I start each screw by tapping it into the board with a hammer before driving it home with a power screwdriver. Drive all screws snug but do not overtighten. If a screw snaps off, drive another within 1 in. Under no circumstances, should you attempt to bury screw heads with a hammer. The blow would probably break the screw and possibly damage the board. The proper screws cut their own clearance as the screw descends into the board.

Use shims or spacers to maintain the recommended expansion gaps (usually ⅛ in.) around the panels. When the lower edge of a CBU terminates on the surface of a tub or shower receptor, leave a ¼-in. gap between the fixture and the board. After tiling, this void will be closed off with flexible sealant and become an expansion joint to allow for movement between the fixture and the tiles (see pp. 102-103).

Kevin Ireton

Fasten backer board to wall studs with corrosion-resistant screws designed specifically for this material.

FASTENING BACKER BOARD TO SUBFLOORING

Attaching CBUs to subflooring requires the same fastening schedule as for wall mounting, with one major addition before the board is placed: The subfloor area to receive the CBU should be covered with thinset mortar made for the purpose (generally, a latex- or acrylic-modified thinset) and spread with a ¼-in. square-notched trowel (consult the manufacturer's instructions for specific application procedures). Stage and cut CBUs away from the installation area to help keep it clean and free of any dust or chips that could interfere with either the board or the bond.

Provide layout lines for multiboard installations, and then vacuum and damp-sponge the substrate to remove any dust and increase adhesion. Locate the boards so that edges terminate above joists, or provide blocking equal in size to the surrounding joists. Stagger the boards so that no more than two corners meet.

The thinset mortar used to bond the board is applied the same way as for tile. Spread the mortar with the smooth side of the trowel first to force the material into the plywood. Press hard against the surface, with the trowel held at about 10°

Sloan Howard

Spread a layer of thinset mortar over the subfloor before installing backer board for a floor-tile installation.

to 30° off the surface (see the drawing on p. 142). Spread the adhesive right up to the layout lines. Trowel on enough thinset to build up a thick, even coat, and then use the notched side of the trowel, held about 45° to 75° off the surface, to build up the ridges. Keep a uniform ridge height by maintaining contact with the substrate. (See Chapter 8 for detailed instructions on spreading thinset mortar.)

Next tip a board on its long edge and slowly hinge it down onto the bed of mortar. It is important to do this while the mortar is still wet and tacky. Walk around the board to seat it in the thinset, align it to the layout lines and secure it with fasteners spaced no more than 8 in. apart. Spacing between boards can be critical, so check the manufacturer's instructions for details. Never butt CBU edges tightly against restraining surfaces such as perimeter walls or pipes, but rather hold edges back at least 1/4 in. (see the discussion of expansion joints in Chapter 6).

Leave a gap between the edge of a board and a perimeter wall to allow for expansion.

FINISHING JOINTS When all the boards have been placed and fastened to the studs or subfloor, the joints must be finished with fiberglass-mesh tape and the same thinset mortar that will be used for setting the tile. The manufacturers of some backer boards claim that joint reinforcement with tape is not required, but I recommend that you use it anyway. Most of the work installing CBUs is in the cutting, thinset laminating and fastening. Proper taping costs very little, requires only a small amount of labor, yet adds a fair amount of strength to the installation.

There are two ways to finish the joints. The first method, which takes a bit longer and is considered to produce stronger joints, entails first filling the joint with a latex- or acrylic-modified thinset mortar, then covering the mortar with a strip of fiberglass mesh (I use 2-in. wide Imperial Type P tape from U.S. Gypsum Industries). Bed the tape with the edge of a trowel, and then cover and smooth with another layer of mortar, using the same general techniques employed for taping drywall. Feather the joints as you go rather than waiting until all the joints are filled.

With the thinset mortar spread, hinge the backer board down into the adhesive.

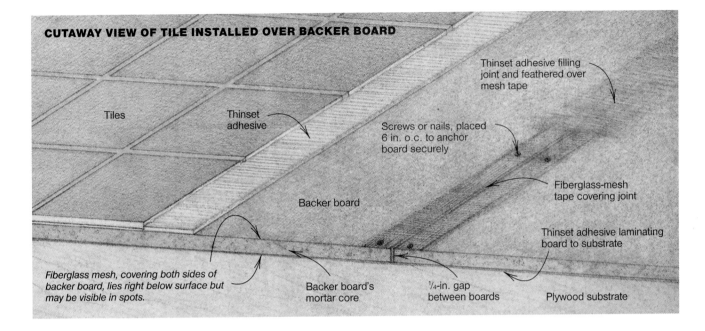

CUTAWAY VIEW OF TILE INSTALLED OVER BACKER BOARD

Tiles

Thinset adhesive

Thinset adhesive filling joint and feathered over mesh tape

Screws or nails, placed 6 in. o.c. to anchor board securely

Backer board

Fiberglass-mesh tape covering joint

Thinset adhesive laminating board to substrate

Fiberglass mesh, covering both sides of backer board, lies right below surface but may be visible in spots.

Backer board's mortar core

¼-in. gap between boards

Plywood substrate

The second method of finishing the joints is to apply gummed mesh to the joints first and then cover with a single layer of thinset mortar (as shown in the photos at right). The strength of the joint can be enhanced by using 4-in. wide exterior mesh tape. Open-mesh tapes are available in a range of widths and weights (see the Resource Guide).

Whichever method you use, I recommend that you schedule taping immediately before you set the tile. This way you avoid having to tile over any hardened ridges of thinset that didn't get flattened (and you also avoid having to mix an extra batch of mortar).

To reinforce corners, the accepted practice is to use three pieces of 2-in. tape: one on the edge of each adjoining board and the third as a bridge between them. Rather than fuss with three pieces of tape, though, I prefer to use a single piece of 4-in. tape (if this size is available). Simply fold the tape in half lengthwise, tuck it snugly against the corner with the edge of a margin trowel, and press firmly to seat both sides of the mesh.

The simplest way to finish a joint between backer boards is to apply adhesive-backed fiberglass-mesh tape to the joint (top left), trowel thinset mortar over the tape (bottom left) and then feather out the mortar for a smooth finish (above).

Kevin Ireton

Drywall

Unpainted gypsum drywall makes an adequate setting bed for wall tile in dry areas and, if properly waterproofed, in light-duty wet areas, too. If radius trim tile is to be used (see p. 20), the drywall can be covered with another layer of drywall or with 1/2-in. backer board (see the drawing below). Doubling up the wallboard strengthens any installation and also offers a quick and economical way to cover drywall that has serious surface flaws, for example, any deep holes left when electrical outlet boxes were removed. If a second layer of drywall is used, bridge over underlying joints and use drywall nails or screws long enough for the task. An option that adds considerable strength is to laminate the two layers with a construction adhesive.

Whether you're using a single or double layer of drywall, leave a 1/8-in. gap between the sheets and cover the resulting joints with open-weave, fiberglass-mesh tape instead of conventional paper joint tape, which isn't water-resistant or strong enough for tile. There are both sticky and non-sticky fiberglass tapes on the market. Because the latter must be stapled or glued in place, I find the sticky tape easier to work with.

After taping, fill the joints with thinset adhesive (don't use mastic) to embed the tape, seal the joint and help minimize cracking. The preparation needed for painting—filling the hammer dimples with joint compound and sanding them—is unnecessary when tiling drywall. Instead, merely dust the surface with a damp rag or vacuum it off and you're ready to go. For dry installations, use as the tile adhesive a latex or acrylic thinset (the best choice), a water-mixed thinset or an organic mastic. For wet installations, add a waterproofing membrane to the surface of the drywall and use a latex or acrylic thinset adhesive. Some building codes allow the use of water-resistant drywall for setting beds in wet areas, but these boards (referred to as blueboard or greenboard) should never be used as a setting bed for tiles.

Plywood

As explained in Chapter 3, plywood is no longer considered an ideal setting bed for tile. Indeed, the TCA *Handbook* includes a caution drawing attention to the limitations of plywood as a substrate for floor tiles (see p. 156). However, if you must use plywood (for reasons of cost, availability, etc.), there are certain installation methods than can help ensure success.

The American National Standards Institute (ANSI) recommends that a plywood setting bed for a floor or counter-top be a minimum thickness of 1 1/8 in. (on wall installations, the plywood must be at least 5/8 in. thick). Instead of putting down a single layer this thick (which can flex and cause tiles or grout joints to crack), build

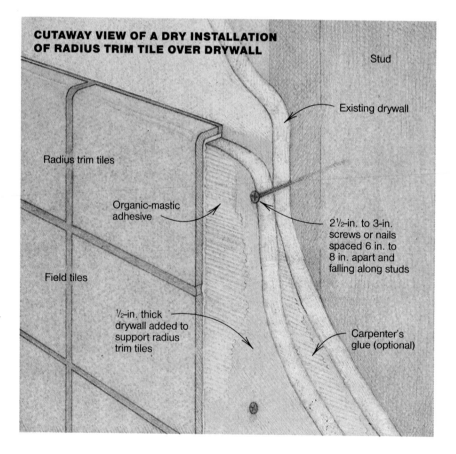

CUTAWAY VIEW OF A DRY INSTALLATION OF RADIUS TRIM TILE OVER DRYWALL

Stud

Existing drywall

Radius trim tiles

Organic-mastic adhesive

2 1/2-in. to 3-in. screws or nails spaced 6 in. to 8 in. apart and falling along studs

Field tiles

1/2-in. thick drywall added to support radius trim tiles

Carpenter's glue (optional)

up the proper thickness by laminating a minimum ½-in. thick plywood underlayment to a minimum ⅝-in. thick plywood subfloor.

When installing plywood over sub-flooring, stagger the sheets so that no joint falls over a joint in the subfloor. Terminate all plywood edges over a joist and provide blocking between joists for sheet ends. Mount the plywood so that the coarser of the two sides is up to give the adhesive a better grip. Also position the sheets to leave a gap between them of no less than ⅛ in. and no greater than ¼ in. These gaps should later be filled with tilesetting adhesive to edge-glue the plywood. (Check the instructions for the adhesive you intend to use for specific underlayment details.)

Laminate the sheets to the subfloor with construction adhesive rated for floor use. Then, with screws or with ring-shank or underlayment nails, fasten the sheets every 6 in., making sure you hit the joists wherever you can (the length of these fasteners should equal about three times the combined thickness of the subfloor and underlayment). The nails or screws that won't hit the joists need only be slightly longer than the combined thickness of the subfloor and underlayment.

When fastening plywood to subfloors or countertops, make sure that the nail or screw heads are sunk below the top surface of the plywood to prevent any tile set over them from cracking under load. If the plywood surface veneer is crushed by the fasteners and wood fibers protrude above the surface, trim them down with a chisel or sandpaper. Once you've vacuumed away any dust, the plywood is ready for tiling.

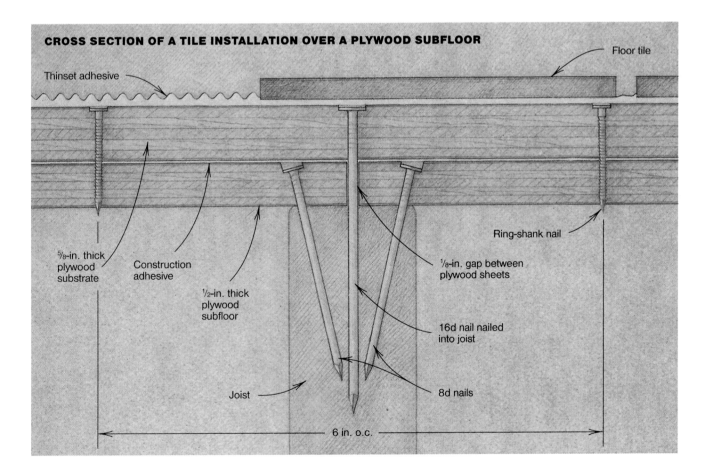

CROSS SECTION OF A TILE INSTALLATION OVER A PLYWOOD SUBFLOOR

Floor tile

Thinset adhesive

Ring-shank nail

⅝-in. thick plywood substrate

Construction adhesive

½-in. thick plywood subfloor

⅛-in. gap between plywood sheets

16d nail nailed into joist

Joist

8d nails

6 in. o.c.

If you're setting tile over existing plywood, sand off any waxes, oils or flaking varnish or paint on the surface before tiling, then vacuum away the dust. I find that an epoxy thinset is the best adhesive to use with a plywood setting bed for a dry installation. My second choice of adhesive would be a latex or acrylic thinset (not all may be suitable for use with plywood), and my third choice an organic mastic. If plywood is to be used as the setting bed for a wet installation, the surface should be properly waterproofed (see Chapter 6). Any tile adhesive used for a wet installation must be compatible with the membrane.

Although there is no ANSI *Standard* or TCA *Handbook* method for using modified thinset mortar on plywood, most manufacturers have adhesive and water-proofing systems especially designed for use with plywood. Many of these systems are multipurpose adhesives and water-proofers appropriate for a variety of conditions. Ask your dealer to explain the range of products in the inventory to fit your application, and be sure to follow the manufacturer's installation instructions carefully (especially in regard to the curing requirements of the material and the placement of expansion joints).

1x or 2x planking

Although many people try to set tile directly on material such as 1x4s or 2x6s, dimensional lumber is not a suitable setting bed. As the lumber expands and contracts with seasonal changes in humidity, the numerous joints will become points of stress for the tiles set over them. If you have this type of subflooring, remove it and replace with a subflooring of plywood and an underlayment of backer board. (If the profile, or height, of the finished installation is not critical, leave the planking in place.) When properly water-proofed (see Chapter 6), this subfloor can be used for a wet installation.

Composition paneling

Composition paneling, or Masonite sheets covered with wood-grain veneer, should not be used for tiling. This paneling is both too thin and too flexible, and using it as a setting bed is only asking for trouble and lots of cracked grout joints. If your walls are covered with this paneling, it should be removed and replaced with backer board, drywall or plywood.

Wainscoted walls

Wooden wainscoting makes a very poor base for tiles. Because the numerous boards making up traditional wainscoting expand and contract considerably, the grout joints of any tiles installed on this surface will probably crack. If you have wooden wainscoting, whether the traditional sort or made from grooved plywood, remove and replace it with drywall or backer board (depending on the installation's eventual use). For backer-board installations, make sure that all board edges are supported by and attached to blocking between studs.

Wainscoting made of tile, however, is an acceptable surface for setting tile, provided the old tile is in good shape and uncracked. (For information on how to prepare a ceramic-tile setting surface, see pp. 85-86.) Choose an adhesive that has been formulated or recommended for this type of renovation.

Masonry walls and concrete surfaces

Most masonry walls (including concrete block, brick and stucco walls), concrete walls and concrete slabs make an excellent base for tile, provided they are flat and free of major cracks. In the case of concrete slabs, a slab finished with a wood float has a coarse surface that works well for tiling, while the surface of a steel-troweled slab is too slick. If a new slab is to be poured, make sure that it will be finished with a wood float. Slabs and concrete walls should be reinforced with wire mesh or reinforcing bar to prevent cracking from seasonal movement (check local building codes for the type and amount of reinforcing necessary in your area). They should also be allowed to cure for 28 days before tile is set (although concrete continues to cure for years after placement, it gains most of its strength in the first 28 days). If your slab was finished with a steel trowel, you'll have to rough up its surface before tiling, either by grinding it with an abrasive wheel or by lightly bush-hammering it with special pneumatic or electric tools.

The one slab over which tile should never be set is that treated with a curing or acceleration compound, or a form-release agent. These chemicals will prevent tile adhesive from bonding. You can test the surface of the concrete for the presence of such chemicals by sprinkling it with water. If the water is not absorbed, a compound or release agent was probably used. While sandblasting may remove the offending material from the surface of the slab, that remaining below the surface may still interfere with the bond of the adhesive.

If the slab or wall is old, remove any wax or oil on the surface, using one of the cleaning preparations listed in the Resource Guide. Then check the slab or wall to make sure that its surface is no more than 1/8 in. out of level or plumb in 10 ft. Be sure to examine the surface of a new slab or wall, too, since new doesn't guarantee perfect.

If the surface is not plumb or level, or too rough to tile, it will need grinding, chipping, filling or other treatments to correct it. On new construction, make certain that the concrete supplier knows the exact requirements.

LEVELING DEPRESSIONS AND MOUNDS

Once you've determined that a slab is level or a wall plumb, check to see that the surface is flat. Do this by moving a long straightedge over the floor or wall. Outline any low spots with a pencil. If the depressions are less than 1/4 in. deep, they can be leveled with latex thinset adhesive and screeded flat with a straightedge, or the tiles could be back-buttered with enough adhesive to allow them to lie on an even plane. Before making such adjustments, however, consider the size of the tile being set. A 1/4-in. depression in a 2-sq.-ft. area may go unnoticed if covered with 12-in. square tiles, but if 1-in. square mosaic tiles are used, the depression is likely to be glaring and definitely needs to be filled and leveled.

If the depressions on a concrete slab are deeper than 1/4 in., brush the surface of each one with latex thinset and then fill it with a latex-modified mortar prepared especially for floors. (The thinset, which should not dry before the mud is applied,

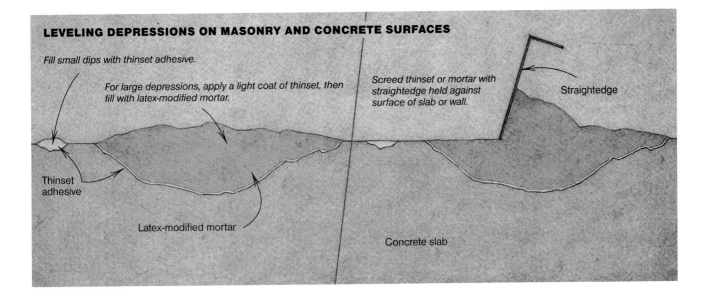

LEVELING DEPRESSIONS ON MASONRY AND CONCRETE SURFACES

Fill small dips with thinset adhesive.

For large depressions, apply a light coat of thinset, then fill with latex-modified mortar.

Screed thinset or mortar with straightedge held against surface of slab or wall.

Straightedge

Thinset adhesive

Latex-modified mortar

Concrete slab

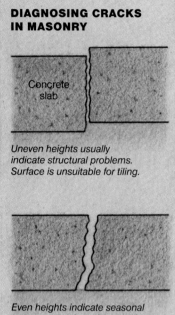

DIAGNOSING CRACKS IN MASONRY

Concrete slab

Uneven heights usually indicate structural problems. Surface is unsuitable for tiling.

Even heights indicate seasonal movement and can be contained with an isolation membrane.

helps the mortar grip the surface of the slab.) Then use a straightedge to screed any excess mud.

Any minor high spots on a slab can be ground down with a rubbing stone or an electric grinder. If the slab's surface is marked with mounds greater than $\frac{1}{4}$ in., lightly coat the entire surface with thinset and float a thin bed of deck mud over the slab to even it out.

Correcting a masonry wall with dips or mounds greater than $\frac{1}{4}$ in. involves a lot more skill than correcting an out-of-level slab. The most practical way to plumb it is with mortar, but this is a job for a qualified professional. Also be aware that dips or mounds greater than $\frac{1}{4}$ in. indicate that there are probably more than just surface problems with the masonry.

CONTAINING CRACKS   To prevent any small cracks in the surface of the slab or wall—or any future cracks that develop—from being transmitted to the tile, install an isolation membrane over the substrate before tiling (see pp. 109-111). The cracks in question are those caused by seasonal movement in the slab or wall (see the drawing at left). Large cracks produced by expanding tree roots, shifting earthquake fault zones or shifting foundations are liable to telegraph to the tile, with or without an isolation membrane. Such cracks can be eliminated only by rebuilding and extensively reinforcing the slab or wall with rebar. If you detect active cracks of any size, you'll need to eliminate the source of the cracking before tiling.

For wet installations, a waterproofing membrane is also needed (see pp. 104-109). Depending on your choice of materials, the isolation membrane itself may also serve to waterproof the installation. Use a water-mixed, latex or acrylic, or epoxy thinset for setting tile on these prepared surfaces.

Plaster walls

Plaster walls make good setting surfaces for tile, provided they are composed of traditionally mixed plaster, and are in good

condition, flat and uncracked. For the purposes of tiling, these walls can be treated just like masonry walls.

Walls composed of plaster made primarily of lime, however, are unsuitable for tiling. This recipe for plaster was commonly used for inexpensive construction about 30 years ago, but it is still occasionally used today. To determine if a wall is made of this type of plaster, poke it with a screwdriver. If the surface is hard, does not crumble and contains no lengthy cracks, it is traditional plaster and can be tiled. Lengthy cracks are those long enough to span two or more studs or wide enough to slip a knife blade into. Such fissures will telegraph to the face of the tiles. If the plaster is soft and crumbles or cracks under the screwdriver test, it should be replaced with drywall or backer board. Keep in mind that tiles installed over any cracks—even hairline cracks—are likely to crack themselves. When in doubt, remove and replace.

Painted and papered walls

Properly prepared, painted walls can be acceptable surfaces for tiling, provided the walls themselves are not composition paneling or any material that flexes more than $\frac{5}{8}$-in. plywood does. Before tiling a painted wall, scrape or sand off any loose or peeling paint, rough up the surface with 80-grit sandpaper and remove any surface dust with a damp rag. Avoid using chemical paint removers, including paint etching compounds, since the residue may react with the tile adhesive.

Because wallpaper adhesives are too weak to support a heavy wall of tile, all wallpaper should be stripped before tiling. (Although some properly attached vinyl wallpapers could theoretically support this weight, I'd remove them, too, and not risk the need for later repairs.) After removing the wallpaper, wash, scrape or sand away any residual glue and remove any surface dust with a damp rag. With papered or painted walls (assuming this is to be a dry installation), I recommend using as the adhesive a latex thinset (first choice), a water-mixed thinset or an organic mastic.

Linoleum and synthetic sheet flooring

Floor tiles in a dry installation can be set over uncushioned linoleum or resilient vinyl or asphalt flooring, provided the existing flooring is firmly attached to the subfloor and is not cracking or peeling. Although this method is common in the trade, it is not an ideal situation. Hidden layers cannot easily be identified or qualified.

Note, however, that tile should not be set over cushioned flooring or multiple layers of sheet flooring, because these layers can compress with the weight of the tile and cause the joints to crack. Instead, all the layers should be removed and a new backer-board underlayment attached to the subfloor. To find out if you have multiple layers of sheet flooring, cut into the flooring at an unobtrusive spot, such as under the refrigerator.

The tile adhesives recommended for this kind of renovation require careful substrate preparation, which always involves removing wax, oils or other contaminants, and may also require abrading the surface. Because of the hazards associated with asbestos, it is important that you identify the flooring you wish to cover. Some building districts may allow asbestos materials to be encapsulated, whereas others may require it to be removed. Either way, your state may have a program to help you determine asbestos content.

Once you have ascertained that the synthetic flooring does not contain asbestos, rough up the surface with 80-grit or coarser sandpaper to improve the adhesive grip. Use an epoxy thinset adhesive on this bed, or a thinset mortar recommended specifically for renovation work. Though I was skeptical when I first heard of tiling over linoleum, I have found that this flooring, when properly prepared and coupled with an epoxy adhesive, will give good service. If the installation is to be a wet one, however, the sheet flooring should be removed and replaced with another suitable, properly waterproofed setting bed.

Plastic laminate

Plastic laminate in good condition makes an excellent surface for setting tile, since it's flat, solid, relatively stable and waterproof. To prepare laminate surfaces for tile, remove grease and any waxy film, then rough up the surface with coarse sandpaper. Epoxy adhesive should be used over plastic-laminate surfaces. Since most laminate surfaces are already waterproof, no additional membrane is needed for waterproofing. In heavy-duty applications, or in situations where the strength or stability of the material is in question and cracked tiles might be anticipated, a crack-isolation membrane applied to the laminate surface might be helpful to lessen any problems.

Ceramic tile

Renovation plans sometimes call for new tiles to be installed over existing ceramic-tile installations. This installation is acceptable as long as there are no structural problems below the existing tiles (such as wood rot from water damage), the existing setting bed can handle the new load, and the old tiles are attached securely to the setting bed.

Note that although it is possible to utilize an existing field of tiles as a setting bed, it may not be wise to assume that such a setting bed does not require additional waterproofing or crack isolation. A major factor in selecting renovation techniques over the more usual remove/redo strategy is often the cost of removing the existing tilework.

If you choose to renovate tiles in a wet area with a floor drain, it is advisable to flood-test the area for leaks first. If flood-testing is not practical, look for signs of leaks in lower ceilings, exposed joists, studs, and so forth. Just because the old

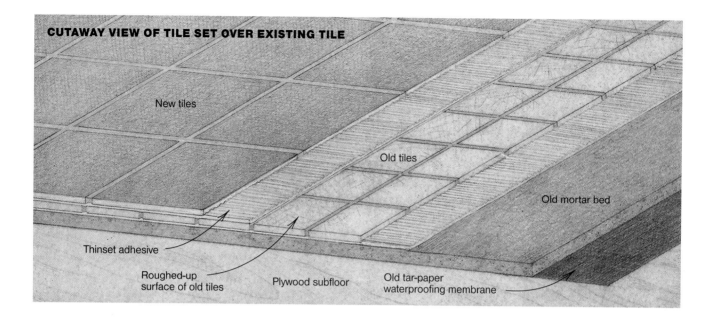

CUTAWAY VIEW OF TILE SET OVER EXISTING TILE

New tiles

Old tiles

Old mortar bed

Thinset adhesive

Roughed-up
surface of old tiles

Plywood subfloor

Old tar-paper
waterproofing membrane

tiles are in good shape does not mean that the old waterproofing membrane is still intact. If there is any doubt, add a waterproofing membrane. If the new tiles are bonded directly over hairline cracks in the old tiles, the cracks, however small, may eventually telegraph through to the new tiles. To help prevent this, a crack-isolation membrane should be used.

Ask your tile supplier for installation products designed for renovation over existing tilework. Normally, the surface of the old tiles will require abrading. On small residential installations, this can be done manually with carbide-grit sandpapers or masonry rubbing stones. On large areas, power grinders and portable shot blasters are a better choice. If your supplier does not carry an adhesive specific for this type of renovation, I recommend an epoxy because of its strong grip. Check the label of the product you want to use to make sure that it's suitable.

If the old tiles have a cushioned (i.e., rounded) edge, the old grout joints may be about 1/16 in. lower than the surface of the tiles. To ensure an even application of

thinset on this type of bed, you may want to fill in and level the grout joints before spreading adhesive over the full bed. Before doing this, however, consider the size of the tile being set. Large tiles can be set over this slightly uneven surface without a problem, but small tiles, such as 1-in. mosaics, will conspicuously highlight the unevenness of the bed. Prepare the surface according to the adhesive manufacturer's instructions and fill in the grout-joint grid with the same adhesive you will use to install the tiles. Use a flat trowel to press the adhesive firmly into the depressed joints, cut away the excess and allow the material to dry thoroughly before spreading fresh adhesive and setting the tiles.

Sheet metal

Unsupported sheet metal normally makes a poor base for ceramic or stone tiles. The sheet metal found on some manufactured fireboxes is backed with a fireproof board similar to cement backer board. If this is the case and the sheet metal does not flex more than a normal tile substrate would, it may be covered with tile (get approval in writing from the sheet-metal manufacturer first). Sand away any paint on the surface down to the metal, rough up any porcelain coating and grind away rust with an abrasive wheel.

If the metal does flex, laminate a piece of backer board with epoxy adhesive to the paint-stripped metal, then set tiles. Allow plenty of room for expansion and contraction and use an epoxy thinset that will bond to the metal and stand up to the heat. (Always use a 100% solids epoxy to avoid rusting metal setting beds.) When grouting tiles that are subject to a hot environment, be sure that all the joints are densely packed. And to ensure greater durability, use a latex- or acrylic-modified grout.

Mortar bed

A bed of mortar makes an excellent surface for setting tiles, though, as explained in Chapter 3, mortar work requires considerable skill. There are two kinds of mortar beds being used today: three-coat beds and one-coat beds. The three-coat method (base, level and bond) is very old and uses a base or scratch coat of coarse mortar floated over a reinforcing mesh, followed by a leveling coat of finer mortar. The tiles are then attached to the still-plastic leveling bed with a bond coat of mostly pure cement. As each section is covered with tile, its joints are usually filled with grout, which can then damp-cure with the rest of the sandwich.

The one-coat method in popular use today produces a mortar setting bed with just one layer of mortar. Tiles can be attached with a bond coat while the bed is still plastic, known as "wet setting"; or they can be bonded to the bed after it has dried, what the trade refers to as "thin-setting." I prefer to allow the mortar to dry before I set tile, since this allows me to concentrate on making the floor, wall or countertop surface as flat and dense as possible without having to fuss with the tiles.

MORTAR MIXES

Mortar is made of sand, cement and water. Varying the proportions of these ingredients and sometimes adding other materials produces different kinds of mortar. The two types of mortar that can be floated to produce a substrate for tiling are deck mud, used for floors and countertops, and wall mud, which, as its name suggests, is applied to walls.

DECK MUD

Deck mud is made, according to the Tile Council of America (TCA), by mixing roughly one part portland cement to six parts sand and approximately one part water (many factors may cause these proportions to change somewhat, including the weather, the characteristics of the sand and the use of additives). There are various recipes for deck mud, but all generally produce a strong mortar that can support the heavy loads a floor will bear. Deck mud should be rather dry and crumbly in consistency and should not spread like plaster.

WALL MUD

Wall mud is made by combining portland cement, sand and water with lime to make a mix that's plastic enough to spread on walls. The TCA recommends making wall mud with roughly one part cement, five parts sand, one-half part lime and enough water to produce a smooth, spreadable mixture. The lime, sold in powdered form in large sacks at building and masonry supply houses, makes this mortar sticky and enables it to grip the reinforcing mesh added to the surface before floating. Because more water is added to wall mud than to deck mud to make it spreadable (and because of the addition of lime), the grains of sand in wall mud are spaced farther apart. The resulting mortar is therefore weaker than deck mud and should not be used on floors.

FLOATING A MORTAR BED The basic process of floating a mortar bed, whether for a floor, countertop or wall, is deceptively simple. On the surface being floated, two strips of wood, called float strips (or sometimes screeds or grounds), are positioned parallel to each other and several feet apart (the distance depends on the size of the area being floated). The strips are securely anchored in columns of mud, with their top surfaces leveled at the intended height of the bed. Mortar is then distributed and compacted between the float strips. Next a third piece of wood or aluminum, called a screed, is positioned to straddle the float strips. This screed is moved side to side and at the same time pulled forward in a sawing motion to scrape away the excess mortar (see the drawing below).

Next any voids left in the surface are filled with mud and leveled with a wood float. The float strips are then pulled into the next area to be floated, and the empty channels are "backfilled" with mortar, compacted and leveled with the wood float. This sequence continues until the entire area being floated has been compacted and screeded.

Once the bed has been floated, it should be allowed to cure, or harden, before tile is set on it. The reason for this is that mud shrinks very slightly for about a week or so after floating, with most of the shrinkage occurring within the first 24 hours. If you're working in 70°F weather, wait overnight before tiling. If the temperature is closer to 50°F, you may need to wait longer for the bed to harden, perhaps two full days. By waiting, you avoid the difficulties involved

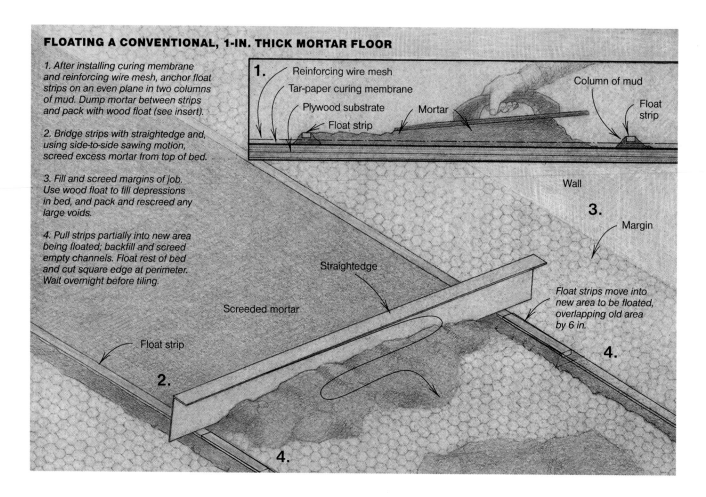

FLOATING A CONVENTIONAL, 1-IN. THICK MORTAR FLOOR

1. After installing curing membrane and reinforcing wire mesh, anchor float strips on an even plane in two columns of mud. Dump mortar between strips and pack with wood float (see insert).

2. Bridge strips with straightedge and, using side-to-side sawing motion, screed excess mortar from top of bed.

3. Fill and screed margins of job. Use wood float to fill depressions in bed, and pack and rescreed any large voids.

4. Pull strips partially into new area being floated; backfill and screed empty channels. Float rest of bed and cut square edge at perimeter. Wait overnight before tiling.

1.
Reinforcing wire mesh
Tar-paper curing membrane
Plywood substrate
Float strip
Mortar
Column of mud
Float strip

Wall

3.
Margin

Float strips move into new area to be floated, overlapping old area by 6 in.

4.

Straightedge

Screeded mortar

Float strip

2.

4.

in setting tile on a wet bed. To take best advantage of a mortar bed's potential, it is important that the bed be given enough time to set up undisturbed, and then be carefully smoothed flat with a wood float.

If the mortar you plan to use does not include a latex or acrylic additive, you will have to damp-cure the bed for 28 days before any tiles can safely be installed. This is a vital step if the bed is to last. Damp curing is messy, time-consuming and schedule wrecking. I heartily recommend you include admixtures that eliminate the need for damp curing (just about all latex or acrylic admixtures do this, but check your brand to be sure). A particular mortar's actual set-up (or curing) time may vary with each batch mixed and will be affected by numerous factors, including the brand of ingredients used and the weather.

Whatever the type of installation, all mortar beds must be placed over a curing membrane (see p. 111) and be reinforced with a layer of wire mesh, theoretically placed in the middle of the bed. Positioning the wire this way is not problematic with floor installations, but for walls the mesh is usually stapled directly to the subwall. Whenever possible, I use galvanized expanded metal mesh. When this is not available, I will use 2-in. by 2-in. welded wire mesh, or even poultry netting. I do not recommend poultry netting (1-in. mesh) for mortars not made with a latex or acrylic, or in areas subject to climate extremes. And finally, mortar beds, like any other tilesetting bed, may require waterproofing and/or crack isolation.

Self-leveling compounds

Self-leveling compounds (SLCs) made specifically for tile are designed for spot leveling or truing up entire floors. Most SLCs are available in sacks in dry form, and require only light mixing with water to become activated. After that, they need only to be poured onto the surface to be leveled. Within minutes, the material spreads out and becomes level. Within hours (for some quick-setting brands), they are ready to receive tiles.

The recommended maximum thickness for most SLCs is around 1 in. If your leveling application requires a depth greater than this, use $\frac{1}{2}$-in. to $\frac{3}{4}$-in. exterior plywood as a filler to reduce the quantity of SLC needed for leveling. Alternatively, you can wait for the first layer of compound to dry and then pour a second layer (check with the manufacturer's specs first). Additional preparations include providing dams or stops where needed, plugging voids with tape, caulk or fiberglass insulation, and providing for plenty of ventilation (which may be difficult in wintertime).

On particularly large applications, it may be more practical to contract with a self-leveling service company (see the Resource Guide). Either way, the SLC must be installed with the same considerations as for any other setting bed. That is, it must be strong enough to carry the expected load, it must be given room to allow for normal expansion and contraction, and it must be used with a waterproofing, crack-isolation or sound-control membrane when required. Make certain you choose the appropriate bagged material for your application, and if you select an SLC contractor to do the work, get a warranty in writing.

As with any other material that is to be used as a setting bed for ceramic tile, the virgin surface of a self-leveling compound is the best base for tile. Don't allow other tradespeople on this kind of floor until the tiles have been set, the grout installed and finished, and enough time given for all the mortars, both adhesive and grout, to harden and cure.

General Room Preparations

Before you begin a tile installation, there may be things other than the surface of the area being tiled that need preparation. You may, for example, need to remove the plumbing fixtures in a bathroom or trim the bottom of a door to accommodate the added height of the tile. The following are general instructions for these preparations, but since each area is a complex subject unto itself and space is limited here, I recommend that you consult a good household-repair book with detailed information on plumbing and electrical work.

Plumbing fixtures

When tiling a bathroom floor, you must work around a toilet and often a sink support. Instead of leaving these fixtures in place and cutting tile to fit around them, they should be removed so the tiles extend under them. The results will be much more attractive and professional-looking, and the job will be easier in the long run. By running the tile under these fixtures, you'll also reduce the number of exposed joints that will need to be maintained over the life of the installation.

REMOVING A TOILET To remove a conventional two-piece toilet, take out the tank and bowl together. Before removing the toilet, disinfect it by pouring a quart of liquid bleach into the tank and flushing. When the tank has refilled, locate the shutoff valve for the water supply line behind the toilet and turn off the water. Then flush again, this time holding the handle down until the tank empties. To remove as much of the water remaining in the bowl as possible, use either a small hand-operated bilge pump to pump the water into a nearby drain (like the tub, for example), or a plumber's helper to push the water through the trap. Stuff some old rags or paper towels into the bowl to keep any remaining water from sloshing around, but make sure you remove them when you replace the toilet!

Before removing the anchoring bolts, disconnect the water supply line from the wall or the toilet with an adjustable wrench. Then gently pry off any porcelain caps covering the two or four bolts holding down the bowl. If there are four bolts, the front two usually will be screwed directly to the floor and the rear set will extend through the toilet base to connect with the closet flange, or connector between the toilet and waste pipe. Often the front bolts will be corroded and break off as you try to unscrew them, but replacement bolts can be bought at a plumbing supply store. The back bolts may also be corroded and snap off when unscrewed, or they may just spin when you try to undo the nuts. If they spin, try gently pushing the tank sideways, which will snug up the lower end of the bolt and allow the nut to unscrew. If you can't budge the bolts, try using Liquid Wrench to dissolve the corrosion, or, as a last resort, saw the bolt in two with a hacksaw blade.

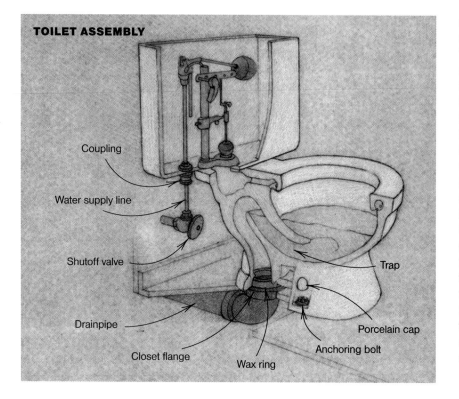

TOILET ASSEMBLY

Coupling

Water supply line

Shutoff valve

Drainpipe

Closet flange

Wax ring

Trap

Porcelain cap

Anchoring bolt

After unbolting the toilet, remove the fixture and carry it to another room to get it out of your way. It's a good idea to get a helper, since the toilet will weigh between 30 lb. and 60 lb. and should be kept level to keep any remaining water in it from sloshing about. Next remove the old wax or plumber's putty ring, which seals the connection between the toilet and the flange. I suggest putting on gloves to do this job. Place a gloved hand into a plastic bag, grab hold of the ring, and, with your other hand, turn the bag inside out to enclose and remove the ring. Then clean and remove the flange below the ring, which connects the bowl to the waste pipe.

After preparing the surface of the setting bed, set tile to within $\frac{1}{8}$ in. of the flange. The top of the flange should be installed flush with or no more than $\frac{1}{4}$ in. higher than the finished height of the tile. If the flange is lower than the tile, this may prevent the wax-ring gasket from sealing properly. In this case, replace the flange to accommodate the new floor height. Then install the new ring, which should be at room temperature when put in place in order for it to seal the connection correctly. Finally, replace the bowl and tank, simply reversing the dismantling process.

REMOVING A SINK There are three basic types of sinks around which you might tile: pedestal sinks, wall-mounted sinks and countertop sinks. For purposes of tiling, pedestal and wall-mounted sinks (the kind with supporting "legs") should be treated just like toilets; that is, they should be removed and the entire floor beneath them tiled. A rimless countertop sink can either be removed before the counter is tiled and then be reinstalled, or it can be left in place and the tiles set over its lip. Tile is often set over self-rimming sinks, too, though it's far easier to remove the sink from the counter-top and reposition it over the newly tiled surface. Almost any sink can be left in place, however, if the situation demands it.

The initial steps in removing any of these sinks are the same. First, cut the water off at the sink shutoff valves and then disconnect the water supply lines from the sink or the

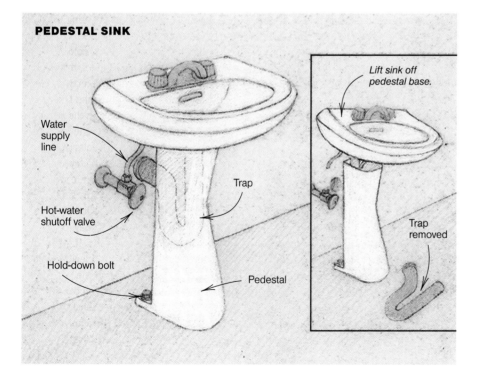

PEDESTAL SINK

Water supply line

Hot-water shutoff valve

Hold-down bolt

Trap

Pedestal

Lift sink off pedestal base.

Trap removed

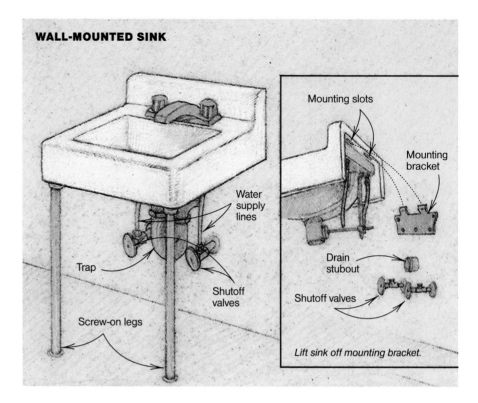

WALL-MOUNTED SINK

Mounting slots

Mounting bracket

Water supply lines

Drain stubout

Trap

Shutoff valves

Shutoff valves

Screw-on legs

Lift sink off mounting bracket.

wall (there's no need to take off the faucet or control valves unless they need replacing). Finally, remove the trap from the sink with a pipe wrench.

To remove a two-piece pedestal sink (see the drawing on p. 91), first unbolt the top and lift it off the base; then unbolt the pedestal and lift it from the floor (you may have to reach around the back of the pedestal to find the bolts). For a single-unit pedestal sink, simply unbolt it from the floor and wall. To dismantle a wall-mounted sink (see the drawing above), first remove any legs supporting the front of the sink. Then dislodge the sink from the wall bracket in which it's mounted and lift it off the bracket. If you will be tiling the wall behind the sink, particularly if you plan to use thick tiles, you may have to remove the bracket and shim it out to compensate for the thickness of the new tile. One way to do this is to mount the bracket to the wall through a plywood "shim." If the bracket

is designed to be installed on a finished surface, it will, of course, need to be removed from the wall and repositioned on top of the new tiles.

If you want to remove any of the several types of self-rimming countertop sinks, including the integral sink and countertop, first unscrew the pressure clips that secure the bowl on the underside of the sink rim or the full sink countertop to the vanity. Then, with a putty knife, cut the sealing material—usually caulk—between the sink and countertop or between the sink countertop and vanity, pry up the sink or countertop and lift it out.

If the faucet and control valves are not attached directly to the bowl of the sink, they need to be removed for tiling the countertop. With the water shut off and the water supply lines disconnected, remove the nuts underneath the counter-top that hold the valves in place. Then tile right to the edge of the mounting hole. If this is to be a thinset installation, the

COUNTERTOP SINKS

RIMLESS SINK

Unscrew clamps on underside of sink and lower it away from countertop.

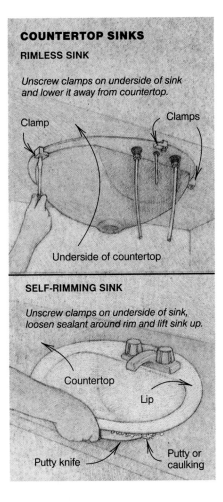

Clamp

Clamps

Underside of countertop

SELF-RIMMING SINK

Unscrew clamps on underside of sink, loosen sealant around rim and lift sink up.

Countertop

Lip

Putty knife

Putty or caulking

shanks on the valves should be long enough to accommodate the added height of the tile. If the tile is to be installed with a mortar setting bed, you may need to install valves with longer shanks. When reinstalling the valves, pack the area around the shanks with plumber's putty, not grout—grout would harden and make any future repairs very difficult.

If you're tiling around the water supply and drain lines in the wall behind a sink, the tile should be set no closer than ⅛ in. to the pipes—¼ in. is better. These joints should later be caulked with plumber's putty or silicone caulk, rather than grouted, because the expanding and contracting pipes will inevitably crack the grout.

REMOVING A SHOWER HEAD Most shower heads are a three-part assembly consisting of a shower head, gooseneck and escutcheon plate (see the drawing at right). The gooseneck screws into a fitting located in the wall, and the escutcheon plate slips over the gooseneck to trim the hole in the wall. When tile is set around a shower head, the gooseneck should be treated just like any other pipe. That is, tiles should be set to within ¼ in. of the gooseneck and the void around it filled with silicone caulk.

If you won't be replacing the walls or adding backer board to install tile and you don't have major demolition work to contend with, you don't have to remove the shower head before tiling. Simply slip a plastic bag over it (freezer bags work best) and tape the end of the bag around the gooseneck. The bag will protect the shower head from stray globs of adhesive. Otherwise, though, I'd recommend removing the entire shower-head unit to prevent damaging its finish. To do this, pull the escutcheon plate away from the wall, and unscrew the gooseneck from the fitting in the wall, using a pipe wrench if necessary (protect the finish of the gooseneck by wrapping it with a rag or duct tape).

When you're ready to install the backer board, screw a pipe nipple into the fitting. A nipple is simply a short length of water pipe, maybe 5 in. or 6 in. long, that's threaded on one end and capped at the other—you can borrow one from your plumber or buy one from any plumbing supply store. The nipple temporarily substitutes for the missing gooseneck and ensures that the hole cut into the backer board for the gooseneck ends up in the right place. It also keeps the fitting threads from getting fouled with adhesive as the tiles are being set. When you're ready to tile, the tiles should then be set to within ¼ in. of the nipple. After the tiles have been grouted, remove the nipple and replace it with the shower-head assembly.

COMMON SHOWER-HEAD, TUB-SPOUT AND FAUCET ASSEMBLIES

In each case, tile to within ⅛ in. to ¼ in. of fitting and fill void with silicone caulk.

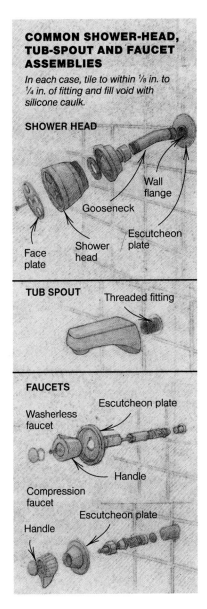

SHOWER HEAD

Wall flange

Gooseneck

Escutcheon plate

Face plate

Shower head

TUB SPOUT

Threaded fitting

FAUCETS

Escutcheon plate

Washerless faucet

Handle

Compression faucet

Escutcheon plate

Handle

Before pressing the escutcheon plate back into place, fill the void around the gooseneck with plumber's putty.

If you're installing a new single-handle control valve in the shower, the unit will come with a plastic setting gauge that shows the exact mounting depth for the valve. This gauge usually will be positioned flush with the surface of the tile and removed after the tiles have been installed. The wall is then tiled to within $\frac{1}{8}$ in. to $\frac{1}{4}$ in. of the gauge. After the tiles have been grouted, the gap around the valve is covered by a chrome or brass escutcheon plate. This plate often has a foam strip adhered to its underside to seal out water between the plate and the tiles. A second foam strip seals the valve handle from water. If the plate has no foam sealing strips, use silicone caulk to do the same job.

TUB SPOUTS Many tub spouts use a threaded pipe to connect with the water supply line, while some newer spouts have a clamp that cinches the spout to a $\frac{1}{2}$-in. copper pipe soldered to the supply line. Either way, remove the spout, and tile to within $\frac{1}{4}$ in. of the pipe. Before replacing the spout, pack the void between the threaded pipe or the copper pipe and the tile with plumber's putty or silicone caulk.

Appliances

Before tiling a kitchen floor, check to make sure that any dishwasher or trash compactor will still fit under the countertop with the additional height of the tile. Tilework should always extend underneath these and any other kitchen appliances, though these are good places to use up cut waste pieces or tiles whose glaze is flawed. If the dishwasher or trash compactor will sit too high to fit under the countertop, either raise the height of the entire countertop, or, if the counter has a lip, notch out this lip to allow the appliances to be slipped in place.

Heating pipes

Some baseboard heating elements and radiators have hot-water delivery pipes that protrude through the floor. When tiling floors with such pipes, tile only up to within $\frac{1}{4}$ in. of these pipes and fill the void with silicone caulk instead of grout. This treatment allows the pipes to move around without scraping noisily against the tiles.

Electrical outlets and boxes

When tiles are set on a surface containing electrical outlets, the utility boxes must be made flush with the surface of the tiles. If you are setting tiles directly on the existing floor or wall, that surface is likely to become $\frac{3}{8}$ in. to $\frac{1}{2}$ in. higher. In this case, you will need to reposition the box to make it flush with the surface of the tiles. Alternatively, you may be able to purchase a box extender from an electrical supply house or hardware store.

If you need to change the position of an electrical box or eliminate it altogether, things get more complicated. In either case, consult a good electrical repair book or hire an electrician.

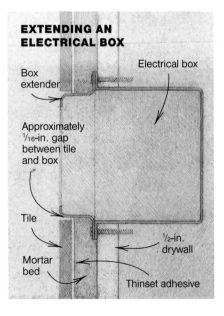

EXTENDING AN ELECTRICAL BOX

Box extender

Electrical box

Approximately $\frac{1}{16}$-in. gap between tile and box

Tile

Mortar bed

$\frac{1}{2}$-in. drywall

Thinset adhesive

Trimming doors

If you raise the height of an existing floor with tile, you may need to trim the bottom of any doors in the room to accommodate the new floor. There are several ways to trim off the bottom of a door, but the method I like is the following: Remove the doors before beginning the tilework. Once the tiles have been set and grouted, measure from a point on the lowest jamb hinge to the top of the tile and subtract ¼ in. from this figure for clearance (see the drawing at right). Then measure down this distance from the corresponding point on the door's hinge, mark a line along the bottom of the door and cut away the door's excess with a power or hand saw. Keep in mind that this system only works when the floor is level.

Thresholds

To create a smooth transition between floors of unequal height or different materials, a threshold can be used. Oak makes a durable threshold that is easily cut on a table saw and installed by screwing it into the substrate. Marble makes an elegant threshold, and most marble dealers can supply one sized to your needs. Install the marble with thinset adhesive. Aluminum thresholds are becoming common at exterior openings because they allow for various weather-stripping details. If you have to install one yourself, screws sunk into the substrate will hold it securely.

Sometimes thresholds can be installed directly over the tile, for example, at a doorway between two rooms that will be tiled. Generally, however, thresholds will be installed directly on the substrate, and the tile will be brought up to the threshold. Thresholds can be installed either before or after tiling. When tiles are to be set up to an existing threshold, they should be kept ¼ in. away from the threshold and the joint filled with silicone caulk. If you can, adjust the layout of the tiles so that you don't end up with a sliver of tile at the threshold.

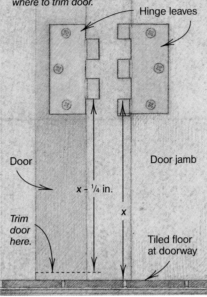

TRIMMING A DOOR TO CLEAR A NEW TILE FLOOR

1. Measure distance from point on jamb hinge to newly tiled floor. Subtract ¼ in. from this distance for clearance.

2. Measure this distance from corresponding point on door hinge to bottom of door to determine where to trim door.

Hinge leaves

Door

Door jamb

x – ¼ in.

x

Trim door here.

Tiled floor at doorway

When you're tiling up to a threshold over which a door will close, the last grout joint should be positioned so that more than just a thin edge of tile is visible when the door is closed. Again, this requires a careful layout before tiling. And if you're tiling between two rooms joined by a door and threshold, remove both fixtures before tiling. The door will, of course, need to be trimmed before it is replaced.

Chapter Six

■ ■ ■

Expansion Joints and Membranes

Because building materials have different rates of expansion and contraction, all tile installations need to be isolated from the inevitable movement caused by daily heating and cooling cycles and from regular seasonal changes. Cushioning the tilework against normal structural movement is the job of expansion joints, which are intentional interruptions in the hard materials used to make up a tile installation. In addition to expansion joints, some tile installations may also require waterproofing, crack isolation, curing or sound-control membranes. This chapter will explain how expansion joints and membranes work and how they can be incorporated into any tile installation.

Expansion Joints

An expansion joint is nothing more than a space provided to allow adjoining materials to expand and contract without damaging themselves or their neighbors. The earliest tile installers unwittingly accommodated the need for expansion space on some installations by attaching and grouting tiles or mosaic chips with asphalt gum; thus the entire installation was able to accommodate movement. Of course, works such as these could support very little weight and in hot weather were quite messy.

Through the centuries, technical improvements in materials and methods led to the development of more appropriate expansion joints. These joints were positioned between rows of tiles—usually at a grout-joint location—and were filled with a resilient material instead of hard grout. Although such joints worked well enough, they tended to look obvious and unattractive. It was not until the recent development of color-matched caulks and sealants that expansion joints could be made to perform reliably and look attractive.

Industry practice would seem to indicate that expansion-joint requirements apply more to large commercial spaces than to residential units. In fact, the TCA *Handbook* (see p. 72) states that rooms less than 12 ft. wide do not need expansion joints within the field of tiles. However, because of other specifications, even a small floor needs, at the very least, an expansion joint around the perimeter of the floor. Here are the minimum requirements:

• Expansion joints are required wherever there is a change in the backing materials, or where tilework meets or abuts perimeter walls, ceilings, curbs, columns, pipes and other penetrations or restraining surfaces.

• Expansion joints are required wherever tilework passes over control, expansion, seismic, cold, construction or other structural joints.

• For interior tilework not exposed to direct sunlight or moisture, expansion joints should be located every 24 ft. to 36 ft. in each direction.

• For exterior tilework, or interior tilework exposed to direct sunlight or moisture, expansion joints should be located every 12 ft. to 16 ft. in each direction.

Placement of joints

Depending on the size of the installation, a tile job may require a network of expansion joints within the field of tile or simply a perimeter joint at the margins (see the sidebar at left for standard industry requirements). The listing below outlines specific expansion-joint locations for the most common residential installations.

FLOORS   On all floor-tile installations, there must be an expansion joint wherever the floor meets a perimeter wall, except on those installations where cove tiles are used around the base (cove tiles require a special joint, as explained in the sidebar on p. 101). On remodeling, restoration or repair jobs where the floor is composed of two different materials (such as a concrete slab used to extend an existing wood subfloor), an expansion joint located directly above the break is required to accommodate the different rates of expansion or contraction of the two backing materials.

Any curbs or columns, whether tiled or finished with other materials, should be isolated from the floor tiles with an expansion joint. Similarly, pipes that penetrate a tiled floor, especially those carrying hot water, must be isolated from the surrounding tilework with an expansion joint. Heating pipes grinding noisily against hardened grout can turn a cozy domestic scene into a house of horrors during cold weather.

As the size of a floor grows, so does the need for expansion joints within the field of tile (see the sidebar at left for specific requirements). On multiroom floor installations, continue the perimeter joint through the doorways at the threshold, as shown in the top drawing on the facing page.

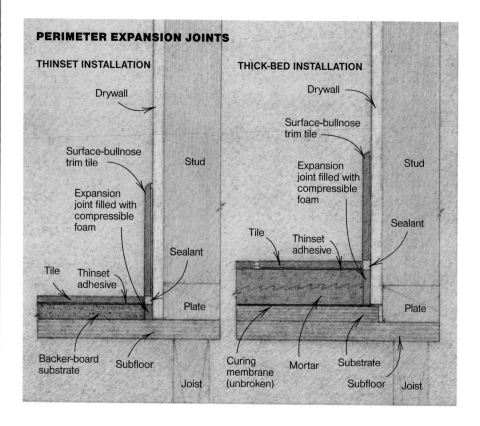

PERIMETER EXPANSION JOINTS

THINSET INSTALLATION

Drywall

Surface-bullnose trim tile

Stud

Expansion joint filled with compressible foam

Sealant

Tile   Thinset adhesive

Plate

Backer-board substrate   Subfloor

Joist

THICK-BED INSTALLATION

Drywall

Surface-bullnose trim tile

Expansion joint filled with compressible foam

Stud

Sealant

Tile   Thinset adhesive

Plate

Curing membrane (unbroken)   Mortar   Substrate

Subfloor   Joist

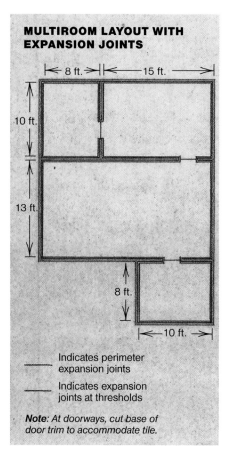

MULTIROOM LAYOUT WITH EXPANSION JOINTS

─── Indicates perimeter expansion joints

─── Indicates expansion joints at thresholds

Note: At doorways, cut base of door trim to accommodate tile.

A floor-tile installation on a concrete slab will require additional expansion joints if the slab was produced with cold joints, control joints or expansion joints. Cold joints are cracks that appear when fresh concrete is poured next to an existing slab (as when a concrete slab is enlarged to accommodate a remodeling project). Control joints are partial interruptions in a slab that are intentionally placed to direct or channel cracks that will eventually appear after the concrete has hardened. Control joints can be formed or molded while the concrete is still plastic or saw-cut after the concrete has hardened. Concrete-slab expansion joints are produced when two neighboring slabs are separated by a resilient filler strip placed before the concrete is poured.

These three types of slab joints are most commonly used on commercial installations, but they may also be found on residential construction. Plans may also include seismic joints in the slab. If tiles are to be applied on slabs that have any of these construction joints, an expansion joint must be incorporated into the field of tile located directly above the joint in the concrete (see the drawing below).

WALLS Most wall-tile installations in North American homes are located on shower walls or backsplashes where plumbing fixtures are mounted. As with floor work, pipes through tile walls need to be isolated with an expansion joint. Another reason for surrounding plumbing fixtures with caulk or sealant is for ease of removal should the fixture need repair or replacement. If the fixture were locked in tight with grout, the surrounding tiles might be damaged during removal of the fixture.

STEAMROOMS A steamroom within a residential stall shower makes excellent use of tile to help protect the rest of the structure from water damage. However, unless the tiles are protected from the extreme heat (and the expansion/contraction cycles it brings to the steam-room environment) with expansion joints, the installation will inevitably fail. Expansion joints are required at all junctions between

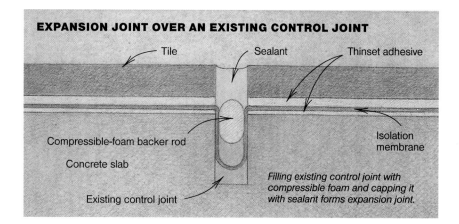

EXPANSION JOINT OVER AN EXISTING CONTROL JOINT

Tile

Sealant

Thinset adhesive

Compressible-foam backer rod

Concrete slab

Isolation membrane

Existing control joint

Filling existing control joint with compressible foam and capping it with sealant forms expansion joint.

DETERMINING THE WIDTH OF JOINTS

The recommended width for an expansion joint differs depending on whether the installation is interior or exterior (interior tilework exposed to direct sunlight should be treated as exterior tilework).

For most residential interior installations (quarry, paver and other floor tile), the expansion joint should be the same width as the grout joint, but no less than ¼ in. For ceramic mosaic tile and glazed wall tile, the joint can be reduced to ⅛ in., though ¼ in. is preferable. Keep in mind that these are minimums. Since most of the installations I design have ⅛-in. grout joints, I double the number of expansion joints within the field of tiles rather than use the recommended ¼-in. width. If you have any doubt, increase the number or width of joints.

For exterior tilework, expansion-joint width is based on the frequency of the joint grid and the temperature difference between winter lows and summer highs. The industry recommendations are ⅜ in. minimum width for joints 12 ft. on center and ½ in. minimum width for joints 16 ft. on center. For each 15°F greater than 100°F between the winter low and summer high temperature range, minimum widths must be increased ¹⁄₁₆ in.

the floor and wall surfaces, at all junctions between the wall surfaces and the ceiling, around all plumbing fixtures penetrating the wall and, especially, around the steam intake. (For more information on steam-room installations, see p. 215.)

COUNTERTOPS Countertops require expansion joints where the deck tiles covering the work surface meet those applied to the backsplash, and also between the deck tiles and any fixtures let into the deck area, such as sinks, cooktops, chopping boards and other built-in appliances (see the drawing below).

Making expansion joints

An expansion joint is comprised of an open slot, a compressible filler or backup, and a capping of caulk or sealant. Making an expansion joint around the perimeter of a floor-tile installation is relatively easy since all that is needed is empty space running from the surface of the tile to the bottom of the substrate. Simply hold the substrate and the tiles a minimum of ¼ in. away from the face of the wall and position the compressible filler approximately half the width of the joint below the surface of the tile. Finish the joint by installing the caulk or sealant after the tilework and grout are dry. Usually the perimeter of the floor is then finished with a baseboard of tile, wood or other material, which covers the expansion joint. For this reason, perimeter joints do not have to resemble grout joints.

Making expansion joints within a field of tiles or at a cove-tile joint, however, requires precision on two fronts. First, the layout of the tiles must place the grout joint used as the tile expansion joint directly above any construction joints below the

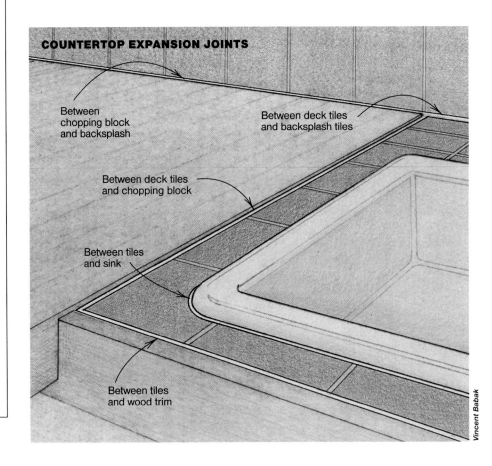

COUNTERTOP EXPANSION JOINTS

Between chopping block and backsplash

Between deck tiles and backsplash tiles

Between deck tiles and chopping block

Between tiles and sink

Between tiles and wood trim

Vincent Babak

COVE-TILE EXPANSION JOINTS

To my eye, no tile installation is more beautiful than a floor finished with cove tile. The gentle curve renders the edge of the floor somewhat invisible and makes for very easy cleaning. Unfortunately, few cove tiles get a proper installation, and the result is invariably a very unsightly crack running along the curve of the tile. A crack appears here because walls and floors tend to move against one another. If the joint between the floor tile and the cove tile is filled with grout, there is no free space to absorb the movement and the cove tile starts to crack midway between the floor and the wall. By filling the joint with resilient material instead of grout, the joint becomes a hinge that allows movement without damage.

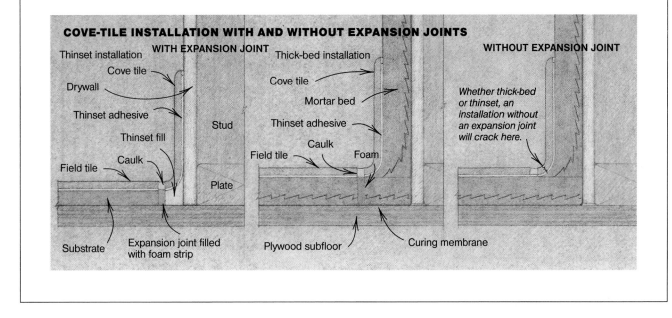

COVE-TILE INSTALLATION WITH AND WITHOUT EXPANSION JOINTS

WITH EXPANSION JOINT

Thinset installation
Cove tile
Drywall
Thinset adhesive
Thinset fill
Field tile
Caulk
Stud
Plate
Substrate
Expansion joint filled with foam strip

Thick-bed installation
Cove tile
Mortar bed
Thinset adhesive
Caulk
Field tile
Foam
Plywood subfloor
Curing membrane

WITHOUT EXPANSION JOINT

Whether thick-bed or thinset, an installation without an expansion joint will crack here.

tilework. (To ensure that expansion joints and construction joints will coincide, it's important to work with the architect and general contractor during the planning stage.) Second, because these expansion joints are visible, they should mimic the appearance of the grout joints so that they do not diminish the look of the finished installation. Here's how I proceed for visible expansion joints.

Once the tiles have been installed and grouted (see Chapter 8), I scour all the expansion joints and slice away any globs of adhesive or grout (using the blunted tip of an old margin trowel to avoid puncturing any membrane below the tiles). After scraping out the excess, I go over the slots with a vacuum cleaner to remove all the debris.

Once all the slots are clean, I install the compressible filler strip. I like to use a filler material called backer rod (see the drawing on p. 99), which is round in cross section and available in a variety of widths for a snug fit in the expansion slot. The backer rod should be positioned approximately half the width of the joint below the surface of the tiles. Here, it controls the ultimate thickness of the sealant used to cap the joint, so that when the sealant has cured it can accommodate maximum movement without destroying itself.

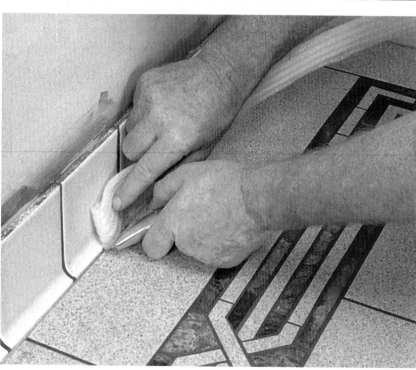

Sloan Howard

Once the expansion slot has been cleaned of debris (top left), install a compressible filler strip (such as sill seal) along the length of the slot (top right). Trim the filler back below the surface of the tiles (above).

If backer rod is not available, I use sill seal, which can be obtained from most building supply companies. I cut the sill seal into strips about 2 in. to 3 in. wide, tuck each strip into the slot with the edge of a trowel, and then trim it back with a sharp knife. As with backer rod, the sill seal should be positioned about half the width of the joint below the surface of the tiles.

CAULKING THE JOINT Sometimes a compromise has to be made when selecting a material to cap an expansion joint. For me, this means choosing between a caulk or sealant that is durable and one that is color-matched to the surrounding grout. The approach I take is to select durable sealants for heavy-duty (commercial) applications. These sealants, such as silicone and polysulfide, are available in a limited color range and are difficult to apply and finish.

For regular-duty, residential applications, I sacrifice durability for invisibility and select a material that closely matches the grout. The material I prefer to use is a caulk that's available in any color (and also sanded or unsanded, so that even its texture will match the grout used to fill the other joints). The brand I use (see the Resource Guide) cleans up easily with water.

As shown in the photos at right, I fill the joint with caulk and then tool it with my finger (you can also use a striking tool). Using the same general technique as for cleaning grout (see pp. 150-153), I then wash the excess caulk with a sponge, making several passes until the excess has been removed and the surface of the caulk is uniformly smooth and even. Since the caulk is somewhat soft, it's important to use a light touch to avoid gouging the joint. Once I've finished sponging the caulk, I remove any excess water from the tiles to prevent any spotting of the drying caulk. After about 15 to 20 minutes—when the caulk has started to stiffen—it's a good idea to check that all the excess caulk has been removed.

Whatever brand of caulk or sealant you use, follow all the manufacturer's instructions regarding preparation of the slot, backing, application temperature and humidity, and curing requirements.

Maintaining expansion joints

When properly made and finished, expansion joints need no special treatment to keep them clean other than wiping spills promptly to avoid staining. Clean with water and a mild detergent, just as you would maintain the tiles.

Because expansion joints move and flex and get abraded and torn, they will eventually wear out. Sometimes the entire system of joints will need replacement; at other times, only a spot repair is needed. Either way, use a sharp knife to cut through the sides of the sealant bead and pull the resulting strip away from the joint (the underlying backer rod may come with it). Trim or scrape away all traces of the old sealant, reline the slot with backer rod as needed, and apply fresh caulk or sealant.

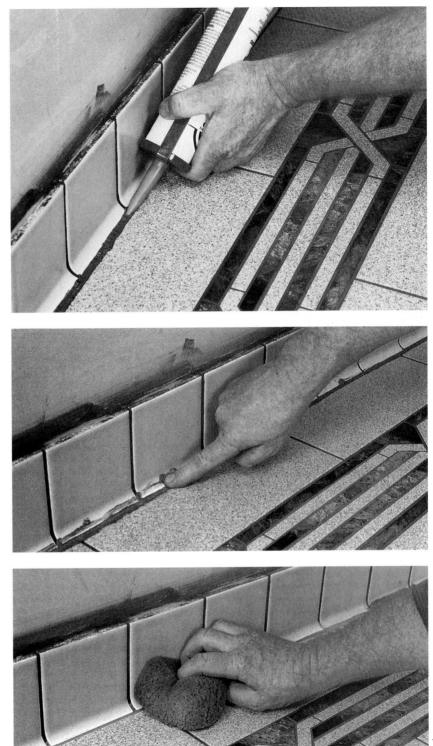

Cap the filler strip in the expansion joint with caulk (top), tool the caulk with your finger (middle) and then clean off the excess with a sponge (above).

Membranes

For thousands of years, all kinds of membranes have been used with ceramic tile. Membranes can be made from a variety of materials, but whether constructed of lowly tar paper or a sophisticated chemical compound, all share the same purpose: They protect the tile installation from damage or deterioration. Membranes are used to combat the problems of water damage to the substrate (waterproofing membranes), unequal seasonal movement of dissimilar materials in the installation (isolation membranes, also called cleavage membranes), premature curing of mortar beds (curing membranes) and noise (sound-control membranes).

Sometimes a single membrane can do more than one job, and its function—or functions—depends on the type of membrane you select. For example, the chlorinated polyethylene (CPE) sheet membrane I recommend (see p. 106) can be used for either waterproofing or crack isolation.

Waterproofing membranes

For years consumers have thought of ceramic tiles as the ultimate protection against water damage to walls, floors and other surfaces. While it's true that ceramic tiles themselves are not harmed by water, they afford little or no waterproofing protection to what lies beneath them. It is the installation as a whole, not just the tiles, that provides, or fails to provide, the protection. Many claims are made regarding a material's ability to resist water. As an installer, you must be able to make a distinction between materials that are water-resistant and materials that can serve as a barrier to water. Many tile installation materials are able to resist water for a time, but without a water-

proofing membrane as part of the setting bed, no tile installation located in a wet area can fully protect the supporting structure from damage.

Water that regularly penetrates an installation can cause serious problems. It can weaken the bond of the tile adhesive and eventually damage the substrate. Moisture seeping through a shower floor to a wood subfloor, for example, will promote rot and provide nourishment for wood-destroying organisms. Additionally, the weakened subfloor will not provide much support for the tile installation, and substantial cracking in the tiles or grout joints will inevitably result. These problems are easily prevented if a waterproofing membrane is incorporated into the installation.

There are several different materials that can be used for waterproofing membranes, and the choice depends on budget, availability and where the membrane is to be located in the installation. When used above the water-line (on shower walls or tub surrounds, for example), the membrane needs only to shed water. When the waterproofing membrane is used below the waterline (on sunken tubs or shower floors, for instance), however, it must be made of a sturdier material so that it can contain and channel water into a drain to which it is attached. (See pp. 211-214 for a full discussion of installing this type of membrane, which is known as a shower or tub pan.)

As a professional installer, I have to select from a variety of materials to suit budget and other requirements. The following list includes those materials that I have used over the years; some are basic and easy to use, while others are high-tech and require considerable patience and dexterity to install, but all have served me well.

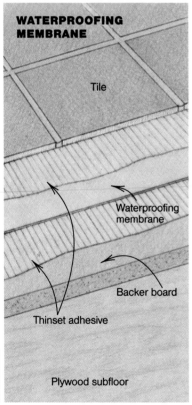

WATERPROOFING MEMBRANE

Tile

Waterproofing membrane

Backer board

Thinset adhesive

Plywood subfloor

Vincent Babak

WHEN TO USE A WATERPROOFING MEMBRANE

Personal experience in the repair end of the tile business has shown me the absolute importance of a waterproofing strategy in residential and commercial tile applications. Rather than make it a nuisance that gets in the way of my tile installations, I take waterproofing seriously and have learned how to blend the artistic with a bit of technology.

Tile and many installation materials are unaffected by water, but that does not mean they will function as barriers to water. In fact, the secret to tile longevity in residential installations is to assume that water will find its way through to the structure.

A tile floor in a dry location (such as a hallway) would naturally be considered a dry installation and require no waterproofing membrane. However, if the owners insist on giving it a daily wash, it should be considered a wet installation. An infrequently used tub/shower in guest quarters is a light-duty wet installation, but if your two kids use it the rest of the time, it's heavy duty. Tar paper or polyethylene film would suffice for the light-duty installation, but the heavy-duty installation calls for a sheet membrane or trowel-applied membrane. Although not every tile installation needs to be built like a diver's watch, it is important that the materials chosen for the job are up to the task.

TAR PAPER   First on the list is tar paper (or tar-saturated felt paper), a staple of most installers and widely available in 1½-ft., 2-ft., 3-ft. and 4-ft. wide rolls in 50-ft., 100-ft. and 150-ft. lengths. Costing only pennies per square foot, this paper will last for about 30 years and requires minimal labor to install. When used to protect walls, tar paper is stapled or nailed directly to studs or drywall (see the photo on p. 106). While many setters use tar paper alone, if the framing is drywalled I increase its protection against water by embedding it in a thin layer of asphalt roofing cement spread with a ⅛ in. V-notched trowel over the entire substrate. To protect large areas, upper layers of tar paper should overlap lower courses by at least 2 in. and for insurance the seam should be sealed with more asphalt. (For a full discussion of installing a tar-paper membrane, see pp. 177-179.)

A modern alternative to tar paper is polyethylene film. Available in a variety of widths, lengths and thicknesses, this material can be stapled or nailed to studs or drywall in one continuous piece and should give good service for 20 years or so. If you select polyethylene film for waterproofing, don't use anything less than 4 mil thick.

One drawback with a tar-paper (or polyethylene) waterproofing membrane is that it should be used only behind setting beds that are completely water-resistant—namely, cement backer boards or mortar beds. If backer board is used, it can be combined with tar paper (or polyethylene) only for wall installations, since the board's manufacturers specify that, when used for floors, backer board must be laminated directly to the subfloor with an approved adhesive. Backer board used for a wet floor installation must therefore be paired with a waterproofing membrane placed on top of, rather than below, the setting surface.

While traditional installation methods have relied on tar paper and tar- or asphalt-based materials, many thinbed applications require more refined waterproofing materials. New waterproofing membranes are being developed continually, but not all are equally effective. Two types

Tar paper is a low-cost, durable waterproofing membrane suitable for use on tub surrounds or shower walls.

fibers, need only be laminated to a substrate with a thin layer of thinset mortar (the same adhesive I use to install the tiles on top of the membrane).

CPE membrane is available in a variety of lengths and widths, and individual pieces can be bonded together to protect large areas (see the sidebar on p. 211). It can be used to waterproof most substrates, including backer board, drywall, plywood, concrete slabs, mortar beds and metal surfaces. The only requirement prior to application is that the substrate must be prepared as it would be for tiling; that is, the surface should be flat, level or plumb, and clean (see the sidebar on standard specifications on p. 72). Although this material is more expensive per square foot than tar paper, its cost is offset by its effectiveness and versatility; CPE membrane is unbeatable when maximum waterproofing is needed.

The membrane is installed by laminating it to the setting bed with latex thinset. Once the substrate has been prepared, comb on a layer of latex thinset with a ⅛-in. or 3⁄16-in. notched trowel (the coarser the substrate's surface, the larger the notch size needed). Next place or unroll the membrane over the adhesive and smooth it out with a standard floor roller. Although the instructions for this material call for a heavy floor roller, lightweight hand rollers and even short straightedges can be used as long as the CPE sheet achieves a 100% bond against the adhesive. To check the bond, pull back a corner of the membrane, as shown in the top photo on the facing page. You should find an even layer of thinset on both the floor and the membrane. If you don't, pull up the sheet, apply more thinset and comb it with a trowel with larger notches.

If the job requires a membrane wider than 60 in. (the standard width), the 2-in. bare edges of two or more sheets can be overlapped and fused with solvent (see manufacturer's instructions for complete details and check the MSDS for proper

of membranes designed specifically for thinbed use that have given me consistently good performance are sheet membranes and liquid (or "trowel-applied") membranes.

SHEET MEMBRANES   Sheet membranes are my personal favorites because their waterproofing qualities are determined by the factory where they are made—not by how thick or thin the installer needs to spread a coating (see below). The sheet membrane I use, a 30-mil thick sheet of chlorinated polyethylene (CPE) bonded between two layers of unwoven polyester

handling and application). If the surface of the membrane is covered with fibers, you'll need to pull these away before bonding the seam (see the bottom photo at right).

Although it is possible to begin tiling immediately after the sheet is installed, I prefer to wait overnight or longer until the thinset mortar has hardened. (Because the sheet is a moisture barrier, it may take longer for a thinset mortar to harden and dry enough to support the tile installation work without becoming delaminated from the substrate).

TROWEL-APPLIED MEMBRANES   Although sheet membranes are my first choice for waterproofing large unbroken expanses of tile, such as a commercial floor, trowel-applied membranes are ideal for smaller, complex installations with lots of plane changes, such as stairways, or for areas where sheet membranes are difficult to work with (as on a tiled ceiling).

Unlike penetrating liquids, which protect only the material being treated, trowel-applied or liquid membranes protect the material and prevent water from passing through it. Trowel-applied membranes are available in a variety of forms, including latex, sand/cement/latex mixtures and single-component urethanes (for a caution regarding single-component urethane membranes, see the sidebar on p. 108).

All are designed to be used with fiberglass, polyester or other types of reinforcing fabric. The fabric should cover the entire substrate to be protected, unless the substrate is cement backer board. Because backer board is already reinforced, fabric is required only at joints between individual boards, at upturns (such as the junction between a floor and a perimeter wall, or between a countertop and a backsplash) and at downturns (such as a step down into a sunken tub).

Although specific installation instructions vary from manufacturer to manufacturer, the process of installing a trowel-applied membrane involves spreading a uniform layer of liquid (or paste) over the surface to be treated, embedding the fabric into the liquid where needed, and then covering the fabric with another coat of liquid (see the drawing on p. 108). After this coat dries, instructions may call for one or more additional coats to complete the membrane.

After spreading thinset adhesive on the area being covered with a CPE membrane, pull back a corner of the membrane to check the coverage (top). If the edge of the CPE is covered with fibers (above), remove them before bonding a seam between two pieces of membrane.

SINGLE-COMPONENT URETHANE MEMBRANES

Unlike trowel-applied membranes made from latex or sand/cement/latex mixtures, single-component urethane membranes can be negatively affected by the presence of too much or too little moisture in the substrate.

Single-component urethanes require a small amount of moisture to cure, which they can obtain from either the air surrounding the installation or the structure itself (from the moisture within a concrete slab, for example). If there is too much moisture present, however, these membranes have been known to foam and expand while curing, which creates air pockets and weak spots within the membrane and can result in cracked tiles. If you choose this kind of trowel-applied membrane, check with the manufacturer for instructions on how to determine and maintain proper conditions.

INSTALLING A TROWEL-APPLIED WATERPROOFING MEMBRANE

Drywall setting bed

Liquid

Fabric

Liquid

Thinset adhesive

Tile

1. Apply a thick coat of liquid part of membrane system to setting bed using a roller, brush or trowel.

2. Cover liquid with fabric, allowing liquid to bleed through.

3. Apply thick top coat of liquid over fabric and let dry 24 hours before tiling.

The trowel-applied membrane I prefer is a ready-to-use latex that requires no mixing before application. It is packaged with a roll of polyester reinforcing fabric and a gauge to ensure that enough material is deposited on the substrate. To install the membrane, I begin by preparing the substrate as I would for tile. I spread the material over the substrate with a notched trowel, using the same technique as for applying a tile adhesive: the smooth side to force the material into the substrate, the notched side to build up the thickness, and the smooth side again to flatten out the ridges (see the top left photo on the facing page).

I use the gauge supplied by the manufacturer to ensure that I am depositing the right amount of material on the substrate. If the gauge indicates that the layer is too thin, I switch to a trowel with larger notches; if it's too thick, I'll use one with smaller notches. Depending on site conditions and the type of substrate, I may use a $\frac{1}{8}$-in., $\frac{3}{16}$-in. or $\frac{1}{4}$-in. notched trowel.

As with all kinds of trowel-applied membranes, it's best to precut and prefit all fabric sections prior to applying any liquid. If you are working alone with large pieces of fabric, roll up the fitted cloth and then unroll it onto a fresh liquid layer. If you are working with a helper, have a hand at each corner of the fabric, stretch it tightly and then lower it onto the liquid layer.

Either way, the cloth will probably need some additional smoothing. Use the edge of a trowel, a wide putty knife or a straightedge to pin the fabric in place, while smoothing out the fabric with another trowel until it is embedded in the liquid. If the cloth gets dredged out of position, tug it back and flatten it with the trowel. If you're applying membrane over backer board and need only install the fabric at the corners, your task will be considerably easier (see the photos on the facing page).

Once the entire area is covered, I allow the membrane to dry (which takes about 30 to 60 minutes for the brand I use). Then I go over the area again with another coat of liquid. To avoid damaging the membrane—and to obtain the maximum adhesion between the membrane and the tiles—schedule tile installation as soon as possible after the membrane has dried or cured (as always, check the manufacturer's instructions). If the tilework must be delayed, cover the fully cured membrane with a sheet of plastic film (4 mil or thicker) to keep dust from settling on the fresh surface, and protect the membrane from other damage by topping the plastic with drop cloths, tarps or protective paper.

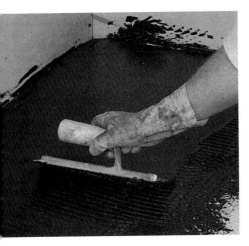

Use a notched trowel to spread the membrane over the substrate (far left) and check thickness with a manufacturer-supplied gauge (left).

Open the floor only to limited foot traffic. For wheeled carts, ladders or extensive activity over a fresh membrane, cover with sheets of plywood or flakeboard until the tiles can be installed.

Crack-isolation membranes

Crack-isolation membranes have been used in tile installations for thousands of years to prevent cracks or joints in the underlying foundation from telegraphing through solid material and damaging the tiles installed above. On many ancient installations, a layer of asphalt between the tiles and the substrate allowed for expected movement. A layer of tar paper beneath a mortar bed is still used for thick-bed installations, but for thinbed work there are other options. Most modern tile membranes can do double duty, and the crack-isolation membranes I use are the same materials (applied the same way) that I use for waterproofing.

Every time I use a crack-isolation membrane, I know I am taking a risk because it is not reasonable to assume that a tile installation can "glue" together a building that has problems. I rely on close observation to determine if the installation is worth tiling, and inform my customer in writing that there are no guarantees. Determining the need for crack isolation is rarely an exact science (see the sidebar

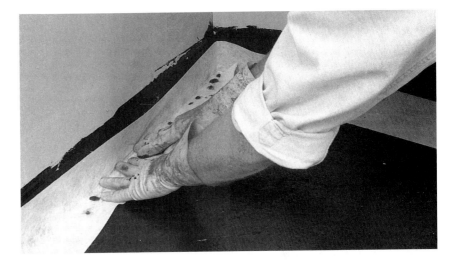

When installing a trowel-applied membrane over backer board, reinforcing fabric is required only at joints between boards and where the floor meets the perimeter wall. Embed the fabric in the liquid (top), allow it to dry and then cover with another coat of liquid (above).

All construction materials, including those used for tiling, undergo a certain amount of internal movement as the climate and seasons change. Oftentimes the movement in one layer of the tile sandwich is slight and only negligibly affects the adjoining layers. At other times, however, the movement in the substrate or setting bed can be significant and produce enough stress in the installation to crack the tiles. To protect against this, an isolation membrane should be used whenever you suspect that movement within the setting bed may cause cracking in the tiles.

If you're tiling over an existing setting bed that seems structurally sound, has no visible cracks and is in a home or building that has fully settled, chances are that no isolation membrane is needed. If you see signs of cracking or you sus-pect minor structural weakness, however, an isolation membrane is called for.

Don't expect any isolation membrane to "cure" a deficient structure—that can be done only by rebuilding. If the setting bed consists of abutting sections installed at different times (a concrete floor with a later extension, for example) or is made of different materials (a plywood floor adjoining a concrete slab, for example), an isolation membrane is essential. In short, any setting bed—whether mortar, concrete, masonry, plaster, drywall, old tiles or some combination thereof—that may crack with seasonal or minor structural movement should have an isolation membrane installed over it to separate it from the tile above.

above), but there are some basic guidelines you can follow when tiling over concrete slabs or wood construction.

OVER CONCRETE SLABS Most savvy building designers acknowledge that concrete is expected to crack. For this reason, long runs of concrete are abbreviated with control joints or interrupted with expansion joints to help control the expected cracking (see p. 99). Nevertheless, even on ideal concrete slabs, a crack-isolation membrane may be required. There may be a risk of cracking on just a portion of the floor, say where it might thin out over a raceway, conduit or pipes. Spot problems like this can sometimes be repaired with an isolation membrane "bandage" (see the drawing on p. 224). For this technique to work, however, all grout joints lying along the perimeter of such problem areas should be filled with an elastomeric sealant, thereby completing the isolation of the tiles

from the anticipated movement. But if cracks begin to appear on a new concrete slab at random, the entire slab should be suspect and completely blanketed with an isolation membrane and carefully located expansion joints.

There are two basic kinds of cracks on concrete slabs—structural and shrinkage (see the drawing on p. 84). Structural cracks, often characterized by a difference in surface height on opposite sides of the crack, usually indicate serious problems within the structure itself, not in the concrete. You should not attempt to install tiles over this kind of crack or expect a crack-isolation membrane to give even marginal results. Shrinkage cracks usually show no difference in height and are usually caused by an improper cure or mix, by changes in temperature or by seasonal movement. Shrinkage and other nonstructural cracks less than $1/8$ in. wide may be controlled with a crack-isolation membrane, subject to the approval of the manufacturer.

OVER OTHER SUBSTRATE The potential for cracking exists in other substrates as well. Plywood is particularly vulnerable because of its active rates of expansion and contraction. On installations where the substrate materials change—conditions often found on remodeling or renovation jobs—a crack-isolation membrane can reduce cracking (see the drawing at right). Another likely spot to include a crack-isolation membrane would be under tiles installed as part of a radiant-heating system. A thin crack-isolation membrane may also be used to reinforce a marginal installation whose height limitations might rule out adding thicker materials.

Prior to settling on a particular membrane, contact the manufacturer or qualified representative and discuss the particulars of your installation. Just keep in mind that no system can completely eliminate cracking. If claims are made otherwise, get them in writing and hope the manufacturer is still in business when you need help.

In some respects, latex- or acrylic-modified thinbed mortars, because of their inherent flexibility, offer some protection against cracking, but when a crack-isolation system is called for, a real membrane that breaks the direct contact between a tile and its substrate should be used. For this reason, my preference for crack isolation is the same CPE membrane I use for waterproofing. Its two outer skins of polyester fabric allow it to be bonded to a substrate, and allow tiles to be attached to its top side. Its inner core of CPE provides the break between the two and prevents movement in the setting bed from telegraphing through to the tiles. Around complicated areas where a sheet membrane might be difficult to install, I use a trowel-applied membrane.

Curing membranes

All mortars (including mortar beds, thin-set mortars and grouts) need to retain moisture for them to cure properly. In the past, curing was accomplished with membranes that isolated the mortar from the drying effects of underlying surfaces or the surrounding air. Permanent curing membranes were placed between the mortar bed and its supporting substrate to prevent moisture from wicking into the substrate. Temporary curing membranes were used to cover fresh mortar beds or freshly grouted tiles (a process known as "damp curing") to prevent moisture from evaporating into the air. Damp curing requires up to seven days and involves misting the fresh mortar with water—a time-consuming and laborious task.

The use of latex and acrylic additives has minimized the need for damp curing, but all mortar beds produced with these additives should still be separated from subsurfaces with a curing membrane (either 15-lb. tar paper or 6-mil plastic film).

Sound-control membranes

As walls and floors become thinner and thinner, many installations, such as multifloor commercial or office space, require sound attenuation beneath ceramic or stone tiles. Sound-control membranes are available in sheet or trowel-applied forms, just like crack-isolation and waterproofing membranes. Some may be multipurpose membranes, while others may be specifically for sound control. Installation is the same as for the other types of membrane described above. As with the other specialty membranes, it is very important to run a projected use by one of the manufacturer's technical representatives for approval.

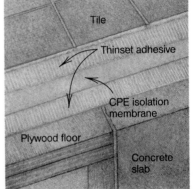

ISOLATION MEMBRANE

An isolation membrane placed on top of setting bed protects tile from stress of seasonal movement in bed, which is exaggerated if bed is composed of two adjoining surfaces made of different materials or installed at different times.

Tile

Thinset adhesive

CPE isolation membrane

Plywood floor

Concrete slab

Chapter Seven

Layout

Tile catalogs were once filled with drawings of ceramic tile and trim in nearly infinite variety. Almost anything imaginable was available in tile, including ceramic window stools, ceramic rosettes and even ceramic crown molding, and rooms were frequently designed around the tile. Tilesetters were involved with the design of a building from an early stage, since it was, after all, tougher to make tile conform to a particular dimension than it was to cut and shape plaster or wood to conform to the tile.

Sometimes I dream of those days. Contemporary setters rarely enjoy the luxury of having the other trades work around them, and the layout of a tile installation must account for the unexpected and the out of square. Although I've never met another setter who lays out tile the way I do (aside from those I've trained), my techniques have proven themselves over the course of many installations.

My training in layout, however, did not begin with tile but in the machine shop at a steel mill. As an engineering student during the day and a machinist apprentice at night, I began my hands-on training at the layout table painting rough castings with whitewash and scribing reference lines to guide the precision machining each one required. When I left steel for tile, I brought the reference-line concept to my tile layouts and the mostly irregular world of construction.

The Importance of Layout

Layout allows me to "see" and plan out the way an installation will look before any tile is actually set. In effect, layout is a dress rehearsal of the real thing, presented graphically with a set of lines marked on the setting bed. Each of these layout lines represents the center of the grout joint between two rows of tile, and together these lines guide the setter in positioning the field of tile. Like an architect's blueprint, the assembled body of layout lines constitutes the tilesetter's plan of action.

For any tile job, there are two basic layout problems to contend with: arranging the tiles accurately in relation to each other, and arranging the entire field of tiles accurately in relation to the surrounding building and its features. Many tilesetters sidestep layout altogether and simply begin setting tile along the longest edge of the installation. Sometimes the results of this approach are fine, but, more often than not, using such an arbitrary starting point dictates an arbitrary look for the entire job. Small, trimmed pieces of tile, for example, may end up positioned at a doorway or another obvious spot, where full tiles would

look much better. By carefully considering the size and shape of the area being tiled and the size and shape of the tile itself, you can easily avoid such problems and produce an installation with the tiles placed exactly where you want them. Since layout is crucial to the ultimate look of the job and involves no expense other than time, I heartily urge you to begin any installation with this step.

I can't stress the importance of layout enough. Not only is it essential for producing a handsome installation, it's also necessary for accurately calculating the amount of tile needed for a particular job (see p. 121). Also, it's vital if you are to set a field of tile correctly on the first try, which is especially important if you're working with an adhesive that sets up quickly. Because layout entails carefully selecting and plotting out the best possible setting configuration before any tile is set, it

Working with a layout grid on a large job, one person can apply the adhesive while the other sets the tiles.

eliminates last-minute surprises, including, in the worst-case scenario, the need to reposition all the tiles on a wet bed.

In addition, the steps involved in layout point out any surface preparation needed before tiling can begin, and they unveil any framing or structural problems that would complicate an installation. A deft layout can also mask structural problems that might otherwise be prohibitively expensive to repair—a tapering hallway, for example.

Layout is especially helpful when you're working on a large job with a helper or crew. With the lines snapped on the setting bed, you can divide the labor—one of you can apply adhesive, while the other sets full tiles (see the photo on the facing page). Moreover, a minimum of verbal instructions to your co-workers will be needed.

Principles of Layout

Because tilework is actually a finishing process for floors, walls and countertops, it should, of course, be as attractive as possible. Many things affect the look of tilework, most obviously the color and shape of the tile selected and the pattern in which it is set. The visual impact of the finished job, however, is also greatly influenced by the physical placement of the individual tiles. Using a wide rather than a thin grout joint throughout a field of tile, for example, will considerably change the look of the installation (see p. 148 for more information on grout joints).

Working with cut tile

Perhaps first among the guidelines for laying out a handsome installation is to use as many full and as few cut tiles as possible. If a job requires that some tiles be cut, these trimmed tiles should be placed, if possible, away from the visual focal points—doorways, thresholds and in front of a fireplace. Only full tiles should be set in these areas. You may encounter situations when this guideline can be abandoned (I'll discuss them later), but the look of most jobs will improve if you minimize the number of cut tiles used.

When cut tile is necessary to fit a specific installation, no tile should be trimmed to less than half-size—a guideline that many architects, in fact, insist upon in their specifications for a job. It may be impossible to avoid small cuts in some L-shaped and multiroom layouts or when

POSITIONING CUT TILE SYMMETRICALLY

An installation will be more attractive if trimmed tiles are placed symmetrically wherever possible. For rows of cut tiles to be balanced, as in example 2, one full tile must be eliminated and size of cut tiles increased.

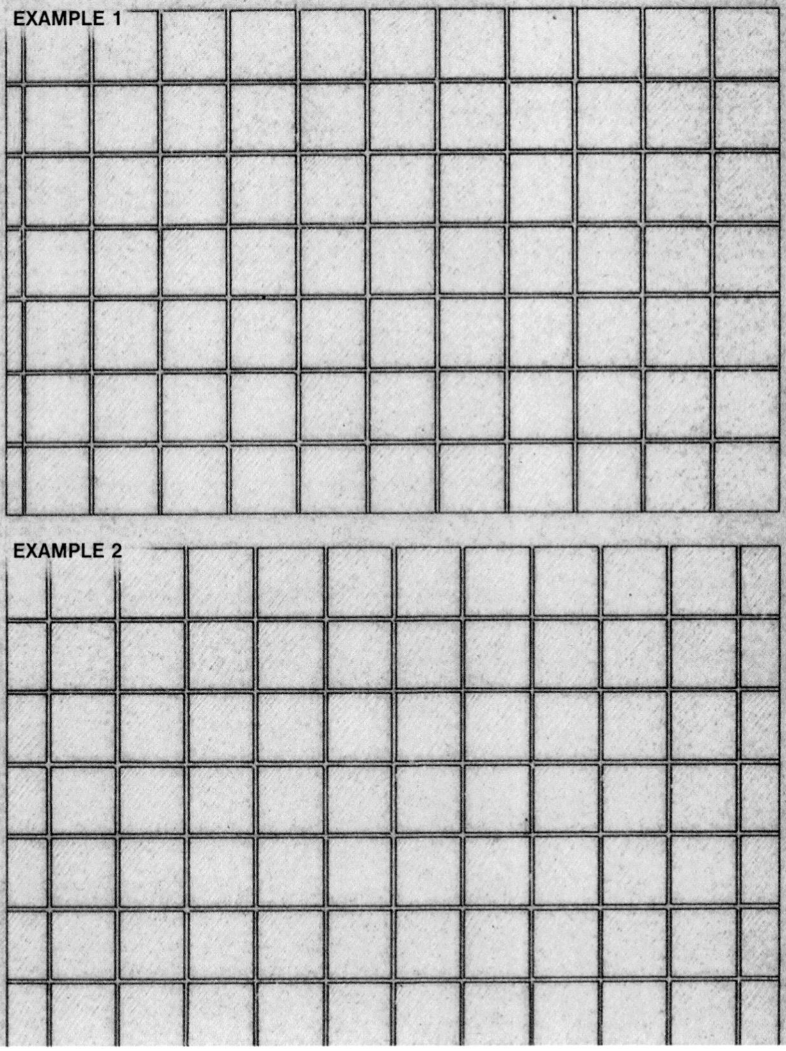

EXAMPLE 1

EXAMPLE 2

masking a particular structural problem, but careful adjustment of the layout will again downplay the visual impact.

When trimmed tile is called for, it should be positioned symmetrically if possible. That is to say, a job requiring a row of cut tile will be more attractive if that row is visually balanced by a second trimmed row on the opposite side of the field. If you find, for example, that 6 in. must be cut from a row of 12-in. square floor tiles where they meet a wall, it's best to cut 3 in. from that row and 3 in. from the row on the other side of the room. The floor will, of course, be covered either way, but the second option looks far better. Using two rows of cut tile means, of course, that the layout of the full tiles will shift, as shown in the drawing on p. 115.

Trimmed tile should also be positioned so that the cut edge is hidden from view wherever possible (see the drawing below). On floor and wall installations, this is easily accomplished, since these unattractive edges are usually masked by baseboard trim and moldings. On countertops, where the surface of the tile is routinely touched, all cut edges should be hidden by trim or buried beneath backsplashes.

Preparing for Layout

Layout is a process akin to solving a puzzle with a variety of solutions. Since each solution is likely to involve compromise, the goal of layout is to explore the various possibilities and pick the one that produces the most attractive installation with the fewest significant compromises.

The basic tools used for layout include an accurate tape measure, a carpenter's square, a spirit level, straightedges, a chalk line and a pencil. In a pinch, I have laid out a job precisely with nothing more than a tape measure and a pencil, but things are considerably easier if you have at least the tools listed above. A jury stick, sometimes called a story pole, is also an extremely useful tool to have. Easily made by the directions on pp. 125-126, this pole provides a quick means of measuring the number of full tiles that will fit into a given area. If your tool kit includes the following items, you might find them handy, too: a machinist's surface gauge for measuring heights, a depth gauge for measuring depth, and trammel points for extreme accuracy in projecting right triangles (needed to determine if a floor is square).

The area to be tiled should be checked to see if it's square (that is, if all its corners measure 90°) and plumb (vertically straight) or level (horizontally even). If the area is only slightly out of square, plumb or level and within the standard tolerance limits

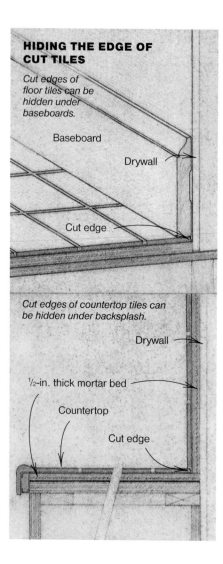

HIDING THE EDGE OF CUT TILES

Cut edges of floor tiles can be hidden under baseboards.

Baseboard

Drywall

Cut edge

Cut edges of countertop tiles can be hidden under backsplash.

Drywall

½-in. thick mortar bed

Countertop

Cut edge

(see the sidebar on p. 72), minor changes in the layout can be made to accommodate these conditions. If the area is more significantly out of square, plumb or level, the process stops for any required structural repairs or surface preparations. If the framing problems are serious, it may not be possible to tile at all.

Checking for square

The object of checking a floor, wall or countertop for square is to determine if the sides of the area being tiled are square to one another and can be used as reference points from which to plot the layout of the tiles. (In the case of a floor, this means figuring out if the walls enclosing it are square to each other.) If the surface being tiled is only slightly out of square, the effect on layout may be negligible. If that surface is more seriously out of square, however, the effect will be obvious (see the drawing below and, again, the discussion of tolerance limits).

Whether a floor or countertop is level or a wall plumb is of less concern than whether the surface's sides are square, because the out-of-level or out-of-plumb condition does not necessarily affect layout

to any significant degree. If the floor or countertop alone is being tiled and it's only slightly out of level, the effect on the job will probably be unnoticeable. Similarly, a single, slightly out-of-plumb wall can usually be tiled without a problem, provided the tile will not be bordered by a starkly contrasting material or a boldly patterned wallpaper (see the drawing on p. 118). If tile is to extend from a considerably out-of-level floor or countertop up the walls, however, or from a seriously out-of-plumb wall to an adjoining wall, the whole installation will look askew. In such cases, the floor, countertop or wall will require repair before tiling, or the setter may want to rethink the decision to extend the tile over the adjacent surfaces.

More often than not, floors, walls and countertops are at least slightly out of square, level or plumb, so the tilesetter should be ready for imperfect conditions. Even the most competent carpenter won't always leave behind square, level and plumb surfaces, so I approach every job as if the structure were totally out of whack—that is, I check all the surfaces to determine the problems. While assessing the extent of the problem is largely a subjective judgment,

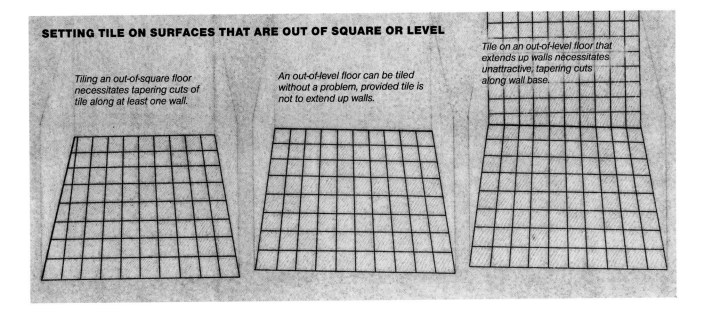

SETTING TILE ON SURFACES THAT ARE OUT OF SQUARE OR LEVEL

Tiling an out-of-square floor necessitates tapering cuts of tile along at least one wall.

An out-of-level floor can be tiled without a problem, provided tile is not to extend up walls.

Tile on an out-of-level floor that extends up walls necessitates unattractive, tapering cuts along wall base.

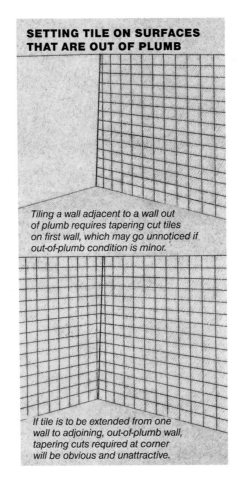

larger room, however, you'll get only a partial reading of the area if you check only the corners, since it's possible for them to be square even though the walls themselves are bowed along their length. To determine if a wall that's not too long is bowed, use a straightedge at least 6 ft. long, holding it against the wall and looking for gaps. For a longer wall, sight down the length of the wall as if you were eyeballing a stick of lumber for straightness. You can also stretch a string across the wall, keeping it about ½ in. from the surface, and compare the gap between wall and string at various points.

If you're tiling a floor that's complex in shape or unusually large, or that extends into several rooms, you can plot a 3-4-5 triangle on the floor to help you check if the walls are square to each other. The 3-4-5 triangle is simply a triangle with a 90° angle at one corner whose proportions are easy to plot in any size (see p. 123). You'll soon see how to use the triangle as a guide to aligning tile, but as an aid to checking a room for square, it acts like a giant, imaginary carpenter's square. (Information on checking for level and plumb is found on p. 73.)

Making a preliminary drawing

The layout process begins on paper, with a drawing of the surfaces to be tiled, showing all critical dimensions and features. Your preliminary drawing of a wall should note, for example, the exact location and size of any windows or doors, the location of electrical boxes, and the location and dimensions of any built-in furniture, particularly shelves and cabinets. Drawing a countertop may seem like a waste of time, but, particularly if you're a novice, the exercise is a valuable one. Note the location of sinks, abutting walls and any other feature that would affect the placement of tile.

Effort spent on a preliminary drawing really pays off when you're tiling a floor. Floor plans generally require the most

the guidelines presented in the sidebar on p. 72 are the industry standards that professional setters use in deciding when to repair walls and floors before tiling and when to forgo tiling altogether.

If a surface is within the accepted tolerance limits, an installer can make minor adjustments to the positioning of the tiles without seriously affecting the appearance of the finished tilework. For quality tilework on any structure beyond these limits, corrective measures should be taken (using a self-leveling compound, floating a mortar bed or rebuilding the surface). If the surface is seriously out of square, level or plumb and cannot be corrected, it should not be tiled—period.

You can check walls for square in a small area like a bathroom by simply holding a carpenter's square in each corner. In a

effort because the spaces to be tiled are larger, and there are many aspects of the room that can influence tile placement (see the drawing below). Your initial sketch should record the dimensions of the area being tiled, trace its perimeter and note everything in the space that will affect the installation, including doorways, thresholds, any obstructions (such as water pipes) and any surfaces that will adjoin the tile. Sometimes it's impossible to repair problem walls, so you should also note on the floor plan whether the walls enclosing the area being tiled are square to each other. Once finished, the preliminary drawing becomes part of your "reference library" for the job, and you'll find that you'll consult it frequently during the layout process.

Making a tile/grout-joint list and layout sketch

Once the preliminary drawing has been done, you can begin figuring out how the tile will fit in the area. While it's possible to

spread the actual tiles out on a floor or countertop (though not a wall) and move them around to try various layouts, this is physically tiring work, particularly on a large job. Besides, at this stage, you may not even have all the tile in hand. So in most cases you're better off figuring out on paper the layout of tile that best suits the space.

Working out a layout on paper involves calculations. Because the odds are good that the combined width of the selected tile and grout joint won't equal a nice, round number of inches, doing these computations in inches and feet can be difficult. Instead, I always compile a tile/grout-joint list, whose basic unit of measurement equals the width of a single tile and grout joint. I make the list long enough to compute the number of tiles needed to fit on the longest segment of the job. This list becomes an invaluable reference that's easy to use and far more reliable than juggling figures in my head. And by comparing this list with the

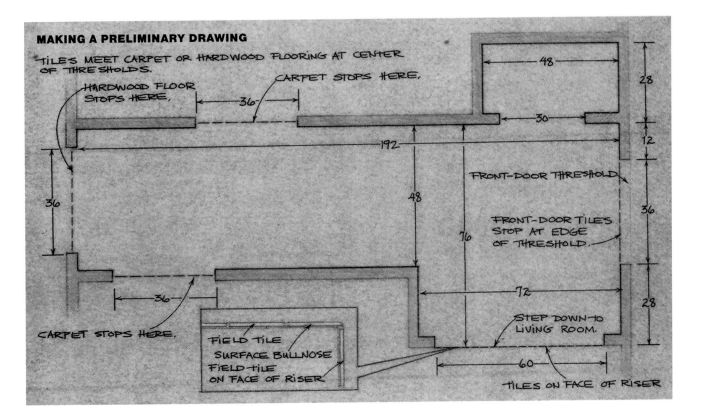

MAKING A PRELIMINARY DRAWING

TILES MEET CARPET OR HARDWOOD FLOORING AT CENTER OF THRESHOLDS.

HARDWOOD FLOOR STOPS HERE.

CARPET STOPS HERE.

48

28

36

30

192

12

36

FRONT-DOOR THRESHOLD

48

76

FRONT-DOOR TILES STOP AT EDGE OF THRESHOLD.

36

36

72

28

CARPET STOPS HERE.

FIELD TILE
SURFACE BULLNOSE
FIELD-TILE
ON FACE OF RISER

STEP DOWN TO LIVING ROOM.

60

TILES ON FACE OF RISER

TILE/GROUT-JOINT LIST

Since the combined width of a single tile (11⅞ in.) and its grout joint (⅛ in.) equals 12 in., the combined width of additional tiles and joints can be calculated as follows:

1 = 12 in.	*8 = 96 in.*
2 = 24 in.	*9 = 108 in.*
3 = 36 in.	*10 = 120 in.*
4 = 48 in.	*11 = 132 in.*
5 = 60 in.	*12 = 144 in.*
6 = 72 in.	*13 = 156 in.*
7 = 84 in.	

dimensions on the floor plan, I can immediately determine if a possible layout will work.

Because tiles vary somewhat in dimension, the only way to make an accurate list is to measure at least a few of the tiles you'll be setting. Thus, ideally, samples of the tile should be in hand before a tile/grout-joint list is worked up. If the tiles are readily available locally, I just purchase or borrow some. But if sample tiles are difficult to obtain—perhaps the tiles are being custom-made—I do the best job I can of estimating the combined dimension of tile and grout joint. If the actual tile turns out to be slightly different in size from the dimension that I used to work up the tile/grout-joint list, I can make up the difference by shifting the layout or running a larger or smaller grout joint. If the difference in size is appreciable, I prepare a new tile/grout-joint list.

To get a better idea of how a tile/grout-joint list is used, let's look at a very simple example, in which, for clarity's sake, I've purposely made the width of a single tile and grout joint equal a whole number of inches. (Later in this chapter I'll give examples of more complicated floor plans and tile/grout-joint dimensions.) Let's suppose a foyer floor measuring 12 ft. 2 in. square is to be tiled with 11⅞-in. square tiles and that the grout joints are to be

⅛ in. wide. The basic unit of measure for the tile/grout-joint list is therefore 12 in. By simple multiplication, I arrived at the list shown at left. This list shows the space required for the width of from one to 13 tiles and grout joints. The list stops at 13 tiles because I wouldn't need more than this many to span the full length and width of the floor.

By looking at the simple floor plan on the facing page and the tile/grout-joint list, I can see that 12 full tiles plus a 2-in. wide cut tile will fit across the floor's 146-in. length and width. Since the specifications for this imaginary job call for no tile less than half-size and since an asymmetrical row of trimmed tiles would be unattractive anyway, I want to avoid having two rows of 2-in.-wide cuts (one row across the width of the foyer, and one across the length). To do this, I need to "remove" both a row of full tiles and the row of cut tiles, then calculate the amount of space freed up (14 in.) and divide this figure by two (7 in.). This 7-in. figure becomes the size of the symmetrically placed trimmed tiles that will be set as the first and last rows across the width and length of the foyer.

On a more complex tile job, such as a large L-shaped room, the tile/grout-joint list allows you to see how shifts in the layout will affect the look of the job. If you want to see how using a slightly different width of

TILE/GROUT-JOINT DIMENSION

Tile,
11⅞ in. square

12

One tile/grout-joint dimension, 12 in. between centers of grout joints

Grout joint, ⅛ in.

grout joint will change the layout, it's easy enough to do another tile/grout-joint list. Over small distances, even a major change in the width of the grout joint may not make much difference in the layout of the tile, but over, say, a living-room floor, the difference could be significant.

Estimating tile

Once you've arrived at a layout on paper, you're ready to estimate the amount of tile needed for the job. Unless the planned layout uses full tiles only, there will be a certain amount of waste that must be accounted for when ordering the tile. This is where the layout sketch and tile/grout-joint list will prove particularly helpful.

The degree of accuracy needed for an estimate for tile depends partly on how complex the installation is and also on how easy the tile is to get—and return. When I'm dealing with a local supplier who has plenty of the tile I'll be using in stock, I can make an approximate estimate. If I under-order (something to be avoided if possible), I can quickly get more tile, though it's a nuisance to break setting stride to make a tile run. On the other hand, if I order too much tile, I can return the excess. An approximate estimate can be made simply by figuring the square footage of the job, adding 8% to 10% to cover waste and unforeseen circumstances, and then ordering enough tile to cover that adjusted square footage.

If the tile is difficult to obtain quickly or costly to return, however, or if the spaces to be tiled are complex, I'll do a more precise estimate. The most accurate way to figure out how much tile you'll need is to count the individual tiles called for in the layout. Often the results of this method are surprisingly different from those obtained with the square-foot method of estimating, and it's the individual-tile method that's more accurate. This discrepancy arises because manufacturers may assign an arbitrary grout-joint width to tile sold by the square foot in order to calculate the area a given amount of tile will cover.

Often the grout-joint size they figure on won't coincide with that planned for your installation, and hence the possible discrepancy between your calculations and the manufacturer's. Also, calculating by the square foot fails to take into account the number of full tiles that will be lost in making trimmed pieces, since each cut more than half-size must be cut from a full tile.

Square-foot vs. individual-tile count

Let's look at these two methods of estimating the amount of tile needed, again using the foyer floor as an example. Since this floor is 12 ft. 2 in. square, the square footage to be covered is approximately 149 sq. ft. (12.17 ft. x 12.17 ft. = 148.1, or, rounded off to the next whole number, 149 sq. ft.). With the combined width of the tile and grout joint being 12 in., I would figure that 149 tiles will be needed to cover 149 sq. ft. If I went to a tile store, though, and bought tile by the square foot (which is how it is often sold), using the manufacturer's coverage recommendations, I might end up with a different number of tiles for this job. I might well find that the manufacturer packaged this imaginary tile 25 pieces to the box, stating that one box would cover 26.6 sq. ft. What this means is that each tile should cover a little more than one square foot, a calculation that assumes about a $\frac{1}{2}$-in. grout joint. Thus, according to the manufacturer, I would need 140 tiles to cover the designated area.

Now let's see what the results are from actually counting the number of individual tiles called for in the layout. In checking my floor plan and tile/grout-joint list, I can see that the main area of the floor requires 121 full tiles, plus 44 tiles to make the rectangular cuts around the perimeter (only one 7-in. cut can be made from each $11\frac{7}{8}$-in. tile) and 4 tiles to make the square cuts in each corner, or a total of 169 tiles,

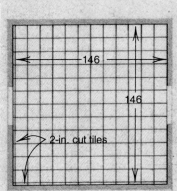

Twelve full tiles plus a 2-in. wide cut tile equals 146 in.

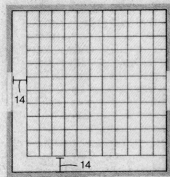

"Remove" cut tile and one full tile from length and width to free up 14 in. of space.

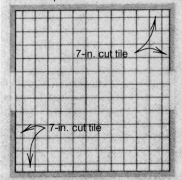

Fill 146-in. space with 11 full tiles plus a 7-in. wide cut tile on each side of field, distributing freed space evenly at edges of layout.

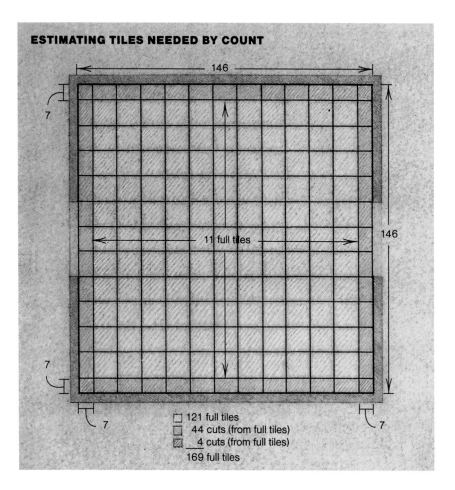

146

7

146

11 full tiles

7

7

7

☐ 121 full tiles
☐ 44 cuts (from full tiles)
▨ 4 cuts (from full tiles)
169 full tiles

Laying Out Floors

The general procedure for laying out floors, walls and countertops is basically the same. In effect, a wall is nothing more than a rectangular or square floor turned on edge, and a countertop is simply a floor made smaller. A floor can be both considerably larger than a wall or countertop, however, and more complex, sometimes extending into several rooms. As the floor's size and complexity increase, so too does the complexity of its layout. For this reason, let's begin with the most simply shaped floor, a square or rectangle, then move to floors with more complicated shapes and finally to multiroom installations. If you can lay out a floor, you'll have little problem laying out anything else.

Plotting reference lines

I've talked to a lot of novice tilesetters and heard a lot of stories about their first tiled floor. Just about every new setter ends up cussing the walls. A setter usually figures that the framing contractor has singled him or her out for some special punishment, because when the floor tiles reach the walls, the hitherto "perfect" layout begins to go awry. Tiles are, more or less, perfect little rectangles; floors and walls are not, and a competent layout minimizes or eliminates awkward results at the walls. Reference lines, the key to layout, represent the transition between a less-than-perfect structure and the relative perfection of the layout lines that are used to guide the placement of the tiles.

Tiles are rigidly geometric, and, to ensure that they look correct in place, they must be aligned with a grid of layout lines oriented at 90° to each other. The easiest way to establish the exact location of the grid of layout lines is to plot a pair of reference lines first. Reference lines are first used to check the room for square. With that done, the reference lines establish the basic 90° relationship necessary from which the grid of layout lines can be plotted.

as shown in the drawing above. This figure takes into consideration the almost 20 sq. ft. of tile waste.

As you can see, it's much more accurate to compute the tile needed by actual count than by the square foot. And once you've arrived at the total number of tiles called for in the layout, add 5% to 10% to this figure to account for breakage in shipment or miscut tiles. For the foyer floor, then, I would probably order a total of 180 tiles. If any tiles remained after the job was completed, I could always store the leftovers in case future repairs were needed.

I find it best to wait until my order arrives before actually chalking layout lines on the setting bed. This way, I can measure a random selection of the tiles to make sure their dimensions conform to my expectations.

THE 3-4-5 TRIANGLE On a small setting surface, such as a bathroom floor or a countertop, a carpenter's square can be used to establish the basic right-angle intersection of the reference lines. But on larger and more complex surfaces, the carpenter's square isn't big enough to establish large, truly accurate right angles. This is where the 3-4-5 triangle comes in handy.

The triangle isn't an actual tool; it's simply a method of establishing a pair of long lines that are perpendicular to each other—that is, reference lines. The method is based on the fact that a triangle with sides in the proportion of 3:4:5 will contain a right angle. That is to say, if the baseline of a triangle is three units, the triangle's height four units and its hypotenuse five units, the triangle is a right triangle. By projecting on the setting bed an accurate 3-4-5 triangle (or a larger triangle with unit measurements in the same proportional relationship—6-8-10, 12-16-20, and so on), the square reference lines needed for layout can be established, whatever the size or shape of the floor being tiled, and the walls can be checked for square. To save time scribing a 3-4-5 triangle, I make the first line to suit my grout-joint list. This first line thus becomes both a reference and a layout line.

To begin making a 3-4-5 triangle, you need one straight line. To establish this line, first consult the layout sketch and the tile/grout-joint list and pick a measurement for a grout joint that will fall several feet away from one of the walls. Then measure this distance from both ends of the wall, mark these points with a pencil and connect the points by snapping a chalk line. If possible, measure from an outside wall, since this wall was built over the foundation and is more likely to be straight than an inside partition wall. If there is no outside wall in the room, take the measurements off the longest wall. Also, if you can see that a baseboard is bowed or uneven, choose another wall from which to measure to avoid introducing error into later measurements.

Next, again consult the layout sketch and tile/grout-joint list to pick a second measurement for a grout joint that will fall several feet away from the adjoining wall. This time measure that distance out from the adjoining wall, first along the reference line you've just drawn and second at another point along the wall. Mark these two points with a pencil and snap a chalk line through them that extends from wall to wall.

Then, measuring from the point where the two lines intersect, make a mark *exactly* 3 ft. away on one of the lines. (If you're working on a large floor, you can enlarge this distance proportionately as long as you follow suit with subsequent dimensions.) Next measure along the other line a distance of *exactly* 4 ft. from the point of intersection and make a mark. Then measure the distance between these two marks. If it is exactly 5 ft., the two reference lines—and the two walls from which they were projected—are square to each other. This is *all* the 3-4-5 triangle tells you, although these square lines can in turn be used to determine if the other walls are square. (To do this, simply measure from both ends of one of the lines to the unchecked wall opposite it and compare the distance. If the measurements are the same at both ends, that wall is square to the neighboring wall, which you already determined was square to the first wall. Proceed in the same fashion to check the remaining walls in the room.)

MAKING MINOR ADJUSTMENTS If you find that the hypotenuse of the triangle is not exactly 5 ft., the walls from which you projected the lines are not square to each other. As shown in the drawing on p. 124, you can use the 3-4-5 triangle to determine the extent of the problem. If the walls are out of square less than ⅛ in. in 10 ft., they will not noticeably affect the layout. Nonetheless, you will need to adjust the reference lines to make sure that the triangle contains a right angle and hence

ESTABLISHING SQUARE REFERENCE LINES WITH A 3-4-5 TRIANGLE

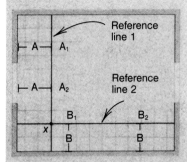

Consult layout sketch and tile/grout-joint list to determine where to place reference lines 1 and 2 so that they fall at what will become centers of grout joints.

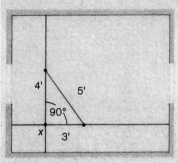

Plot a 3-4-5 triangle on reference lines to determine if walls from which lines are projected are square to each other. If triangle's hypotenuse equals exactly 5 ft., walls are square.

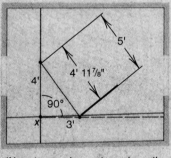

If hypotenuse does not equal exactly 5 ft., walls are out of square. To square up reference lines, pivot one line at point of intersection to correct length of hypotenuse.

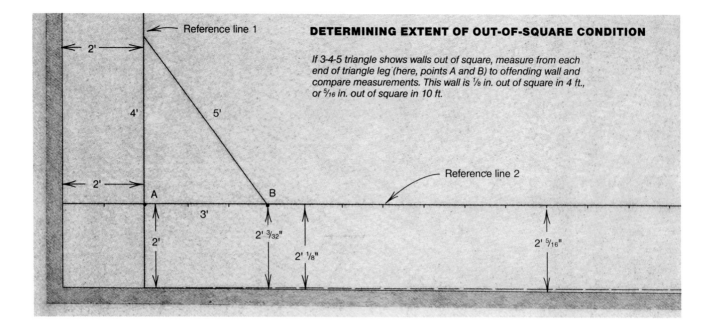

DETERMINING EXTENT OF OUT-OF-SQUARE CONDITION

If 3-4-5 triangle shows walls out of square, measure from each end of triangle leg (here, points A and B) to offending wall and compare measurements. This wall is ⅛ in. out of square in 4 ft., or ⁵⁄₁₆ in. out of square in 10 ft.

Reference line 1

Reference line 2

that the reference lines intersect at a 90° angle. This will mean that the triangle will not be square to both walls, only to one wall. If you need to adjust the triangle, square it up to a wall containing the most obvious focal point—a fireplace, a threshold, maybe a bay window. This is a compromise, but if you can't align the tile perfectly with every wall, it should at least be aligned with the wall people will look at first.

After deciding which wall to square up the triangle with, make the adjustment by moving the reference line perpendicular to that wall. Note that the first snapping point for this line (point x in the drawing on p. 123) remains unchanged, and the line is pivoted at that point until the hypotenuse equals exactly 5 ft. Once the hypotenuse is corrected and the reference lines are square to one another, the grid of layout lines can be chalked on the setting bed, as described below.

MAKING MAJOR ADJUSTMENTS If the bases of the walls prove to be out of square by more than ⅛ in. in 10 ft., you'll have a decision to make, which, I'm afraid, is a judgment call. Either you'll have to fix the

walls to make them square to each other, or you'll have to live with a tile layout that features obviously angled, cut tiles at one wall and maybe at other walls as well. This is when you'll need to draw on all the insight you can muster. Scrutinize the room for places where the angled tile will be least noticeable. Sometimes this means putting it along a wall that's broken into shorter lengths by built-in furniture, or along a wall with windows covered by floor-length drapes.

The basic layout rule of using no tiles less than half-size will also minimize the visual problems associated with setting tile in problem rooms. Imagine a floor of 6-in. square tiles in which the setter allowed a row of full tiles against one wall and a row of 1-in. wide cuts along the opposite wall. If the latter wall happened to be ¾ in. out of square along its length, the tiles against one end of the wall might be a full 1 in. wide, but against the other end of the wall they'd be only ¼ in. wide—making the out-of-square condition glaringly obvious. But if the layout were adjusted to use a 3½-in. wide cut on both opposing walls, tiles on the one wall would taper from 3½ in. to 2¾ in. Even though the amount of taper is unchanged, it will be far less noticeable on the larger portion of tile. As a general rule, larger tiles will mask an out-of-square condition better than smaller tiles will. Given uncorrectable, out-of-square conditions, you'll have a better-looking job with larger tiles. Again, though, let me stress that the best-looking jobs are those where effort has been spent to correct problems, not disguise them.

If you're dealing with a real problem room in which no corner is really square and whose problems you can't correct—and you insist on setting tile—the reference lines will be particularly important. Even if nothing else in the room is square, the reference lines must be square to one another. They will serve as the benchmark from which to measure everything else. If you can visualize the entire tiled floor shifting every time you shift the reference lines, you'll understand how to use the lines to plan the tile job.

MULTIROOM INSTALLATIONS   Another situation that points up the importance of reference lines is a multiroom installation where the tile needs to look continuous. In this case, reference lines plotted throughout the series of rooms enable the setter to position the tile so that, wherever possible, the grout lines run uninterrupted from one room through the doorway into the next room, as shown in the bottom drawing on p. 129. For the layout of such an installation, reference lines are plotted first in one room—usually the largest or most complex in shape—and arranged so that one leg of the 3-4-5 triangle can be extended to pass through a doorway into the next room. This line will then serve as the basis for plotting another 3-4-5 triangle in the new room. Depending on the complexity of the job, you may need to plot a series of 3-4-5 triangles in this fashion. You may also find that you have to adjust the multi-triangle layout to correspond to differences in the squareness of each room. The important thing to remember in this case is that adjusting or moving one triangle means similarly altering the others as well.

Making a jury stick

Once reference lines have been established, the next step in layout is determining where to chalk layout lines on the setting bed to guide the actual placement of the tile. A jury stick will considerably speed up this task.

This tool is a sort of measuring stick that uses as its unit of measure the average width of a single tile and grout joint, rather than inches or centimeters. It eliminates the need for a tape measure and calculator at this stage of tiling, enabling the setter to locate layout lines quickly and accurately and determine exactly how many tiles will fit into a given area.

A jury stick is usually 6 ft. to 8 ft. long and can be made out of any dimension of wood stock, provided the board is straight (I use ripped-down plywood or scrap lumber, especially pine lattice). When I'm working with a multiroom layout, I find it convenient to have two jury sticks, a short one for hallways and other narrow places and a long one for large rooms.

To establish the jury stick's basic unit of measure, line up 10 tiles against the stick. If the tiles are self-spacing, that is, if they have built-in spacing lugs, butt the lugs tightly against each other. If you plan to use tile spacers, be sure to include them when lining up the tiles (see the photo on p. 126). If the tiles don't have lugs and you're not using spacers, just space the tiles with a scrap of wood cut to the thickness of the planned grout joint. Then mark the location of each grout joint's center on the stick.

The jury stick now provides a quick means of figuring out how many full-size tiles will fit into a given area. By starting at one side of the area and measuring with the jury stick across to the other side, you can determine what adjustments will be needed in layout to produce the visual

To make a jury stick, a simple tool that speeds up the process of marking layout lines, line up 10 tiles against a straight piece of stock and mark the center of each grout joint.

Again, you will need to consult the layout sketch and the tile/grout-joint list to figure out the exact distances from the reference lines at which layout lines should be plotted. Because the series of layout lines are projected off the reference lines, they, too, will be square to one another. And if one or both reference lines were positioned to coincide with grout joints, they now become part of the grid of layout lines.

The purpose of layout lines is to prevent the grout joints—and tiles—from wandering off square and running at an angle. Imagine a large living-room floor, for example, and the problems you would have keeping tiles running straight across 15 ft. or 20 ft. of space without layout lines. Even self-spacing tiles, if their lugs are covered with adhesive, can veer off course quickly, so you can't depend on them to do the thinking for you. Layout lines provide a guide to work by, ensuring not only that the tiles run straight but also that each tile ends up exactly where you want it. If you want to avoid having to cut tiles at a threshold, or if you want a particular grout joint to line up with, say, the edge of a built-in cabinet, layout lines are essential.

Layout lines also allow the setter to cut tiles to size where necessary before the actual setting begins. If you're setting tile on a large floor, for example, and you have a section of it spread with quick-setting adhesive, you don't want to spend time measuring the cuts and dashing back and forth to the wet saw. Instead, by using a layout line to separate cut tiles from full tiles, you can measure and make all the cuts at once ahead of time. That way, once it's time to set the tile, you can concentrate on this step alone.

And if you're not yet convinced of the importance of layout lines, consider another advantage they offer. By using layout lines to break up a large surface being tiled into smaller sections, you can spread adhesive and set tiles in the small areas one by one. Working this way divides

results you want. You're doing basically the same thing as you did when you worked with the floor plan and the tile/grout-joint list to produce a layout sketch on paper, but this process is more accurate because it deals with the actual floor, rather than a representation of it. Using the jury stick accomplishes the same thing as physically laying out all the tiles on a floor to develop the correct layout—but, believe me, it's a lot easier.

Marking layout lines

With the reference lines marked on the floor and the jury stick made, you're ready to snap layout lines on the setting bed to guide the actual positioning of the tile.

the job into manageable segments, ensures that every portion of each small "box" is comfortably within your reach, and also reduces the possibility of spreading adhesive over a larger area than you can cover before the adhesive sets up. I like to divide the setting bed into small sections about 3 ft. square. Of course, the exact size of these areas depends on the size of the tile I'm working with.

The steps for establishing layout lines involve deciding the number and location of the lines needed; using the jury stick to project measurements from the square reference lines established on the setting bed; and, finally, snapping chalk lines (or using pencil and straightedge) to mark the layout lines on the bed.

HOW MANY LAYOUT LINES? The number and position of the layout lines depend on the size and complexity of the installation, the size and shape of the tiles, the speed with which the adhesive will set up and the skill of the setter. Generally speaking, small, simply shaped installations need fewer layout lines than large, complex jobs, and large tiles necessitate fewer lines than small tiles do. Also, machine-made tiles of uniform size and shape, self-spacing tiles and tiles to be set with spacers require fewer layout lines than irregularly shaped, handmade tiles do. Slow-setting adhesives allow you to work larger areas at any one time, so fewer layout lines are necessary. And, finally, an experienced setter will probably need fewer layout lines than the novice. But since it never hurts to put in more layout lines than you'll actually need, don't skimp on this step.

All of the above factors mean that a small, rectangular floor may require only a pair of intersecting lines for layout, while a large, complex floor extending into several rooms may need a dozen or more layout lines. And in a few rare instances—when you're working with very irregularly shaped,

handmade tiles or unusual tiles, for example—it may be necessary to mark a layout line for every grout joint.

Rectangular floors and single-room layouts

Let's look at some examples of floor layouts, the first being a bathroom floor, 5 ft. by 8 ft., set with self-spacing, 6-in. square tiles, as shown in the drawing below. Because of the floor's small size and simple shape, it's easy to check the room for square by putting a carpenter's square to the corners, rather than going to the trouble of chalking reference lines and a 3-4-5 triangle on the floor. Assuming that the room is square, a pair of layout lines will suffice to guide the placement of the tile. These two lines, which, of course, fall in the center of grout joints, divide the floor into four sections, in each of which all the tiles, both full and cut, are within easy reach. Because the floor is small and requires relatively few cut tiles, I wouldn't bother adding another layout line to separate the cut tile from the full tile—the

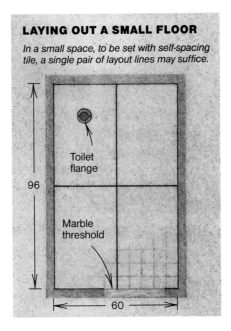

LAYING OUT A SMALL FLOOR

In a small space, to be set with self-spacing tile, a single pair of layout lines may suffice.

Toilet flange

96

Marble threshold

60

time saved cutting the tiles in advance would be negligible. I would begin positioning full tiles at the point where the lines intersect, working from the center of the room outward and cutting the trimmed pieces as needed to complete the layout.

On a large floor being tiled with hand-made Mexican pavers, which have a somewhat irregular shape, a layout line should be drawn to mark the rows of cut tiles around the perimeter, and a grid of layout lines should be plotted to enclose all the full tiles in sections no more than about 3 ft. square, as shown in the drawing below. With the rows of cut and full tiles separated, the cuts can be accurately measured and trimmed before setting actually begins. And the grid breaks the job into manageable segments.

After marking the joint separating the cut and full tiles on this floor, which is 11 ft. 2 in. by 15 ft. 8 in., I plotted additional layout lines every 36 in. across the floor's length and width. This produced a grid of twelve 36-in. square boxes, each containing nine tiles, as well as one horizontal row

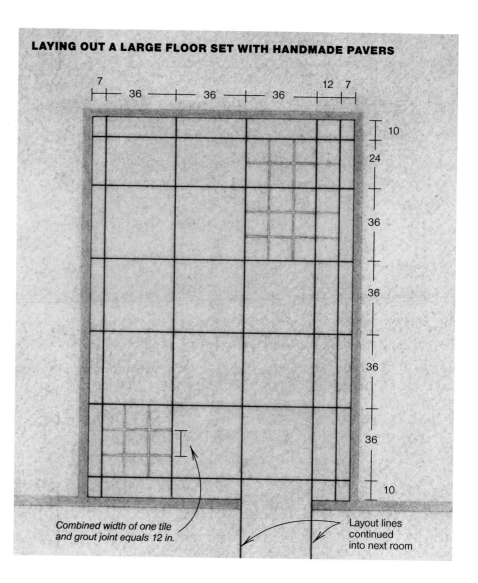

LAYING OUT A LARGE FLOOR SET WITH HANDMADE PAVERS

Combined width of one tile and grout joint equals 12 in.

Layout lines continued into next room

of boxes, 24 in. by 36 in., which would each accommodate six tiles, and one vertical row, 12 in. by 36 in., into which three tiles would fit. In each of the boxes, all of the tiles were easily within my reach.

L-shaped floors and multiroom layouts

L-shaped floors are simply composed of two parts, whether square or rectangular, and they are no more difficult to lay out than a simple square or rectangular floor. The trick in laying out this type of floor is to project the reference lines from the longest walls and to position the lines so that one falls in each leg of the L, as shown in the drawing at right.

In doing a multiroom layout, the key is not to lay out each room individually, but rather to connect the layout from room to room with one of the initial pair of reference lines. Additional reference lines can then be plotted in each room from the original pair, and the entire surface being tiled can then be treated as one continuous installation.

When plotting the original pair of reference lines for a multiroom installation, make sure, if possible, to project the lines off a wall that extends to the connecting rooms. In the case of the example shown below, line 1, plotted the full length of the installation, was projected off the west foundation wall that stretches along three rooms. Line 2 was projected off the full width of the installation, and a 3-4-5 triangle was plotted to establish this pair of reference lines as square. Line 3 was then projected off line 1, and line 4, the next longest line, off line 2. Then line 5 was

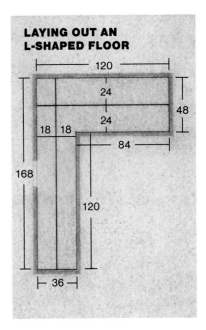

LAYING OUT AN L-SHAPED FLOOR

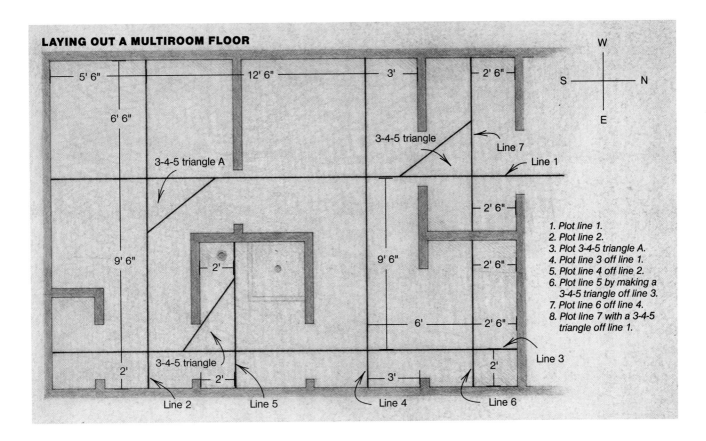

LAYING OUT A MULTIROOM FLOOR

1. Plot line 1.
2. Plot line 2.
3. Plot 3-4-5 triangle A.
4. Plot line 3 off line 1.
5. Plot line 4 off line 2.
6. Plot line 5 by making a 3-4-5 triangle off line 3.
7. Plot line 6 off line 4.
8. Plot line 7 with a 3-4-5 triangle off line 1.

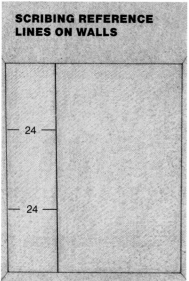

Measuring from an out-of-plumb wall to scribe a vertical reference line will result in duplicating out-of-plumb condition of wall.

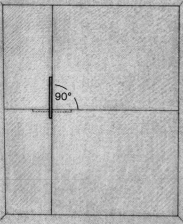

Instead, use a level, positioned first vertically and then horizontally, to draw a pair of reference lines from which to project layout lines.

projected off line 3 with a 3-4-5 triangle. Line 6 was projected off line 4, and line 7 off line 1 with a 3-4-5 triangle. Once these reference lines were plotted throughout the installation, I could project layout lines to divide the larger areas into manageable segments. Then, as with all the layouts shown, I began positioning tile in the center of the installation and worked outward toward the perimeter. (For further information on laying out and installing tile on floors, see Chapter 9.)

Laying Out Walls

Laying out walls is much easier than laying out floors. One reason is that to check a wall for plumb and square, you need only use a spirit level. Hold the level vertically against the wall to determine if it's plumb. Then place the level on the adjoining horizontal surface to be tiled—the floor or a countertop—to see if that surface is level. If the wall is plumb and the horizontal surface is level, the two surfaces are square to one another. Walls are set to the same tolerances as floors: if the surfaces are out of square more than 1/8 in. in 10 ft., corrective action should be considered. And as with floors, the kind and size of tile you plan to use will figure into your decision about correcting the problems or living with them. Crisp, rigidly uniform Italian tile might exaggerate the out-of-square conditions, but the natural irregularities of Mexican tile might disguise them.

Reference and layout lines should never be projected directly from adjoining walls or floors. Instead, use a level positioned on the wall first vertically and then horizontally to establish a pair of square reference lines, as shown in the drawing at left. As when laying out floors, try to place each of the reference lines in what will become the center of a grout joint. The two reference lines can then later serve as layout lines.

While setting tile on walls is in many ways like tiling floors, working on a vertical surface introduces the added concern of dealing with gravity. The inevitable pull of gravity on the tiles means that you must work quickly when tiling walls, and on large walls you can speed up the setting process by using plenty of layout lines. On most small walls, however, I usually divide the wall only into quadrants. In addition to these layout lines, I also add a line, if needed, to separate the field tile from any trim tile around windows, doors or other features. The drawing on the facing page shows a typical layout for a tub/shower surround with a window in the back wall, using 3-in. square tiles. Let's look at each of the layout lines and what it denotes.

Lines 1 and 2 mark the outer vertical limit of the field tiles and the grout joint between these and the trim tiles. Lines 3, 4 and 5 mark the upper horizontal limit of the field tiles and the joint between these and the trim tiles. Lines 6 and 7 and lines 8 and 9 split each of the side walls into four easily managed sections of field tiles. Note that line 7 is positioned to clear the spout, shower-head and control-valve holes, and that lines 6 and 8 are continuations of line 10.

Lines 10 and 11 divide the back wall into manageable quadrants. Line 10 is located below the row of field tiles abutting the trim tiles on the window sill (in this case, there would be no room for the line between field and trim tiles). Lines 12, 13 and 14 denote the grout joints between the field tiles on the header of the window and jambs and the trim tiles on the window's face. With all of these lines in place, I would not need to use a level during the actual setting of the tile, which eliminates the constant bother of having to clean adhesive off this tool.

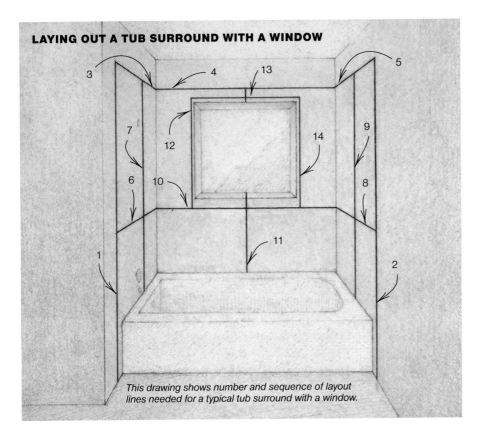

LAYING OUT A TUB SURROUND WITH A WINDOW

This drawing shows number and sequence of layout lines needed for a typical tub surround with a window.

Had a mortar setting bed been used for this tub surround, I would have also placed layout lines to note the outer limits of the mortar bed on the substrate (the other layout lines would, of course, have been chalked on top of the mortar bed once it was dry). This first set of lines would have facilitated the installation of the tar-paper curing membrane and the reinforcing wire mesh necessary with a mortar bed. For further information on laying out and tiling walls, see Chapter 10.

Laying Out Countertops

Countertops are the easiest installation of all to lay out. Because you're working with relatively small, narrow surfaces, there's less chance of positioning the tiles askew.

Before beginning the layout, check the countertop for level and square. Then also make sure that the cabinets are securely fastened in place, since any wobbling might cause the countertop to move or flex, which will likely result in cracked tiles or grout joints.

The principal rule in laying out a countertop is to place full tiles at the front edge of the countertop and position any required cut pieces at the base of the backsplash where they will be less noticeable and probably covered by the backsplash tiles. When installing backer board as a setting surface for a countertop, it's a good idea to use the factory edge for the front edge. Use the cut edge to accommodate any irregularities in the backsplash wall.

FITTING A COUNTERTOP TO AN UNEVEN BACK WALL

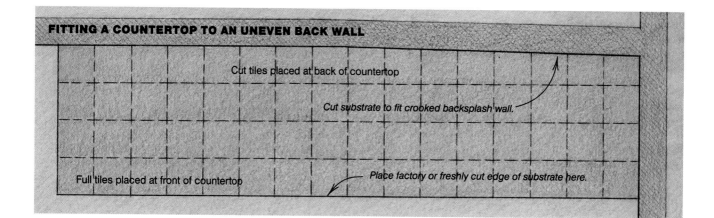

Cut tiles placed at back of countertop

Cut substrate to fit crooked backsplash wall.

Full tiles placed at front of countertop

Place factory or freshly cut edge of substrate here.

LAYING OUT COUNTERTOPS

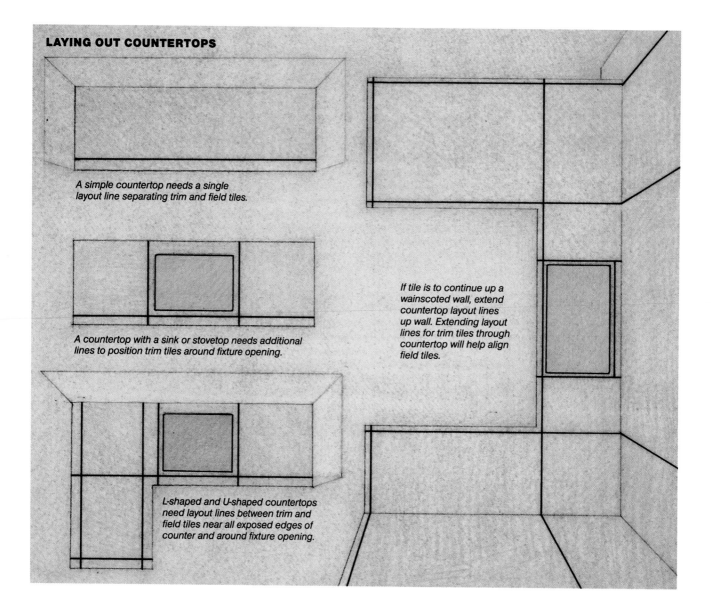

A simple countertop needs a single layout line separating trim and field tiles.

A countertop with a sink or stovetop needs additional lines to position trim tiles around fixture opening.

If tile is to continue up a wainscoted wall, extend countertop layout lines up wall. Extending layout lines for trim tiles through countertop will help align field tiles.

L-shaped and U-shaped countertops need layout lines between trim and field tiles near all exposed edges of counter and around fixture opening.

You needn't plot reference lines on a countertop—the front edge of the countertop *is* a reference line. But layout lines, projected from the edge of the countertop, can be helpful. If the countertop is a simple rectangle bordered on both ends by walls, the only layout line needed is one to separate the field tiles from the trim tiles used at the forward edge of the counter, as shown in the bottom drawing on the facing page. If one end of the countertop is not bordered by a wall, or if the countertop is L-shaped or U-shaped, additional lines are needed to position the trim tiles on the counter's other exposed edges. And if the countertop contains a sink or stovetop, several lines are also needed to mark the position of the trim tiles around these fixtures. Finally, if the tiles are to continue up the wall as a backsplash, remember to plot the layout lines on the wall with a level to make sure that they're perfectly vertical. For a good-looking job, always line up the grout joints on the countertop with those

on the wall. (For further information on laying out and installing countertop tiles, see Chapter 11.)

Laying Out Irregular Tiles and Setting Patterns

While it's a relatively simple task to lay out square or rectangular tiles in similarly shaped spaces, laying out irregularly shaped tiles or laying out standard tiles in unusually shaped spaces can present more of a challenge. Keep in mind, however, that all consistently shaped tiles, no matter what their contour, have points of reference that can be used to align them, and that any space can be inscribed with reference and layout lines to aid in setting these tiles.

In the case of hexagonal and octagonal tiles, the flat sides and pointed corners both offer places for alignment. Each of

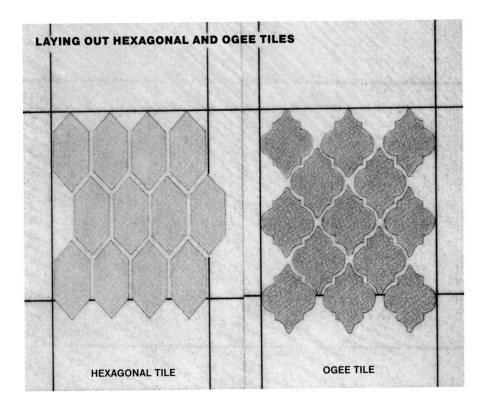

LAYING OUT HEXAGONAL AND OGEE TILES

HEXAGONAL TILE

OGEE TILE

these tile shapes can be aligned to the same kind of layout lines described earlier, that is, a grid of layout lines intersecting at right angles. In fact, even penny-round tiles can be set to the 90° grid. When it comes time to set irregularly shaped tiles, however, the grid won't offer as perfect a guide for spreading adhesive. Because of their shape, the tiles won't butt up against the layout lines along their full length or width. This isn't a big problem, just something to bear in mind. Also keep in mind that tiles in any shape other than squares or rectangles will overlap the layout lines. If you have trouble following the layout lines, just lay a straightedge on top of the already set tiles to "bridge" parts of the lines covered by tile. While more complex in shape, ogee tiles nonetheless have repeating points that can be used for aligning them with layout lines formed into a 90° grid.

LAYOUT ON THE DIAGONAL   When setting floor, wall or countertop tiles on the diagonal, keep all the layout lines at a true 45° angle to the edge of the installation. There are various ways to do this, but I start by snapping a pair of intersecting reference lines to form a 90° angle, as I would for any installation. Then, starting from the intersection of the lines, I measure out equal distances in three directions, as shown in the drawing at right. Connecting the points and extending the lines forms a large X on the setting floor, and these lines become the new reference lines. Layout lines can then be projected as needed from the new reference lines.

Setting tile on the diagonal has long been popular, especially for floors, but many setters shy away from this pattern because of the numerous cuts required at the perimeter of the installation and the often unattractive look of these cuts, as shown on the left side of the drawing on

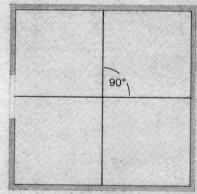

1. Plot two reference lines, square to area being tiled.

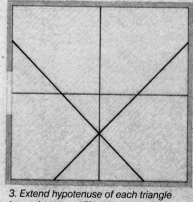

2. Plot two neighboring isosceles triangles at point of intersection.

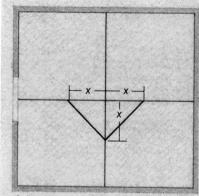

3. Extend hypotenuse of each triangle to produce two 45° angled lines from which to plot a regular grid of layout lines.

DIAGONALLY SET TILE, WITH AND WITHOUT A BORDER

Vincent Babak

Adding a border to a field of diagonally set tile can help avoid unattractive cuts at perimeter.

this page. To give this kind of installation a professional, finished look, try using the standard border treatment employed by old-time setters. After diagonally setting a field of full tiles only, they cut enough tiles in half on the diagonal to fill in the remaining spaces around the perimeter. Finally, they bordered this square or rectangle of diagonally placed tile with a row of full or, if need be, cut tiles set square to the field. The border tiles can even be a different kind of tile, as long as they are compatible in thickness and durability with the field tiles.

To achieve this kind of layout, I usually plot a standard diagonal layout grid on the floor, wall or countertop using a jury stick. Once this is in place, it's not too hard to see how big the field should be in order to leave a single row of tiles between the field and the edge of the installation. A straight-edge is generally all I need to guide the placement of the bordering trim tiles. It takes a bit of figuring, but the results are well worth the effort. Because the border serves as a decorative element in the installation, a continuous pattern can be attained on checkerboard layouts by beginning at the corners with a quarter diagonal. Chances are that in setting any other arrangement of tile you can imagine, a 90° grid of reference and layout lines will do the job.

■ ■ ■

Chapter Eight

Basic Application Techniques

When I started out in the tilesetting trade, most of the tiles I installed were set over plastic beds of fresh mortar, a process known as wet-setting. The tiles had to be soaked overnight in water, the setting beds had to be floated quickly and the adhesive was a runny paste made from portland cement and water. Grout was also applied as a thin paste, and it had to be installed on the same day as the tiles. Thankfully, those days are past, because, in my opinion, wet-setting methods were tedious at best, required extensive training and dedication on the part of the installer and yielded rather inferior results compared to the thinbed methods presented in this book.

Thinbed methods are relatively simple to learn, allow a more relaxed pace and can produce superior strength and performance. I stress "can" because the process does not automatically guarantee results—you must carefully prepare the areas to be tiled, choose the right materials, use the proper techniques and safeguard the installation until the adhesive, grout and sealants have cured. Apart from the handyman skills you will need to prepare the substrate, you will also need two specialized skills for installing tile: mixing and spreading adhesives, and mixing and placing the grout.

Mixing Powdered Adhesives

For the past 25 years, I have used hundreds of tile adhesives, both ready-to-use and site-mixed. There are many dependable ready-to-use mastics on the market, but for the performance and flexibility of use that I demand, I prefer to work with site-mixed thinset mortars. If you choose mastic for your installation, make

Unlike thinset adhesives, organic mastics require no preparation or mixing, but there are certain precautions you should take when working with these adhesives.

SAFETY

Solvent-based mastics demand particular caution. Their vapors are potentially explosive and can be hazardous when inhaled. Before opening the can or bucket, put on a charcoal-filter mask and check to see that there are no open flames nearby (including pilot lights on a stove) and that the work area is well ventilated. Although water-based mastics are considered safer to use than their solvent-based counterparts, I prefer not to take chances with any mastic and always observe these precautions.

STIRRING MASTICS

When you first open a fresh can of mastic, you may notice, depending on the product's composition, an oily-looking or watery puddle floating on the surface. This puddle, which results from the mastic's lighter ingredients separating and rising, should be stirred back into the mixture with a stick. If you have a problem doing this, it may be because the mastic sat on the store shelf too long (in which case, you should return the can to the store for a replacement).

EXTENDING THE LIFE OF MASTICS

If you've used the can before and find that the mastic has begun to harden when you open it, throw it out. Never, under any circumstances, try to thin a mastic. I've found that leftover mastic will harden quickly in the can, even if it has been closed tightly. Keeping the can out of direct sunlight and in a cool place will help lengthen a mastic's life. You can also extend the life of a solvent-based mastic by covering the adhesive with a few inches of water before closing the lid. The water prevents air from reaching the mastic, and the vapors in the mastic from evaporating. (Pour off this water before using the adhesive.) Note, however, that adding water to the top of latex-based mastic before closing the lid will only dilute the adhesive and render it useless.

USE

With regard to using mastics, the individual product label will tell you the product's open time (how long the mastic takes to begin to "skin over," or lose its bonding ability, after being spread) and set-up time (how long the mastic takes to begin curing once applied to a surface). The label should also recommend the size of notched trowel to use in spreading the mastic.

CLEANUP

Both solvent- and water-based mastics must be cleaned up promptly, using, in most cases, paint thinner or water, respectively. Since there are now some mastics with solvent ingredients that can be cleaned up with water, however, check the individual product label for instructions. If the mastic on tile and tools is still soft, it can be removed with a rag dipped in thinner or water. For partially dried mastic, use a white Scotch-Brite scouring pad and thinner or water. Once the mastic has hardened, it must be scraped or sliced off with a razor blade or paint scraper. Since it's difficult to get dried mastic out of the tiny grooves of a spreading trowel, I heartily recommend cleaning up while the mastic is still soft.

sure to select one that is appropriate for your needs and expectations, and follow the manufacturer's instructions to the letter. Mastics require no mixing, and their basic application is the same as for thinset mortar (see the sidebar above for additional information on mastics).

Mixing thinset mortar

To prepare regular or polymer-modified thinset mortar (see pp. 40-41), first make sure that all the ingredients—wet and dry—have been conditioned to normal room temperatures. Any water required should be clean enough to drink, and all buckets and other mixing containers should be thoroughly cleaned. Never mix a new batch of adhesive in a container that holds the soft residue of a previously mixed batch, because the residue can cause the new batch to begin curing (setting up) prematurely.

When making up two gallons of thinset adhesive or less, I prefer to mix it by hand with a long-blade margin trowel. For larger amounts, a mixing paddle chucked in a drill is more efficient (see the photo on p. 54). Be sure to use a paddle designed for mixing mortar rather than paint.

Although there are no fumes to worry about when mixing thinsets, dust is a problem, so a fitted dust mask is recommended when you're working with any thinset. Because thinset is both caustic and very difficult to clean off your skin once it has dried, it's also a good idea to wear latex gloves when mixing and working with thinsets. If you find that you must take the gloves off for precise work, make sure to have a bucket of clean water nearby and occasionally wash off your hands.

Mixing any thinset by hand is a straightforward process that simply requires a bit of care. I like to pour the liquid into the bucket first and then add the powder gradually. Once all the dry ingredients have been stirred into the liquid, about 90% of the lumps can be eliminated with the trowel. At this point, it is important to allow the mixture to slake, or rest, for about 10 minutes to allow moisture to penetrate the remaining lumps and make them easier to eliminate. Restirring the mixture just before use should render it lump-free and ready for spreading.

If you're mixing thinset with a paddle, keep the speed below 300 rpm and be sure to keep the paddle submerged to prevent air from being whipped into the mixture. The presence of air bubbles will reduce the number of solid particles per cubic inch and can weaken the adhesive's bond strength by as much as 50%. Once the thinset is thoroughly mixed, let it slake for 10 minutes and then remix before using it.

GETTING THE RIGHT CONSISTENCY Thinset mortar that is ready to use is wet enough to adhere instantly to both tile and substrate, but if it's too wet, it can be difficult to apply. To determine if a thinset mortar is the proper consistency, I use a very simple test. I reach into the bucket with a margin trowel, load the trowel with mortar and then hold the trowel upside-down. If the mortar runs off easily, the mix is too loose. If this is the case, add more powder and remix. If the mortar stays put without too much sagging, it's ready to use. (For another way to test adhesive consistency, see pp. 143-144.)

Remember that heat and humidity can affect the consistency of the mixture, as can the type of tile being set. Heat or low humidity requires that a thinset be mixed slightly wetter than it would be in cold weather or high humidity. Also, when setting nonvitreous tile, which readily absorbs water, mix a thinset adhesive a bit wetter than for vitreous tile, which absorbs little moisture. When mixing the thinset mortar I normally use, I know that the liquid/powder ratio is slightly variable to account for application differences— sometimes I need the mix a little stiffer than usual, while at other times I may need a slightly thinner consistency.

If you are concerned that high heat may prematurely dry out the thinset mortar you are using, do not use extra liquid in the mixing in an attempt to overcome this heat because the liquid will only weaken the mix and render it ineffective. If a prepared thinset begins to set up on the job, it should never be thinned with water. Instead, the old mix should be discarded and a new batch made.

Mixing epoxy adhesive

Mixing epoxy adhesive is the same as for regular or polymer-modified thinset mortars, with two exceptions. First, all mixing should be done by hand to avoid the potential heat caused by power mixing. This heat can trigger the chemical reaction that turns epoxy mortar into stone. Second, the proportion of wet to dry ingredients should never vary from the manufacturer's mixing instructions. As always, check the manufacturer's instructions for specific details and procedure.

When mixing epoxies, proportioning the liquid ingredients is critical. Those adhesives specifying equal parts of resin and hardener are simple enough to mix, but those requiring unequal amounts require real care in measuring. Coffee cans with indented rings make good measuring cups, but if you're mixing more than a gallon or two, make a dip stick marked off in inches to measure the proportions. Before pouring either of the two liquids into a mixing bucket, stir each ingredient with a separate clean stick or margin trowel. (Be sure you don't contaminate the contents of one container with that of the other, or the liquids will begin to harden irreversibly.) Then pour the liquids into the mixing bucket and stir or paddle them until they're thoroughly combined. Next mix the filler powder into the liquid a little bit at a time. If the initial mix is too dry, thin it with a properly portioned mixture of the liquid ingredients, which you should prepare in a separate container. Under no circumstances should you add anything to the epoxy adhesive to thin it once it has begun to harden. As with any thinset that starts to cure before use, discard it and prepare a new batch.

SAFETY All the usual precautions concerning vapors and dust should be observed when working with epoxy adhesives: Wear a charcoal-filter mask, make sure that the work area is well ventilated and check the product label for any additional safety precautions. Anyone with sensitive skin may be particularly bothered by epoxy. And because the hardened stuff is extremely difficult to remove from skin, it's a good idea to wear rubber gloves while mixing and working with epoxies.

CLEANUP Cleanup with epoxies varies from product to product, depending on the ingredients. Some are water-soluble when still wet and easily cleaned up; others require a solvent and a bit more work (cleanup information for a particular product will be provided on the label). As with any adhesive, cleanup is considerably easier if it's begun before the adhesive dries.

Spreading Adhesives

Whenever you're working with any adhesive, the ideal temperature at the job site is between 65°F and 75°F. I've installed tile successfully in 50°F and in 95°F weather, but in more moderate temperatures there are fewer problems. For example, at 35°F to 50°F readings, the adhesive will take a long time to set up (from four to eight hours, or even longer), and in freezing weather, the water in thinset adhesives will turn to ice, rendering the adhesive useless. When the thermometer goes above 90°F, and in the direct sun no matter what the temperature, all adhesives will "cook," meaning that the moisture will be driven out of them too quickly for them to cure properly. The resulting adhesive might seem like it is holding fast, but eventually its initial grip will begin to decrease rapidly.

If you're working indoors in cold weather, adjust the heat or use supplemental heating to regulate the room's temperature through-out the installation until the tile is set and the adhesive has dried. In hot weather, however, avoid using an air conditioner to cool down the room, as the unit's dehumidifier may draw essential moisture from the adhesive (or grout or other mortars, for that matter). The result will be the same as if the moisture were heated out of the mixture. If need be, wait to spread the adhesive and set tile until the evening or early morning when the temperature has fallen. If excessive heat

Don't start any tile installation unless you're sure that you have all the materials needed. Gather all the tools required for the job and put them in a convenient spot. Keep a bucket of water and a sponge handy to clean up tools or spills quickly. Spread tarps or drop cloths over finished areas you want to protect, cover up kitchen cabinets with plastic or protective paper when tiling countertops, and use tape or other masking devices on wood, papered or painted surfaces to keep grout contained to the tiles. (Don't leave masking tape in place for too long, though—it can pull up the wallpaper, paint or finish on woods if it stays in place for a long time.)

Before you begin work, plan the sequence of areas to be tiled so that you will be positioned at or near the door to the room when you finish. Don't tile yourself into a corner! If, however, you need to walk on a freshly tiled floor for whatever reason, keep handy some plywood squares, 2 ft. square by ¾ in. thick, to serve as a walkway over the floor. Make sure as you exit the room to remove each square, and check to see that you haven't disturbed the position of the tile below.

or cold cannot be moderated, contact the adhesive manufacturer or representative for advice, and as a final precaution in hot weather, reduce the amount of adhesive you spread before covering with tile so the adhesive will not skin over and render the bond ineffective.

Before you begin applying adhesive, you should clean the setting bed a final time to eliminate any dust that has settled and that may interfere with the adhesive's bond. When working with a thinset or a water-based organic mastic, wipe the bed with a damp sponge. If you're using a solvent-based mastic, use a painter's tack rag or sprinkle a cloth with a small amount of paint thinner or other solvent that is compatible with the adhesive.

Application

All adhesives, whether ready-to-use mastics or site-mixed thinset mortars, are generally applied in the same way. They're first spread on the setting surface with the unnotched edge of a V-, U- or square-notched trowel. Then they're "combed" with the notched side of the trowel, which, if the trowel is held at a consistent angle, produces ridges of uniform height. Generally speaking, ⅛-in. to ³⁄₁₆-in. V-notched trowels are used for thin tiles (glazed wall tiles, for example),

¼-in. square-notched trowels are used for larger tiles (6-in. to 8-in. floor tiles, for example) and deep U-notched trowels are used for large tiles (12 in. and up) and irregular tiles (handmade Mexican paver tiles, for example).

A well-equipped tile installer will carry a complete range of notched trowels to suit conditions. To make sure I apply enough adhesive, I generally use square-notched trowels whose teeth are ¼ in. wide. I keep three trowels in my tool kit—one with teeth slightly less than ¼ in. deep, one with teeth about ¼ in. deep and another with teeth ⅜ in. deep. I usually buy ⅜-in. deep trowels only. As each begins to wear down, I replace it with a fresh trowel and use the partially worn trowel for installations requiring less adhesive.

The adhesive should be spread with the unnotched edge of the trowel held at an acute angle of about 30° to the setting bed, which helps force (or "key") the adhesive into the pores of the bed (see the drawing on p. 142). Then enough material should be applied to cover the immediate area being worked, and its depth should equal at least the height of the trowel's notches. The layer of adhesive between the tile and the setting bed needs to be at

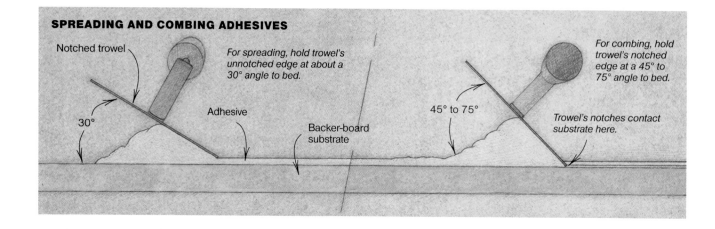

SPREADING AND COMBING ADHESIVES

Notched trowel

For spreading, hold trowel's unnotched edge at about a 30° angle to bed.

30°

Adhesive

Backer-board substrate

For combing, hold trowel's notched edge at a 45° to 75° angle to bed.

45° to 75°

Trowel's notches contact substrate here.

Dump enough adhesive on the setting bed to cover only the area in which you're immediately working.

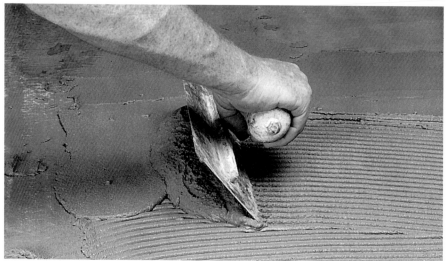

Spread the adhesive with the unnotched edge of the trowel held at about a 30° angle (top). Then comb the adhesive with the trowel's notched side held at an angle of from 45° to 75° (above).

least ³⁄₃₂ in. thick for the adhesive to reach its full bond strength. If the initial application with the smooth edge of the trowel is too thin, there will be insufficient material to produce fully formed, uniform ridges.

The area you choose to work with can be anywhere from 4 sq. ft. to 20 sq. ft., depending on the size of the installation and the temperature at the job site (the hotter the temperature, the faster the adhesive will begin to skin over or set up). If you try to cover the entire area being tiled, chances are the adhesive will set up faster than you can set all the tile. I rarely spread and comb more than 10 sq. ft. at a time.

To comb out the adhesive, hold the notched side of the trowel at an acute angle of from 45° to 75° to the bed—the larger the angle, the higher the ridges will be. While combing, it's crucial to keep the angle of the trowel consistent. Maintaining the trowel's angle will produce uniform ridges, and thus a level setting surface. It doesn't matter whether you make sweeping strokes or parallel passes as you comb, provided you maintain the trowel's angle and leave no stray globs of adhesive anywhere on the surface. Precise workmanship at this stage will reward you later with a nice, flat bed of tiles.

TESTING ADHESIVE CONSISTENCY If you are working with a thinset, you need to make sure its consistency is correct before spreading a lot of it on the bed. (Since organic mastics are premixed to the correct consistency, they don't need to be checked.) One method of testing consistency is mentioned on p. 139. Another method is to follow the manufacturer's mixing instructions and then spread and comb the thinset on a small area of the setting bed. Next press a single tile firmly into the adhesive and then remove it. By "reading" the back of this tile, you can ascertain the adhesive's consistency, and you'll also be able to decide if the layer of adhesive is the correct thickness.

When the tile is removed from the setting bed, its entire back should be covered with adhesive. If the adhesive was mixed to the correct consistency and spread to the right thickness, half of its depth will remain on the setting bed and half will have adhered to the tile back. If the adhesive was mixed too wet, you would have noticed that the ridges produced by combing would not hold peaks. If the

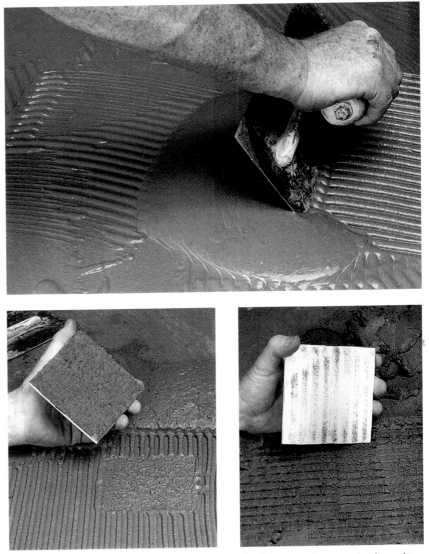

When using a thinset adhesive, you must mix it to the right consistency so that it can be combed into fully formed ridges and will completely cover the back of the tile (above left). If mixed too wet, thinset will not hold combed ridges (top). If too dry, it will not adhere to the tile (above right).

adhesive was mixed too dry, it will have formed full ridges but will not have properly wet the tile, and very little will have adhered to the tile. Should you need to adjust a thinset's consistency, add more dry or wet ingredients to the mix very gradually and test it after each adjustment until its consistency is right.

If you find only parallel lines of adhesive lifted from the tops of the combed ridges, the thinset's consistency is correct, but the layer of adhesive is combed too thin. In this case, apply more adhesive and comb it with a larger-notched trowel. Conversely, if

the tile's back is so filled with adhesive that it has oozed up the sides into what will be the grout joint, the layer is too thick and needs to be combed with the angle of the trowel reduced or with a smaller-notched trowel. As a rule of thumb, pick a notch size equal to about two-thirds the thickness of the tile being set.

BACK-BUTTERING Button-backed tiles, handmade tiles with very uneven backs, sheet-mounted mosaic tiles and some small cut tiles and stone tiles may need additional adhesive buttered on the back with a

For spreading adhesive, the trowel's notch size must be paired to the size of the tile. The deep ridges produced by a large-notched trowel appropriately cover the back of large and button-backed tiles, but cause adhesive to ooze up into the joints between small tiles (top right). Conversely, a small-notched trowel yields ridges suitable for small tiles but too shallow to cover large or button-backed tiles fully (bottom right).

If you are installing tiles 12 in. square or larger, particular care should be taken when combing out the adhesive. Tiles this large can sometimes trap air between the combed-out ridges, which reduces the overall grip of the adhesive (the problem is exacerbated as the size of tiles increases). For tiles smaller than 12 in. square, you can spread and comb in just about any direction as long as the overall amount of material is consistent. For large tiles, however, greater adhesion results if you comb the ridges in one direction only. This provides an escape route for all the air sitting between the combed-out ridges.

When installing tiles 12 in. square or larger, the adhesive should be combed in one direction only.

Sloan Howard

margin trowel to ensure full adhesive contact between the tile and setting bed. Back-buttering should supplement, not replace, spreading adhesive on the bed. Insufficient or unevenly applied adhesive produces a poor bond, and leads to cracked tiles and grout joints.

ADHESIVE COVERAGE The amount of adhesive needed to cover a given area can vary considerably from job to job, depending not only on the differing physical properties of the adhesive but also on the choice of setting bed and tile, the force used to spread the adhesive, and the weather. More adhesive is absorbed by a relatively porous mortar setting bed, for example, than by a concrete slab, and by porous nonvitreous tile than by vitreous tile. Hot weather tends to evaporate the moisture in thinset adhesive or mastics, requiring more to be applied to the setting bed than would be needed at normal room temperatures. Because these variables preclude a reliable

adhesive coverage table, I recommend consulting the instructions for the adhesive you have chosen. If there is no coverage table, call the manufacturer or your tile retailer to estimate your needs for a particular installation.

Setting the Tiles

Once you begin spreading thinset, get the tiles bedded quickly to maximize the bond. Depending on job-site conditions, I may set all the full tiles before dealing with the cuts (my usual procedure on large installations), or I may choose to install cut tiles as needed. If your tiling experience is limited, you'll probably find it easier to set full tiles first even on smaller areas. Concentrate on getting the full tiles installed in one day. The next day, when the adhesive has dried, prepare all the cut pieces, mix up a fresh batch of thinset and position the cuts. The job will take a bit longer, but you can put your energy into the finishing details rather than racing the clock.

Regardless of how you proceed, make sure that you don't install any tiles over thinset that has skinned over, which would minimize the bond between the tile and the substrate. If the adhesive should skin over, scrape it away and reapply fresh thinset.

Cleaning up excess adhesive

After the tiles have been positioned, it's imperative to clean up both excess adhesive on the face of the tile and any that has oozed up into the grout joints. Adhesive left in the joints will cause problems when the tiles are grouted. First, grout applied over uncleaned joints may eventually crack, since it's thinner there than at other places. Second, globs of adhesive protruding through the grout are unsightly. And third, if colored grout is used in a joint clogged with adhesive, the thinner grout over the adhesive will take a slightly different cure than the surrounding material and become a different shade as it dries. The grout will, in effect, appear spotted.

A grout saw can be used to cut away excess adhesive that has hardened, but I prefer to use a utility knife while the adhesive is still soft (see the photo at right). If you opt for the knife, slide the blade along the edge of each tile and flick out adhesive between the tiles with its tip. Cleaning excess adhesive while it is soft is a normal part of the installation process. Cleaning the excess after it has hardened is difficult at best and hopeless at worst. If you have to remove hardened adhesive, use the grout saw to cut through the center of the joint and the knife to scrape or slice any remaining dried debris from the edges of the tile, and then clean the tile with a white Scotch-Brite scrubbing pad as needed. Finally, vacuum the joints to pick up loose particles.

Kevin Ireton

Use a utility knife to clean out the excess adhesive between tiles while the adhesive is still soft.

Allow the adhesive to cure at least overnight before grouting (check the label of the product you're using for instructions on precisely how long to wait). If you apply grout over wet or damp adhesive, the grout may discolor.

Grouting

Although grouting is not a particularly difficult job, it does take time, a bit of skill and some patience. It's worth the effort to become an adept grouter, however, since a sloppy grout job can ruin the appearance of an otherwise commendable tile installation. It's a maxim in the tile industry that a good grout job can mask a less-than-perfect tile installation, while a bad job can ruin a perfect installation.

Before you begin to grout, the grout materials should be brought to job-site temperature, which, as for adhesives, should ideally be between 65°F and 75°F. All the same temperature considerations for adhesives apply to grout as well, and the same recommendations should be followed (see p. 140).

To ready the tile for grouting, remove any plastic spacers used to align the tiles. The manufacturers of some spacers state that they can be left in the joint and covered with grout. But the thinner layer of grout above the spacers will cure to a different color, and ghosting will mar the appearance of the grout.

If you're working with vitreous tile, grouting can now begin. If you're setting nonvitreous tile, sponge the tiles with water first, dampening the surface and the sides of each tile to prevent the bisque from sucking too much moisture from the grout. Some commercial tile crews use a garden sprayer to mist the tiles with water. Whichever method you choose, don't overdo it. Puddles of water left on the tile or in the joint will ruin the grout. (If in doubt about the procedure, check with the grout manufacturer.)

Mixing and applying grout

Grouting involves several steps. At each step, as the grout is mixed, allowed to slake, remixed, spread and cleaned up, it changes slightly in consistency, and these changes signal when the next step should begin. Briefly, when first mixed, the grout should be wet enough so that it could be spread with a grout trowel but not so wet that it runs. After slaking for 10 minutes, the grout will be slightly stiffer. Before you add any more liquid to the mixture, however, restir the grout, which will "loosen" it up a little. If it's still too stiff—if it won't stick to the sides of the tile—add a little more of the grout's liquid ingredient, mix thoroughly, and then slake and remix again.

Grout that's ready to use will not pour out of the bucket but rather needs a slight shove, and it should be stiff enough to hold peaks when spread. After the grout is applied, cleanup should begin when the grout residue on the tile's surface is starting to firm up but not completely dry.

The grout within the joints should also be firm or starting to firm, but care should be taken to avoid deforming it with the cleaning sponge.

MIXING GROUT Regular grout can be mixed either with water or with liquid additives as a replacement for the water; dry-polymer grouts must be mixed with water only. Whatever liquid you use, add only enough to render the mixture plastic and spreadable. This point is very important, since too much liquid will weaken the grout (follow the proportioning ratios found in the instructions printed on the container). The mixing bucket should be clean and dry, and if water is used as the liquid element, it should be clean and pure enough to drink.

I mix grout by gradually adding the dry ingredients to the liquid, beginning with only about three-quarters of the liquid needed. Then after all the dry ingredients have been mixed into this liquid, I very gradually pour in the remaining liquid, checking the grout's consistency with each addition. As with any mortar, many factors affect the amount of liquid required, including temperature, humidity, the product used and, in the case of grout, whether it's colored. For these reasons, the ratio of dry ingredients to wet should allow for some adjustment. Mixing grout or any mortar requires care, patience and a bit of trial and error, but with experience, you'll begin to know instinctively when the grout is the right consistency. (With grouts made with a factory-added dry polymer, mixing proportions may be critical—check the label instructions for specific details.)

Use a margin trowel or a power mixing paddle to mix the grout. If you use a paddle, make sure to keep it submerged, as you would for mixing adhesives, to prevent air from being whipped into the grout and weakening it. Keep the blade speed below 300 rpm to reduce air in the mixture. After the ingredients have been

GROUT-JOINT WIDTH

The width of the grout joint is in part a matter of personal preference, and I tend to favor narrow joints. Joints that are too wide will visually overpower the tile. With 4-, 6-, 8-, 10-, 12- and even 24-in. square tiles, I think a ⅛-in. wide grout joint looks crisp and clean. Irregular tiles are set off better with a wider joint, but I tend to make them no more than ½ in. Remember that as the width of the joint increases, so too does the possibility of cracking. Unless you increase the particle size of the sand in the grout, joints larger than ½ in. wide can be troublesome—although increasing particle size doesn't always prevent cracking either. (Another factor that contributes to cracked or powdery grout is using too much liquid when mixing grout.)

It is equally important not to make grout joints too narrow, because they will be difficult to pack and fill properly, resulting in joints that permit substantial water penetration. I feel more confident about an installation when the joints are wide enough to take full advantage of the properties of latex- or acrylic-modified grouts: their ability to cushion the tiles against expansion and contraction, and their increased strength and water resistance. In my opinion, these abilities diminish to negligible levels when the width of the joint is less than ¹⁄₃₂ in.

mixed initially and most of the lumps have been eliminated, let the grout slake for 10 minutes. Slaking allows the dry ingredients, in particular those in clumps, to be thoroughly wetted by the liquid. Then restir the grout to get out all the lumps.

If you need to mix several batches of grout for a job, make sure they're all identical. (When buying more than one package of grout, check to see that the lot numbers are the same.) Not only should the proportions of the ingredients be consistent from batch to batch, but also the order in which the ingredients are combined, as well as the length of the mixing time and the speed of the mixer. To ensure uniformity of color on large installations, dispense grout from several bags for each batch.

APPLYING GROUT   When you're ready to begin grouting, dump a pile of grout on the surface of the tile (tip the bucket if you're doing floor work, scoop out the grout with a margin trowel for wall tiles). To spread the grout, use a grout trowel (available in floor or wall versions) rather than a steel trowel. Hold it at an angle of about 30° to the tile, as you would to spread an adhesive. Grout over the entire area you're working two or three times, not just dabbing the grout into the joints but pushing and pressing it between the tiles so that you feel resistance as each joint is packed. The greater the resistance, the more densely packed and stronger the joints will be. The idea is to cram grout into all the nooks at the tiles' edges and into voids left around the tiles by insufficient adhesive. The process also forces some of the liquid out of the grout, so that the joints are as fully packed as possible with sand and cement particles—a solid, if you will, rather than a slurry with suspended particles of cement and sand.

Rather than grouting an entire installation all at once, spread only a small section at first—about 10 sq. ft. to 20 sq. ft.— until you see how quickly the grout sets up. This way, if you happen to be working with a grout that sets up fast, you won't get ahead of yourself and end up with a tough cleaning job. Sometimes it is possible to

After dumping enough grout on the tile to work a small section (top left), begin spreading it with a grout trowel held at a 30° angle (above). When you've forcefully packed the joints in this area, cut away the excess grout with the trowel held at almost a right angle (left).

grout 100 sq. ft. of tile or more before cleanup must begin; at other times only a small area can be covered. A trial patch will tell you how to pace your work.

REMOVING EXCESS GROUT When all the joints are filled, hold the trowel at almost a right angle to the surface of the tile and cut the excess grout off the surface. As you do this, also make sure to move the trowel diagonally across the joints to prevent the tool's edge from dipping into the joints and raking out grout. (If this does happen, simply refill the divot with fresh grout material and recut with the edge of the

trowel.) Once the excess has been removed, let the grout begin to set up before you start cleaning. As you're grouting and cleaning up, of course, the grout in the bucket will also be setting up. For this reason, occasionally restir the grout in the bucket to loosen it up before applying it in a new area.

USING A GROUT BAG If the tile you're working with has a surface that will be particularly difficult to clean up after grouting, for example antique brick-veneer tile, use a grout bag to fill the joints. This bag looks and works much like a cake-decorating bag (see the photo on p. 65). A metal tip the approximate width of the grout joint is placed on the end of the bag. The bag is filled, and then folded and squeezed to force grout into the joints.

When working with a grout bag, hold the tip of the bag at the top edge of each joint and move the bag along the edge as it's filled. For greater efficiency, run the entire length of the joint—not just around an individual tile. I generally fill all the joints along the x axis and then fill those along the y. Without overdoing it, squeeze a bit more grout into the joint than appears to be needed. After letting the grout harden slightly, compact this excess into the joint with a striking tool or simply a piece of smooth metal tubing whose diameter is wider than the width of the joints being filled. Let the packed grout harden for a half hour or so, and then whisk away any extraneous material with a stiff brush or broom.

Cleaning and finishing grout joints

After the dry cleaning with the edge of the grout trowel (which removes the bulk of the excess grout from the tiles), each tile installation requires a certain amount of wet cleaning. The time grout needs to set up before this part of the cleaning process varies from job to job. It may set up within five minutes, or it may take 20 minutes (or longer). The weather as well as the type of setting bed, adhesive and tile used all affect the rate at which moisture evaporates from the grout.

Keep in mind that the grout residue on the surface of the tile can harden fairly quickly, whereas the grout in the joints may take considerably more time. Use the sponge to judge when the surface of the tile and the grout joints are ready to be cleaned: Wring out as much moisture from the sponge as possible, and then test a small area by sponging over the surface of

the tile. The grout in the joints should be resilient and firm but not hard. If the grout has set up too much, the tiles will need to be scrubbed heavily, which can disfigure the joints. On the other hand, if the sponge pulls grout out of the joints, the grout hasn't set up sufficiently. Wait a few minutes and test again. When grout in the joints is not so easily disturbed, cleanup can begin.

If you've waited too long to begin cleanup and the grout has dried on the surface of the tile, scrub each tile with a white Scotch-Brite pad. (Unlike some other scouring pads, this pad should not scratch the surface of the tiles—to be sure, test first on a scrap tile.) After scrubbing, go over the entire area once or twice with a thoroughly wrung-out sponge.

There are many techniques for cleaning grout, some of them rather unusual. Some setters, for example, sprinkle dry grout powder over the joints (to help dry out the wet grout in the joint), while others use sawdust to collect moisture and clean excess grout particles. Many of these methods weaken or otherwise affect the grout joint, however, so I don't recommend them. I use a combination of approaches that have proven effective on both commercial and residential installations. The key to all techniques is to use an absolute minimum of water during cleanup to prevent weakening the grout.

STARTING THE WET CLEANUP   To clean up grout by my method, you'll need only a sponge and a bucket of clean water. (The sponge I use is roughly 5 in. by 7 in. by 3 in. and has rounded rather than square edges, which are less likely to gouge the joints.) Work only a small section at a time (10 sq. ft. to 20 sq. ft.), rinsing the sponge often to wash out the grout particles that collect in the pores.

When rinsing the sponge, always wring as much water from it as possible, ensure that the loose grout particles are flushed from the pores of the sponge, and remember to shake the excess water from your hands. Surprisingly, unless the installation is larger than 100 sq. ft. or so, it's not necessary to keep changing the water in the rinse bucket. It's the way you use the sponge, not the cleanliness of the water, that determines how well the tiles are cleaned (of course, on some commercial projects, providing fresh water is a full-time job). The residual haze left drying on the surface of the tiles should be your guide.

My process of cleaning grout involves several steps. An initial, quick scrubbing with the sponge takes up most of the unwanted grout from the surface of the tiles; a second going-over neatens the grout joints themselves; and a third, careful cleaning removes any grout residue from the surface of the tiles. After these steps, the grout is left briefly to harden in the joints. Then any remaining grout haze on the tiles is wiped off with cheesecloth.

Begin cleaning up the grout on the surface of the tiles by gently sponging in a circular fashion to loosen the sand and cement particles (see the photo below). Be careful not to gouge grout out of the joints. Turn the sponge as soon as its pores fill with grout and rinse it often, remembering to wring it out well. If you haven't waited too long before starting to clean up, you should be able to remove the excess grout from the surface of the tiles in two or three passes.

Turn next to cleaning and shaping the joints themselves. Make passes with the sponge that are parallel to the joint, gently shaving down any high spots and stopping to fill any voids with a fingerful of grout (wearing snug-fitting rubber gloves). The joint's actual shaping depends on the type of tile used and the treatment the factory or tile maker has given the top edge. If that edge is sharply squared off, the grout should be flat and flush with the top of the

Begin cleaning up the grout by sponging the tiles with a circular motion. Remember to rinse the sponge often and wring out all the excess water from it.

To remove the grout residue and shape the joints, make slow, short, parallel passes, pulling the sponge toward you. Rinse the sponge frequently and thoroughly.

tiles. If the top edge is rounded, the setter must decide how high to make the joint. Whatever height is selected, ideally the joint should be flat on top, not convex, although most will end up being slightly concave, which is fine. The important thing is to give all the joints a consistent shape and depth.

REMOVING THE CEMENT RESIDUE Once the joints in the field of tile have been shaped, the surface of the tiles should be carefully cleaned again. First rinse and wring out the sponge. Then make a straight, vertical pass of about 3 ft. with one side of the sponge, pulling it toward you slowly—more slowly than you think you need to—and without stopping. (If you pull the sponge quickly toward you or move it in stages, grout will streak across the surface of the tiles.) After the first pass, turn the sponge over to the clean side, make a similar pass parallel to the first, and then stop and rinse the sponge. Use a freshly rinsed side of the sponge for one pass only.

Continue this procedure throughout the full area being cleaned, being careful again not to dig into the joints with the sponge. At the same time, watch to see if the sponge pulls grout from the joints. If it does, the grout is either too high in the joints and needs to be shaved down farther, or there's too much water in the sponge. This cleaning should remove almost all of the grout residue from the face of the tiles, and they should be left alone for about 15 minutes.

During this pause, the moisture left on the tiles from cleaning will evaporate and any cement particles suspended in the water will be deposited on the surface of the tiles. If the tiles you are grouting have a high-gloss glaze and the corners are smooth and crisp, this grout haze should be easy to remove by rubbing the surface promptly with cheesecloth or a soft, clean rag. If the tiles have a matte finish or rounded corners, the grout haze may require an additional pass with fresh water and the sponge.

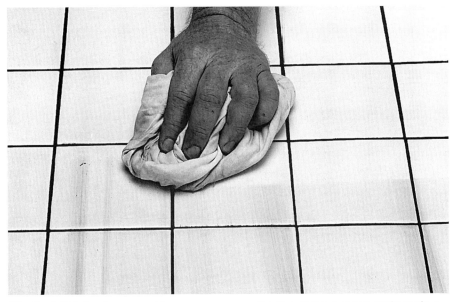

After the initial cleaning, a grout haze may appear on the tiles as the moisture on the surface dries. If you don't wait too long, you can usually clean off this haze by rubbing the tiles with cheesecloth.

If the residue still resists cleaning, you may not have cleaned the surface of the tiles adequately the first time around. Lingering grout residue may also be caused by latex or acrylic additives that cause the grout to grip the surface of the tiles more tenaciously than regular grouts. Whatever the cause, the longer the haze remains on the tiles, the harder it becomes to remove it. If scrubbing with a damp, white Scotch-Brite pad does not remove the residue, you may have to use a special grout-haze cleaning solution, or, in a worst-case scenario, resort to acid cleaners (see p. 229).

If you have determined that special cleaners or acid must be used, keep in mind that the grout should be allowed to cure fully before this kind of cleaning can take place. Nevertheless, don't wait for the grout to cure before completing the last stage of the grout cleaning—removing all traces of grout from the expansion joints (see the sidebar at right).

Grout sealers and impregnators

Grout can be protected from staining by cleaning up spills promptly and by regular maintenance. Using latex or acrylic additives or polymer-modified grouts can reduce staining, but supplemental sealers or impregnators provide the best protection. These are liquids applied to the tile, the grout or both after the grout has cured (refer to manufacturers' instructions for complete application details).

I prefer to use an impregnator that was developed to minimize the effects of urban graffiti on natural stone (see p. 31). Experience has shown it to provide considerably better protection than silicone-type grout sealers. This impregnator lasts longer, too, but it is considerably more expensive than silicone sealers (see the Resource Guide for a source for this product). Nevertheless, when maintaining an installation is important, the treatment is rather inexpensive in the long run.

EXPANSION-JOINT CLEANUP

When applying grout, it may be difficult to prevent grout from clogging joints earmarked as expansion joints (see pp. 97-103). These include joints at inside corners, around sink rims and where tiles abut any nonceramic materials (such as wood trim, porcelain and stainless steel).

Don't worry, however, if grout does stray into expansion joints, since it can easily be sliced away from the sides of a tile with a trowel or utility knife while it's still soft. In fact, it is much easier to remove stray grout after it has begun to set up (but before it gets too hard!). Grout in this condition easily crumbles into particles that can be removed with a vacuum cleaner.

When all the unwanted grout has been removed, go over the expansion joints with a damp sponge to remove any excess that may have found its way to the surface of the tiles.

■■ ■■ ■■

Chapter Nine

Floor Installations

Floors account for the majority of all tiles installed. Inviting entry halls, hard-working mudrooms, low-maintenance kitchen and bathroom floors, elegant hallways and courtly terraces are just a few examples of how tiles can be used to finish, protect and decorate floor areas. Ceramic and stone tiles can readily beautify any floor space, but for the tiles to perform as expected, the entire installation—from tiles and materials to setting methods—has to be carefully considered.

Thinbed Floors vs. Mortar-Bed Floors

Not too many years ago, practically all floor tiles were installed over thick beds of mortar. Beneath those mortar beds could be found wooden substructures that, by today's standards, would be considered massive. Also, the quality of the lumber used was excellent, with little or no warping, bowing or twisting. A thick bed

of mortar needs this kind of strong and unyielding structure to keep the tiles from cracking.

Today, most buildings are quite flexible—the exact opposite of what is required for traditional mortar-bed tile installations. Fortunately, the tile industry has worked very hard to perfect materials and methods that permit tiles to be installed with confidence on the new, thinner substrates. That is not to say that mortar beds are no longer used. Quite the contrary. Mortar beds can be seen on many residential, commercial and industrial applications. I use mortar beds regularly for special installations, but I also rely on them on problem jobs where no other material or method will give satisfactory and economical results. Mortar beds, whether for the simple or the extravagant, are indeed special installations requiring patience, understanding and skill. (For information on installing a mortar-bed shower floor, see pp. 208-219.)

The TCA (Tile Council of America) *Handbook* is the industry benchmark for ceramic-tile installation methods. A number of the methods presented in the *Handbook* include a "caution" message, as shown in the drawing at right (taken from TCA *Handbook* F142). These cautions are included to underscore the potential problems related to certain substrate materials, such as plywood and gypsum board, when they are used on wet installations. The caution message reads:

The performance of a properly installed thin-set ceramic tile installation is dependent upon the durability and dimensional stability of the substrate to which it is bonded. The user is cautioned that certain substrate materials used in wet areas are subject to deterioration from moisture penetration.

Therefore, while every effort has been made to produce accurate guidelines, they should be used only with the independent approval of technically qualified persons.

If you are planning to use plywood (or gypsum board) as a wet-area setting bed, contact the manufacturer of the adhesive you intend to use for a project review. The manufacturer's technical representative will help you determine whether the substrate can stand alone or will require a waterproofing membrane.

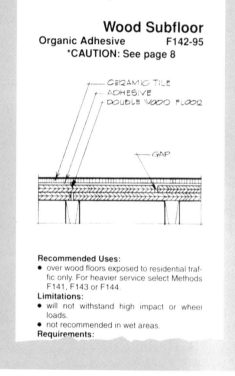

FLOORS, INTERIOR

Wood Subfloor
Organic Adhesive   F142-95
*CAUTION: See page 8

— CERAMIC TILE
— ADHESIVE
— DOUBLE WOOD FLOOR

— GAP

Recommended Uses:
- over wood floors exposed to residential traffic only. For heavier service select Methods F141, F143 or F144.

Limitations:
- will not withstand high impact or wheel loads.
- not recommended in wet areas.

Requirements:

In my business, I install floor tiles on mortar beds, cement backer boards (CBUs), concrete slabs, existing fields of ceramic tile, and other surfaces—even plywood. Because I never set tiles over soft mortar (I wait until the mortar bed has hardened), all my installations use thinbed materials and methods. This means that the skills to do the necessary work are quite simple to master, and beyond the ability to hammer a nail, drive a screw, use a tape measure, read a level and cut along a straight line, all that is required is the ability to mix and spread an adhesive, and to mix and install the grout. These techniques are described in Chapter 8.

A Kitchen-Floor Installation

Although I am always looking for perfection on the job, and thoroughly enjoy working over surfaces produced by skilled craftsmen, I have never worked on any job that had so much to tell an interested reader as the tile-over-plywood installation described in this chapter. Although I shy away from plywood installations nowadays (much preferring CBUs), I have completed hundreds of plywood floors like this one with excellent results. What makes this particular floor such a good example is that there were so many problems: The floor was way out of level, the subfloor was poorly prepared, the wrong materials were chosen initially, and not enough fasteners were used—the kind of problems most professional installers face every day.

Also at stake in this job was a budget that had already been stretched. Making the right material and method choices is crucial to any successful installation, but when the budget is pinched, the choices become even more important. The owner wanted ceramic tile—no other floor covering would do. This particular floor required more compromises than I normally make, but in the end, the kitchen was finished with a durable tile installation that attractively masked the problems.

Tiling this floor was part of a kitchen remodeling job that was under way before I was called in. The owner had halted work on the floor after another contractor had nailed down, over two existing layers of vinyl flooring, a layer of 1/8-in. thick lauan plywood as a setting bed for the tiles. The customer had noticed that the plywood was springy in places and that there was no clearance to install tiles below the dishwasher. She phoned the office and asked if I could take a look at the job.

Sizing up the job

When I went to the house to measure the job, the situation was worse than I thought. The whole first floor of the house sloped from west to east, leaving the kitchen floor out of level 2 in. in the space of 10 ft. Of the three doorways leading into the kitchen, two were located on the high side of the room and one was on the low side. New kitchen cabinets had already been installed on two walls and were perched on 2-in. high shims on the room's downhill side. This arrangement meant that the cabinet's rough toe kick, which the customer wanted tiled, was suspended in midair at one end.

Normally, a condition like this could be remedied by floating a mortar bed to level up the floor. But in this case that would

have left a 2-in. high step down into the living room from the doorway on the low side of the kitchen. A step might not be objectionable, except that since none was needed at the two doors on the high side, this solution would awkwardly point up the house's structural problems. (And in some households, a step can be hazardous.) The only other way to even out the floor would be to correct the framing or the foundation, an expensive prospect that was far beyond the customer's budget.

The owner had grown accustomed to sloping floors throughout the old house. For her, this condition was acceptable. I did

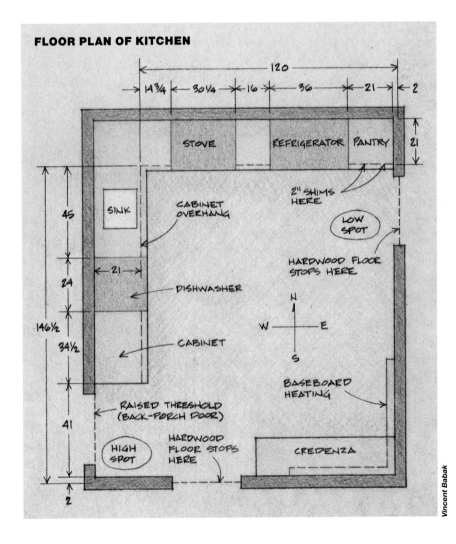

FLOOR PLAN OF KITCHEN

When out-of-level floors are neither quaint nor desirable, there are a number of options you can use to correct the situation. The option you select will depend on the availability and cost of materials, the skills required for the fix, and any height limitations. Determining the height limitation is the best place to start.

HEIGHT LIMITATIONS

Height limitations are especially critical in a kitchen because appliances may be restricted by existing cabinetry. First, measure the available head space above built-in or roll-in appliances. Then locate the highest point on the floor and extend this height into the appliance area. Add to this the thickness of the tile and the adhesive and any membrane planned for the floor. Then compare this amount to the available head space, which will tell you whether you can use a simple fix , like a self-leveling compound (SLC), to correct the floor or something more complex, like extensive carpentry to rebuild and level the subfloor.

SELF-LEVELING COMPOUNDS

If height limitations are not a problem, determine the highest and lowest points on the floor. If the difference in height is less than 1 in., most self-leveling compounds can be used in a single pour (see p. 89). If the difference is greater than 1 in., SLCs can still be used by employing two or more pours (or "lifts"), allowing each to harden and cure before the next is applied.

OTHER ALTERNATIVES

Applying a self-leveling compound is the easiest way to correct an out-of-level floor, but it may also be the most expensive material to use. Plywood and dimensional lumber are not exactly inexpensive, but if you have the tools and the skills and the time is your own, carpentry may be a better option. The materials for producing a reinforced mortar bed may be less expensive than lumber or SLCs, but the skills and labor required are considerable.

---

not like the slope, but since this would be a dry floor (and not have to channel water to a drain), it was the owner's call. However, the owner was willing to compromise on the 12-in. tiles she had originally selected. I knew that some of the corners and edges of these large tiles would protrude above the plane of the floor, because it undulated as it went from the high side to the low. A better way to mask this condition would be to use a smaller-size tile. The owner agreed to select a tile no larger than 8 in. square.

One thing I could not compromise on was the material used for the setting bed. Lauan plywood is all right for resilient flooring or as a base for carpeting, but it should never be used under ceramic or stone tile. I would have preferred to use a cement backer board (see the sidebar on the facing page), but the cost of the board and its layer of laminating thinset mortar was too steep for the budget. This left plywood—not my first choice, but given the rather modest demands that would be made on the finished installation, it was acceptable.

First, however, I needed to reduce the profile (height) of the floor. To do this, I would need to remove the rest of the existing flooring down to the subfloor. I am concerned about removing some kinds of resilient flooring that may contain asbestos. Tiles can be installed over sound single-layer resilient flooring, thus effectively encapsulating the asbestos, but not over two layers. As luck would have it, however, I was able to contact the dealer who had supplied both layers. After his assurance that neither layers contained asbestos, I proceeded with the work while the owner went off to select a new tile.

If the budget for the kitchen floor presented in this chapter had not been so tight, I would have used cement backer boards as the setting bed and laminated them to a ¾-in. plywood subfloor (½-in. subflooring is the industry standard, but I prefer to upgrade to ¾ in.). Here's how I install a backer-board setting bed (see also pp. 77-79):

To laminate the backer board, I begin by spreading and combing latex-modified thinset mortar onto the subfloor with a ¼-in. square-notched trowel (working one sheet at a time). This mortar, which must be compatible with the plywood, is the same thinset I use to install the tile. Next I position the backer board over the bed and hinge it down into place.

To seat the backer board in the bed of fresh mortar, I either use a beating block and a hammer or simply walk around the board. Then I align the board with the layout lines and secure it with screws.

After all the boards have been installed (with an ⅛-in. gap between boards and a ¼-in. gap between the boards and any restraining surfaces), I cover all the joints with open-mesh fiberglass tape. The joints within the field could be filled and finished with thinset mortar at this point, but I prefer to wait until it is time to install the tiles so there are no bumps or ridges of hardened material to tile over.

Once I have established the tile layout and am ready to set tiles, I fill the joints with thinset mortar (working one layout square at a time), feather the joints and then proceed to spread and comb the thinset for the tiles.

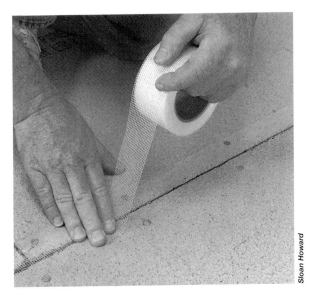

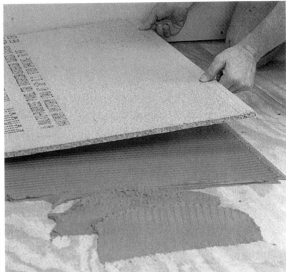

Hinge the backer board down into the thinset adhesive.

After screwing the backer board to the subfloor, mesh all the joints between boards (top). Finish the joints by troweling on the adhesive and then feathering it out (above).

Removing the old materials

The first step on this job was to disconnect the water supply and electrical lines to the appliances and move them out of the kitchen. Next I took the baseboards off the walls and then tore out the lauan plywood with a pry bar and hammer. To make it easier to remove the vinyl flooring and particleboard underlayment, I cut through the flooring along the toe kick with a small-diameter sawblade mounted in an electric hand grinder.

I also made several cuts with the saw a few feet away from the kick so that I could easily pry up the old layers of the floor. Because the sawblade is only 4 in. in diameter and can cut only ¾ in. deep when mounted in my hand grinder, I didn't have to worry about sawing into the joists.

When I yanked a piece of the lauan plywood off and pried up a section of the two sheets of vinyl, I found that the first sheet was glued to a ½-in. thick particleboard underlayment, which, in turn, was nailed to 1x8 subflooring. The subflooring was fine, but the particleboard, an inappropriate substrate for tiling, would need to be removed.

Choosing installation materials

I decided to replace the particleboard with ½-in. thick, AC exterior plywood for the setting bed, which would strengthen the floor but still leave room to tile underneath the dishwasher once the old flooring layers had been removed. Because this installation would not get wet, other than an occasional washing, no waterproofing membrane was necessary, and the tile could be set directly over the plywood.

For a plywood setting bed like this, an organic mastic rated for use with plywood could be used, but I prefer a suitable latex thinset or an epoxy for floors because these adhesives are stronger than mastics. In this case, a strong adhesive was especially important because the floor had a crown, or hump, in the middle, produced by structural forces that might still be at play. After considering an epoxy adhesive, I opted for a latex thinset because of the client's budget and the extra expense she had already borne for the first contractor's efforts. While the compressive strength of the adhesive I wanted to use is not as high as that of an epoxy, its greater flexibility made it better suited than epoxy to the plywood underlayment.

Although this would not be a wet installation, I suggested that vitreous tiles be used because of their strength and durability. Knowing that the floor would undoubtedly be subject to slippery spills from time to time, the customer wanted a tile with a non-slick glaze. She selected four samples that she liked, and tested their practicality by grinding her heel into each to see how well it would stand up and, in turn, clean up. In the end she picked a sand-colored, Italian floor tile $7^{15}/_{16}$ in. square. She chose to pair the tile with a tan-colored, sanded grout, specially formulated for joints wider than ⅛ in. Although I generally prefer a ⅛-in. wide joint, we had agreed on a ³⁄₁₆-in. wide grout joint to help mask the presence of the floor's crown.

Surface Preparation

When plywood underlayment is installed as the setting bed for tiles, the joints between the underlayment sheets should be staggered over the joints in a plywood subfloor. But in this case, the existing subfloor was made of 1x8s. The ceiling below this floor was finished, and without access to the joists (where I could nail in additional support to catch the edges of full sheets), I would have to cut down the underlayment so its edges terminated along the middle of joist.

After thoroughly vacuuming the entire floor, I installed the new underlayment by working in the following sequence: I started in one corner of the room and cut a piece of plywood to fit, with about a $\frac{1}{8}$-in. gap planned between sheets. (These gaps would be filled with adhesive when the tile was set, effectively edge-gluing the sheets; the $\frac{1}{4}$-in. gap that I allowed at the perimeter of the floor would not be filled.) With the plywood laid in position, I snapped chalk lines on it to indicate the location of the floor joists, which I determined from the placement of the nails in the surrounding subfloor. Then I picked up the plywood sheet, turned it on edge, and caulked a bead of construction adhesive (rated for floor use) around the perimeter of the sheet and in parallel lines down its length about every 8 in.

Once I had relaid the sheet, I secured it by hammering in a few 1 $\frac{1}{2}$-in. ring-shank nails, starting in one corner and working toward the opposite corner. Next I nailed down the sheet every 6 in., then went back to the chalk lines and used 3-in. nails every 6 in. to anchor firmly into the joists. Finally, I ran my hand over all the nails and hammered down any whose heads stuck up (these might crack the tile). I moved all my tools onto the first installed segment of underlayment, and proceeded sheet by sheet to cover the floor.

In the process of installing the plywood, I came across one sheet that was slightly warped. To counteract the warping, I turned the sheet concave-side-down before measuring and cutting it. I also added a little extra construction adhesive to this sheet and nailed in a few more nails once it was in position to ensure that it would lie flat.

Estimating Tile and Materials

On my initial visit to the client's house, I had sketched in my notebook a floor plan of the kitchen, showing room dimensions with the baseboards removed and with indents for the dishwasher, stove and refrigerator, since each cutout was to be tiled (see the drawing on p. 157). I also noted where the cabinets overhung the floor, where the baseboard heating elements were located, where the tiles met hardwood flooring in other rooms and where there was a raised threshold at the back door to the porch. All these factors would affect the eventual layout. Once I knew the size of the tile and grout joint selected, I could proceed to work out the layout on paper and to calculate the amount of tile needed for the job.

Working out the layout

I used $\frac{1}{8}$-in. graph paper to do a detailed floor plan because it's easy to scale out a drawing on this paper and to lay out a floor fairly accurately. Each graph-paper square represents a 6-in. square floor area (I didn't worry about fractions of an inch on this drawing). Although I usually have to make some adjustments on any job once I begin to check the room for square and to do the actual layout, working things out on paper beforehand helps speed up this process. Next I made up a list of tile and grout-joint dimensions, which I would refer to when doing the layout.

This list, shown at right, begins with the combined width of a single tile and grout joint (8 $\frac{1}{8}$ in.) and ends with the combined width of 18 tiles and grout joints (146 $\frac{1}{4}$ in.), because this measurement was nearest the room's longest dimension.

Since the door on the east wall led from the living room into the kitchen and the tiles abutting the hardwood floor at the doorway would be very visible, I wanted to

TILE/GROUT-JOINT LIST

Since the combined width of a single tile (7$\frac{15}{16}$ in.) and its grout joint ($\frac{3}{16}$ in.) equals 8$\frac{1}{8}$ in., the combined width of additional tiles and joints can be calculated as follows:

1 = 8$\frac{1}{8}$ in.   *10 = 81$\frac{1}{4}$ in.*

2 = 16$\frac{1}{4}$ in.   *11 = 89$\frac{3}{8}$ in.*

3 = 24$\frac{3}{8}$ in.   *12 = 97$\frac{1}{2}$ in.*

4 = 32$\frac{1}{2}$ in.   *13 = 105$\frac{5}{8}$ in.*

5 = 40$\frac{5}{8}$ in.   *14 = 113$\frac{3}{4}$ in.*

6 = 48$\frac{3}{4}$ in.   *15 = 121$\frac{7}{8}$ in.*

7 = 56$\frac{7}{8}$ in.   *16 = 130 in.*

8 = 65 in.   *17 = 138$\frac{1}{8}$ in.*

9 = 73$\frac{1}{8}$ in.   *18 = 146$\frac{1}{4}$ in.*

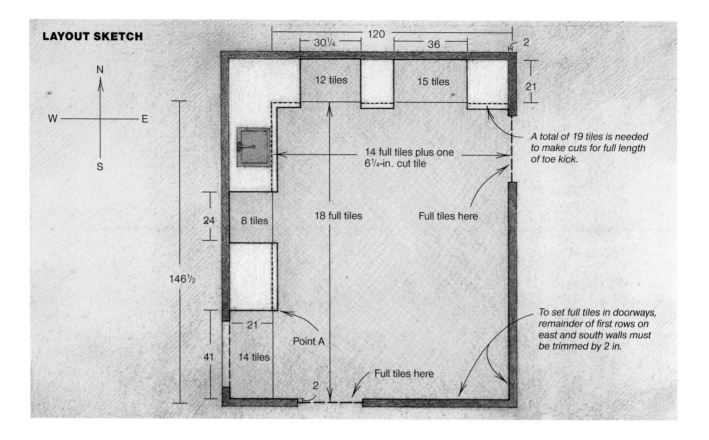

LAYOUT SKETCH

120

30¼   36   2

12 tiles   15 tiles

21

A total of 19 tiles is needed
to make cuts for full length
of toe kick.

14 full tiles plus one
6¼-in. cut tile

18 full tiles   Full tiles here

24   8 tiles

146½

To set full tiles in doorways,
remainder of first rows on
east and south walls must
be trimmed by 2 in.

21

Point A

41   14 tiles

2   Full tiles here

use full tiles at this point. To calculate the
number of rows that would fit from this
doorway to the back of the toe kick under
the cabinets on the west wall, I checked
the room dimensions on the sketch and the
tile/grout-joint list. The width of the room
at this point was 120 in., which meant that
14 full tiles would fit, with a 6¼-in. wide
cut tile tucked under the overhanging
cabinets. The cut tile was to be more than
half-size, so it would not detract from the
floor's appearance even if there were no
overhang. Except for the tile at the
doorway, the remaining tile in the first row
along the east wall would have to be
trimmed by 2 in. to accommodate the
width of the wall. Since this cut, like that
across the room, would be more than half-
size, it would not be visually distracting.

Looking next at the length of the room
from the toe kick on the north wall to the
doorway on the south wall, I saw that the

tile would again abut a hardwood floor at
this door and I wanted to use full tiles here,
too. Within the 146½-in. length, I found
from my list that 18 full tiles would fit, with
a ¼-in. space left over. This gap would be
hidden at the back of the toe kick, but even
if there were no toe kick, it would still be
obscured by the overhanging cabinets.

Having established the crucial spots
where full tiles had to be used, I wanted to
check the rest of the room to see if the
proposed layout would work. The one area
that concerned me was the floor at the
corner of the cabinet near the door to the
back porch (point A in the drawing above).
The distance from point A to the threshold
at the south door was 43 in., into which I
could fit 5 full tiles with a 2⅜-in. space left
over. This meant that there would need to
be a strip of cut tiles 2⅜-in. wide along the
base of the cabinet. Shifting the layout
2⅜-in. north would eliminate the cut tiles

at the cabinet, but would produce a gap of the same width at the threshold. Since there was no other alternative and a compromise had to be made, I chose to place the cuts along the base of the cabinet, where they would be far less obvious than at the threshold. This layout also meant that the first row of tiles along the south wall on either side of the threshold would need to be trimmed by 2 in.

The areas beneath the dishwasher, stove and refrigerator would be hidden once the appliances were repositioned, and I was therefore not too concerned with the layout there. In fact, these locations were just the place to make use of leftover cut tile and any tile with surface blemishes.

Once I had settled on a layout, I could calculate the number of tiles needed. This can be done either by calculating the square footage covered and then ordering the tile by the square foot (it's usually sold this way), or by adding up the number of individual tiles called for by the layout. Since the latter method is more reliable (see pp. 121-122), I referred to the floor plan and layout to do the count, as shown in the drawing below.

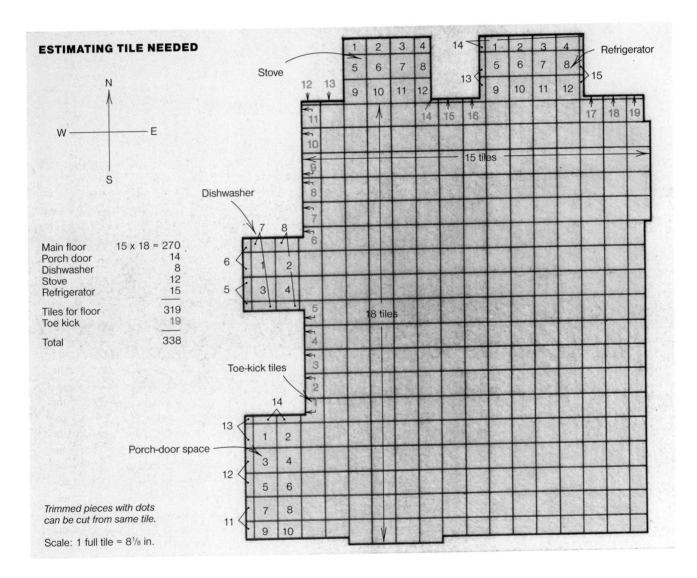

ESTIMATING TILE NEEDED

Main floor	15 x 18 = 270
Porch door	14
Dishwasher	8
Stove	12
Refrigerator	15
Tiles for floor	319
Toe kick	19
Total	338

Trimmed pieces with dots can be cut from same tile.

Scale: 1 full tile = 8 1/8 in.

For each east-west row in the main portion of the floor, a total of 14 full tiles and a 6¼-in. tile cut from a full tile would be needed, that is, 15 tiles in all. Each north-south row here required 18 full tiles. The number of tiles needed for the main area of the floor was therefore 270 (15 x 18 = 270). The count of tiles needed for the other sections of the floor and for the vertically installed toe kick was 68 (see the drawing on p. 163). The total counted number of tiles needed for the floor was thus 338. To be on the safe side, in the event that some tiles arrive at the scene broken or I miscut one or two, I always order more than needed. On this job I added 10 tiles to the count and ordered 348 in all. The customer could store any leftovers in case any future repairs were required.

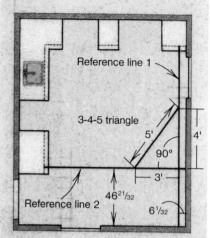

CHECKING FOR SQUARE

If hypotenuse of 3-4-5 triangle equals exactly 5 ft., reference lines and walls from which they're projected are square. If walls prove slightly out of square, reference lines must be adjusted before layout. For information on adjusting these lines, see pp. 123-125.

Layout

Doing the actual layout on this floor was simple. In effect, I had already figured out the position of the layout lines when I did the layout on paper and calculated the number of tiles needed. Since the planned layout would work only if the walls and cabinets at the job site were square to each other, however, I needed to check this before chalking any layout lines. Two reference lines on the floor were required, from which I could measure the cabinets, toe kick and other areas to determine if the room was square.

Checking for square

Inasmuch as I had planned my layout with full tiles at the east and south thresholds, I decided to use these points to help me establish the reference lines. To begin, I measured out from the edge of the east threshold a distance of one tile and one grout joint, subtracted half the thickness of the grout joint and made a mark. This mark would give me a point representing the center of a grout joint. From my earlier

layout on paper I knew that tiles along the east wall would have 2 in. cut from them, so I measured out from the wall a distance identical to the one I had measured at the threshold, subtracted 2 in. and made another mark. Then I connected the two marks with a snapped chalk line to get a line parallel to the east wall, which represented the center of a grout joint between the first and second rows of tile.

I would have repeated the process on the south wall for the second line, but because it would be difficult to work beneath the built-in credenza, I made my measurements so that they would put this reference line between the sixth and seventh rows of tile. By positioning the reference lines in the center of what would become grout joints, I could later use these lines, once established as square, as layout lines. (I could theoretically locate the reference lines anywhere on the floor, but the above technique saves time and eliminates confusion for me.)

With these two lines in place, I could begin to check the room for square by plotting a 3-4-5 triangle on the reference lines. If the east and south walls were square to one another, a triangle plotted on the lines with a base of 3 ft. and a height of 4 ft. would have a hypotenuse of 5 ft. (see p. 123). If the hypotenuse were shorter or longer than 5 ft., I would know that these walls were out of square and I would have to adjust the reference lines. Unless the walls were drastically off, this adjustment would only slightly affect the outermost row of tiles along these two walls and would keep the tiles in the rest of the room properly in square.

To begin making the 3-4-5 triangle on the two reference lines, I measured north 4 ft. on the first line from the point where the two lines intersected and penciled a mark. Next I drew a mark on the second line 3 ft. west of the point of intersection. When I measured the distance between the two marks, completing the triangle, I found that it was exactly 5 ft., which meant that the east and south walls were square to one another. (For information on adjusting the reference lines if the walls prove not to be square, see pp. 123-125.)

Next I wanted to check to see if the cabinets on the west and north walls were square to each other. If the toe kicks on these walls proved parallel to the first and second layout lines, respectively, I would know that the cabinets were square. To check whether each kick was parallel to the opposing line, I simply measured the distance to the line from each end of the kick and then compared the measurements.

The west toe kick turned out not to be parallel to the east reference line—it angled out from the line about ½ in. at the south end of the cabinets. This discrepancy meant that the tiles along this kick would have to be cut to fit the angle. Since I had

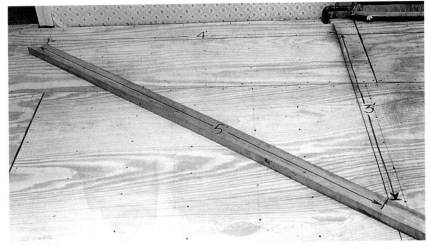

After projecting a pair of layout lines off the east and south walls, the author made a 3-4-5 triangle to see if the walls were square.

planned to cut these tiles anyway, however, and since the kick tiles would largely hide the tapering cuts, this was not a problem.

If the north toe kick was not parallel to the south reference line, however, it would cause problems. If the kick angled away from the line, the ¼-in. space planned in the layout to fall between the last row of tiles and the kick would increase and need to be filled with slivers of tile. Since this would be an unattractive solution, I could instead solve the problem by shimming out the kick's depth with plywood equal in thickness to the width of the taper.

If, on the other hand, the toe kick angled toward the line, the tiles at the kick would need to be trimmed. Though this was not an ideal solution, it would not detract too much from the visual effect of the entire floor. After taking the necessary measurements, I was pleased to find that the north kick was parallel to the reference line.

Plotting layout lines

With the room checked for square, I was ready to snap layout lines on the setting bed. Ordinarily in a room this size, I would probably need only two layout lines to keep the tiles straight, provided I could get tile spacers long enough to extend beyond the rounded corners of this tile. (I would want

LAYOUT LINES

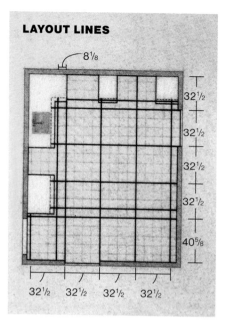

to use more layout lines with smaller tiles, regardless of whether spacers were available.) Unfortunately, I couldn't get the spacers I needed quickly because the local supplier had none in stock, so instead I added more layout lines.

For the sake of accuracy, I projected all the layout lines off the two reference lines used to check the room for square. I wanted enough layout lines on the setting bed to allow me to set the full tiles quickly and accurately and also to separate these tiles from the cut tiles. First, I chalked lines that were parallel to the two reference lines and spaced 32½ in. apart (see the drawing above). This layout produced a series of boxes, most of which would hold 16 tiles each, all of them comfortably within my reach. Then I snapped additional lines around the north, west and south walls to mark the grout joint between the full tiles and the cut tiles. While setting up this layout grid obviously takes time, I am firmly convinced that it saves time in the long run, because the actual setting goes much more quickly and efficiently than it would otherwise.

Staging the Installation

Because the thinset adhesive I would be using sets up in about 30 minutes (faster than is usual), I gathered and arranged all the tools and materials needed on the job before starting to tile. I also took time to trim all the cut tiles so I wouldn't have to keep stopping once the tiling was under way. I figured the size of the cuts by subtracting ³⁄₁₆ in. (the width of one grout joint) from the distance between the toe kick or wall and the nearest parallel layout line. This would give me some space between the tile and the toe kick, as well as some space at the layout line. The space between the tile and the kick or wall would be filled with caulk instead of grout to allow the floor to expand and contract freely (see the discussion of expansion joints on pp. 97-103). If this space were grouted, the floor would have no room in which to expand and, when it did, might cause the tiles to crack (and might also damage the walls and cabinets).

SETTING SEQUENCE

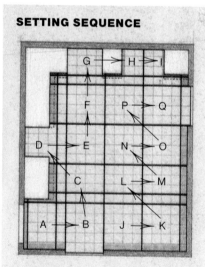

Margin tiles (shown in blue) were set first. After all cut tiles had been set, sections of full tiles were installed in above sequence.

Once everything was ready and I had staged the cut tiles around the perimeter of the room, I had to decide where to start setting tile. Since I was working alone and there were a number of cuts to set, I decided to begin with these and then to move on to the full tiles. Given the many layout lines, I could start setting full tiles anywhere on the outermost row of one of the large layout squares, provided I could eventually work my way out one of the doors. Because I had set my wet saw up just outside the east doorway and I always like to have quick access to it when tiling, I decided to start in the southwest corner of the room and work toward the east door. The setting sequence is shown in the bottom drawing on the facing page.

I next hauled six boxes of tile into the kitchen, leaving the rest outside the door to keep them out of the way. I checked the coverage table on the adhesive's label and estimated how much thinset to mix to complete about a fourth of the floor. I didn't want to mix more than I could use in the half hour the thinset would take to set up. By starting out slowly, I could check the adhesive's actual set-up time under the conditions on this job and, if I wanted, adjust the amount I mixed for the rest of the floor.

Spreading the adhesive

After preparing the thinset, I used a damp sponge to clean off the first area of the setting bed I wanted to cover with adhesive. Then I spread the adhesive with the unnotched edge of a ¼-in. square-notched trowel, covering the first layout square with a layer of adhesive that was ¼ in. to ½ in. thick. (For detailed instructions on applying adhesive, see pp. 140-145.)

I next combed the thinset with the notched edge of the trowel to produce ridges of uniform height. To make sure that the adhesive was the right consistency and the layer of adhesive the right depth, I set and removed one tile and checked it. Since the underside was correctly covered with thinset (to judge this, see the photos on

A number of cut tiles had to be set around the perimeter of the installation, so the author decided to stage and set these tiles first (top). After sponging down the perimeter of the installation, he spread and combed adhesive and then back-buttered the tile with the pipe cutout before setting it (center). With the cuts at the perimeter of the floor set, he installed the cuts on the face of the toe kick, using wedges to keep the tiles in position until the adhesive had set up (bottom).

p. 143), I proceeded to set the cut tiles around the perimeter of the room. Then I set tiles on the face of the toe kicks, using wedges to hold them ⅛ in. off the floor tiles until the adhesive had set up.

In spite of my planning for the cut tiles, I still needed to perform some additional cutting on the wet saw. Since the pipe cutout shown in the middle photo above took several minutes to execute, the thinset mortar already combed out might have started to skin over. To ensure full wet mortar contact, I back-buttered this tile with a thin layer of thinset mortar. I do this with any tile I cannot place immediately into freshly combed mortar. Usually, it takes less time to apply a thin layer of mortar to the tile than it does to remove and recomb the area to be tiled.

Setting full tiles

With the cut tiles set, I staged the full tiles around the room and sponge-cleaned the setting bed in the first layout square along the west wall. Then I spread the adhesive in this square (making sure to spread it just up to the layout lines so that the lines would remain visible) and started setting the tile. I laid down all the tiles in one square and then began aligning them by butting the first vertical row snugly against a long straightedge, positioned half the width of a grout joint from the layout line. I worked my way across the square, adjusting each vertical row in relation to the first row and then aligning the rows horizontally in the same fashion. As I completed positioning the tiles in each square, I placed a beating block over each one and gave it a few light taps with the hammer to ensure full contact of the tile and thinset.

After beating in the tiles, I rinsed the sponge, wrung it out well and cleaned up spilled adhesive from the face of the tiles. At the same time, I readjusted any tiles that had been nudged out of position by the sponge or the beating block.

Checking alignment

At the beginning, I set the tile quickly to keep the thinset from setting up in the bucket. Then, as I approached the bottom of the bucket, I slowed down to look over the tiles set and make sure that they were all properly aligned and cleaned.

As I inspect the tiles, if I spot one that sits a bit too high, I wiggle it down by hand or with a straightedge if it is out of reach. If I spy a tile that sits too low and needs repositioning but which is beyond my reach, I cover the path to it with $3/4$-in. plywood rectangles measuring about 1 ft. by 2 ft. so that I can walk over the newly tiled surface. I then back-butter the offending tile with thinset and seat it properly. When doing this, it is important not to squirm around too much. Walking boards can help keep tiles from breaking, but their use can disturb the alignment of the tiles below. If you have to use walking boards, check the tile alignment after the boards have been removed.

I continued tiling until I had used up every bit of the thinset in the bucket. What I could scrape from the bucket was not enough to comb out an entire square, so instead of spreading it around, I left the pile of scrapings in the layout square. It was fresh enough and could still be used, but I did not want it contaminating the new mortar I would mix for the rest of the floor. For this reason, rather than slow down to clean the old bucket, I switched to one already cleaned (I keep a stack of them handy). If fresh buckets are not available, clean out all traces of thinset mortar to prevent any old, hardening thinset from contaminating the next batch and causing it to set up prematurely.

On a small floor like this, I will set all the cut and full tiles in a day. If you can do only a portion of the floor in one day, make certain that you double-check tile alignment —both the x and y axis—and the height. You will not be able to move these tiles around or change their height when you resume work the next day. When the entire floor is finished, let the tiles sit undisturbed overnight to allow the adhesive to set up sufficiently before grouting.

Working in one square of the layout grid at a time, the author spread and combed adhesive (top), then set the full tiles (center). After initially positioning the tiles, he straightened each row horizontally and vertically by butting the tiles against a straight-edge, which was long enough to reach into the neighboring section of tiles already aligned (bottom).

Grouting and Finishing

Although I am very careful to remove excess thinset while it is still soft, I've never done an installation yet that did not need some final preparations before the grout could be applied. If there is any stray thinset on the tiles, I use a white Scotch-Brite scrubbing pad, moistened with water, to remove it. (For further discussion of cleaning up adhesives, see p. 146.) Next I use a utility knife to pare down any adhesive that clogs the grout joints (a grout saw would also work).

Ideally, the adhesive should be pared down to the bottom of the tile, but this is a lot of work that's not absolutely necessary. Instead, I concentrated on removing any thinset in the joints that was higher than the ridges of adhesive. I also cleaned away any thinset clinging to the sides of the tiles and between the tiles and the walls and cabinets. The gap between the cut tiles and the walls and toe kicks would later be caulked to allow for expansion of the floor. Finally, I vacuumed the floor to remove any loose particles of adhesive from the joints.

The grout for this job was a sanded grout with which I mixed a latex additive to help prevent staining, which is likely in a kitchen. By consulting the grout manufacturer's coverage table, I estimated that the floor would need about 30 lb. of dry grout, which I mixed, allowed to slake and mixed again. (For more information on mixing and applying grout, see pp. 147-149.)

To avoid kneeling on fresh grout, I wanted to grout the room in the same sequence that I had tiled it. So I began in the southwest corner, spreading grout over an area of about 10 sq. ft. To ensure that the density of each grout joint would be consistent, I followed the same grouting procedure throughout the room. As I worked each section of floor, I first dumped on more grout than I would actually need, since the weight of the grout mass would help fill the joints. I spread the grout, holding the grout trowel at about a 30° angle to the floor. To make sure that each joint was fully packed, I spread grout over the area twice, working the trowel from two different directions and firmly pushing the grout into each joint. When I felt that each joint was densely packed, I held the trowel at a 90° angle to the tiles to cut away the excess grout, scraping diagonally across the joints to keep the trowel from gouging them.

At this point I moved from the first 10-sq.-ft. area into the next and began grouting it. When I reached the same stage in the grouting sequence in the second section, I went back to the first to see if the grout had begun to set up. By working in this fashion, I was able to have the final cleaning keep pace with the spreading. This sequence was important because the additive I used with the grout made it very sticky and difficult to remove when dry. Since the temperature in the room was in the mid-70s this day, I found that I could spread quite a bit of grout before needing to clean up. In fact, I was able to pack a 3-ft. wide strip of tiles from the southwest corner of the room along the full length of the west wall before cleaning.

Cleaning the grout residue from the surface of the tiles takes patience. The method I use, described in full on pp. 150-153, keeps the work to a minimum. After I had cleaned the first 3-ft. wide strip of tiles, I checked the grout in the bucket, which I found had begun to stiffen up. I stirred it with the margin trowel to loosen it up, and then grouted and cleaned another 3-ft. wide strip next to the first. Then I changed direction, grouting a 3-ft. wide strip east to west at the south wall, so that I could eventually grout my way out the door on the east wall. At the same time that I cleaned the joints, I shaped them with the sponge, making them slightly concave on top.

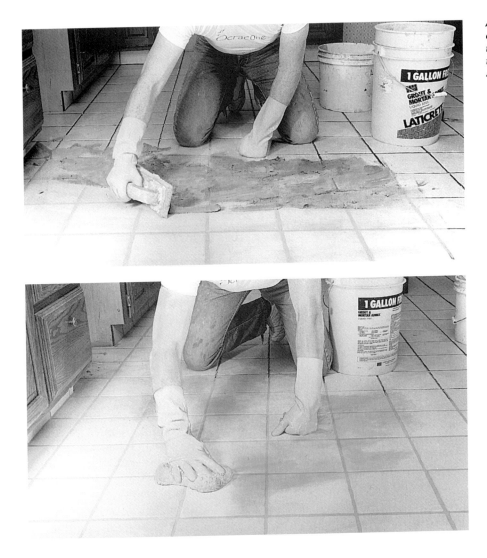

After letting the adhesive harden overnight, the author began grouting the tile, spreading and cleaning up the grout in about a 10-sq.-ft. area at a time.

After the floor had been grouted and cleaned, I waited 15 minutes for the moisture on the surface of the tiles to dry and the grout to set up. At that point, a cement haze appeared on the tiles, which I rubbed away with a soft cloth. If the haze had not come off easily, I would have used a barely dampened sponge. The important point is to clean the grout haze as soon as possible, before it becomes extremely difficult to remove.

After the grout had dried and hardened for almost three days, I filled the joint at the walls and cabinet sides with a color-matched caulk. I also filled the joint between the base of the toe kick and the tiles with caulk. If there is any movement between the cabinets and the floor, the caulk will allow the movement to occur without any crack showing. Finally, after all the open joints had been capped with sealant, I moved the appliances back into the kitchen and reconnected the plumbing fixtures.

Chapter Ten

Wall Installations

Although there are many similarities between floor and wall installations, the effects of gravity introduce an important difference: Floor tiles tend to stay where you put them, but wall tiles are always trying to move downward. Wall installations can be a challenge even for a professional, so if you are a first-time tile installer, you might want to read the entire chapter and assess your skills before starting.

In my own work, I like to float mortar as a setting bed for wall tiles; mortar beds offer the greatest accuracy and are unmatched for durability. However, unless you have had some practical experience floating mortar on walls, and have the tools, the time and the determination (you will need all three in abundant quantities!), you will probably get better results if you use cement backer boards as the setting bed for your project.

Mortar beds are sometimes the only way to get an attractive wall finish. If you are working with a defective surface that is beyond acceptable limits, carpentry cannot correct the problem and you still wish to install tiles, I would advise you to hire a reputable tile mechanic to produce the mortar bed. Although I have seen a number of first-time efforts that are beautiful examples of the tilesetter's craft, I have seen far more disasters when novices insist they are ready for mud work.

A Tub-Surround Installation

The wall installation discussed in this chapter—a tiled tub surround set over backer board—was part of a bathroom that required complete renovation as a result of water leakage and termite damage. After the wall studs had been replaced and all new plumbing installed, I tackled the tile installation.

Ordinarily, when tiling a tub surround, I would float a mortar bed as the setting surface because I like the performance of a mortar job and the look of the radius trim tile it requires. This client, however, wanted the flatter, more streamlined look of surface-bullnose trim, applied directly to the wall (see pp. 19-21). I thus decided to install backer board for the walls of the tub surround, applying it directly to the studs. The thickness of the backer board would ensure that the finished tiles would sit just slightly proud of the adjacent drywall surfaces.

Backer board itself is unaffected by water, but water can penetrate the joints where two boards meet, even when these joints are "sealed" with thinset adhesive. Because water can also get through surface cracks and around nails or screws, a waterproofing membrane is necessary. Given this tub shower's history and the fact that it would get regular use by two exuberant young boys, I wanted the most effective waterproofing possible and suggested a chlorinated polyethylene (CPE) membrane or a trowel-applied membrane (see pp. 106-109) on top of the backer board. But because the client was concerned about cost, we agreed on a tar-paper waterproofing membrane, which is quite effective for residential jobs.

Installing the tar-paper membrane beneath the backer board would be the first step of the job. But before any work could start, I needed to do a layout sketch and estimate the amount of tile and other materials required.

Making a Layout Sketch and Estimating Tile

The client had already chosen some hand-made tile and placed an order before I became involved with the installation. After I had quickly assessed the situation, I realized he had not ordered enough. To calculate how much more tile would be needed, I first had to figure out the combined width of one tile and grout joint and then make a layout sketch.

The tile my client had chosen was sold as 3-in. square tile, though it actually ranged in size from $2^{13}/_{16}$ in. square to $2^{15}/_{16}$ in. square. Since the tile manufacturer recommended a $1/_8$-in. wide grout joint, I figured that if I mixed the different sizes of tile and alternately set larger and smaller tiles, I could assume an average tile/grout-joint dimension of 3 in. This was a nice, whole number to work with, so I dispensed with making my usual tile/grout-joint list (see pp. 119-121). I could also do the layout sketch on graph paper on which each square represented one tile and grout joint.

Finding the focal point

To start the layout, I measured and noted all the dimensions of the tub surround, figuring in the thickness of the backer board that would later be put in place. After determining the measurements of the three walls of the installation, I needed to locate its visual focal point. It was clear that the window was it and that, aesthetically, full tiles just beneath the sill were mandatory. I therefore began my layout here by dividing the wall's $82^1/_4$-in. height into two segments: the first one 29 in. from the top of the tub to the sill, and the second $53^1/_4$ in. from the sill to the ceiling. Vertically, 9 full tiles plus a 2-in. cut tile could fit in the first section, and in the second, 17 full tiles plus a $2^1/_4$-in. cut at the ceiling. Although the tiles at the ceiling and the tub would not be full tiles, the size of the cuts would be roughly the same, and visually the job would be fairly well balanced.

Back-wall layout

With regard to the horizontal alignment of tiles on the back wall, I wanted any cut tiles to be equally distributed at either corner. I could have centered all the tile on the slightly off-center window, but I decided that it wasn't worth the trouble in this case. Instead, I cut the bullnose tiles on either side of the window to different dimensions. Across the $59^1/_2$-in. width of the back wall, I could fit 18 full tiles plus a $2^3/_4$-in. cut at each side.

LAYOUT SKETCH

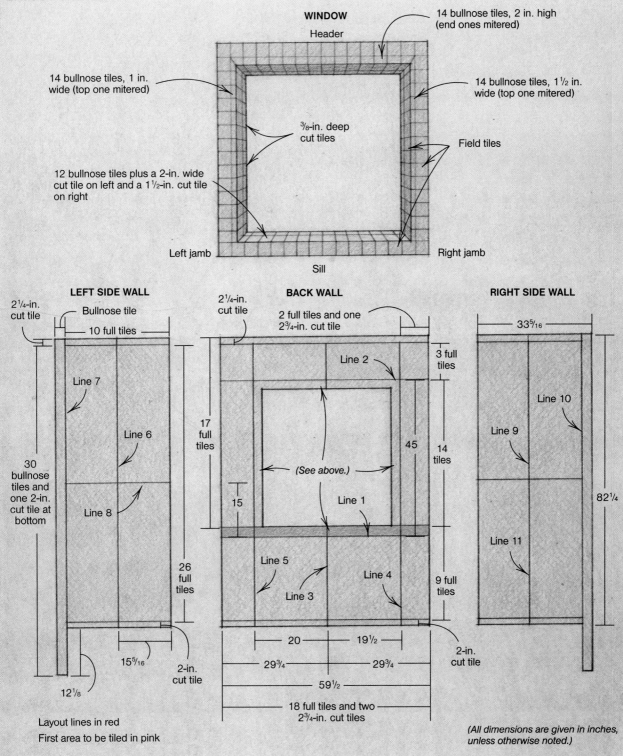

WINDOW

Header

14 bullnose tiles, 2 in. high
(end ones mitered)

14 bullnose tiles, 1 in.
wide (top one mitered)

14 bullnose tiles, 1½ in.
wide (top one mitered)

⅜-in. deep
cut tiles

Field tiles

12 bullnose tiles plus a 2-in. wide
cut tile on left and a 1½-in. cut tile
on right

Left jamb

Right jamb

Sill

LEFT SIDE WALL

2¼-in.
cut tile

Bullnose tile

10 full tiles

Line 7

Line 6

30
bullnose
tiles and
one 2-in.
cut tile at
bottom

Line 8

26
full
tiles

15⁵⁄₁₆

2-in.
cut tile

12⅛

BACK WALL

2¼-in.
cut tile

2 full tiles and one
2¾-in. cut tile

Line 2

3 full
tiles

17
full
tiles

45

14
tiles

(See above.)

Line 1

15

Line 5

Line 3

Line 4

9 full
tiles

2-in.
cut tile

20   19½

29¾   29¾

59½

18 full tiles and two
2¾-in. cut tiles

RIGHT SIDE WALL

33⁵⁄₁₆

Line 10

Line 9

Line 11

82¼

Layout lines in red
First area to be tiled in pink

*(All dimensions are given in inches,
unless otherwise noted.)*

Vincent Babak

I wanted the window sill set with surface-bullnose trim tiles that would overlap the top edge of the field tiles beneath the window. Arranging the tiles this way, rather than setting the bullnose on the face of the wall, eliminated a grout joint on the sill that might collect water. If I did the same thing on the jambs, however, the visual result would be a grout joint encircling the window opening. So instead, I decided to set the bullnose around the jambs rather than on them—outside the window opening, rather than inside.

The tiles on the sill would have to be aligned with those on the face of the wall to make the grout joints line up. This meant that I could fit 12 full bullnose tiles along the width of the sill, with a 2-in. cut tile on the left side and a 1½-in. cut tile on the right. The inside surface of the head jamb would require the same number of tiles as the sill, while the header's face would need fourteen 2-in. cut bullnose tiles, with the two tiles at each end cut diagonally to accommodate the corners.

Given that the window was ⅜ in. off-center to the right, I decided to make up the difference at the bullnose tiles on the face of the side jambs by cutting them to slightly different sizes. The 14 bullnose tiles to be set on the face of the wall at the left jamb would need to be 1 in. wide, while those at the right jamb would be 1½ in. wide. On both jambs the top tile would be mitered to fit the corner. To cover the jambs' 3½-in. depth, I would need one full tile and a ⅜-in. cut tile (½ in. minus the thickness of the grout joint). Although I generally try to work with cut tiles larger than half-size, this would have visually "split" the jambs and sill with an unattractive grout line.

Totaling up the tiles required for the back wall, I calculated that the base of the wall would need 20 tiles across the width (18 full tiles, 2 cut tiles) x 10 tiles from the sill to the top of the tub (9 full tiles, 1 cut tile), or 200 tiles (remember that the rows of trimmed tiles on the bottom and top of the wall must be cut from full tiles). Each segment of the wall beside the window, from the sill to the ceiling, would require 18 full tiles (17 full tiles plus a 2¼-in. cut) x 3 full tiles across its width, or 108 tiles for both sides. Next, the portion of the wall above the head jamb would need 4 tiles along its height (3 full tiles plus a 2¼-in. cut) x 14 tiles across its width, or 56 tiles. Finally, I would need 31 full tiles to make the cuts around the inside of the jambs, plus 38 full tiles for the rest of the inside of the jambs. I would therefore need 433 full tiles for the back wall and 56 bullnose tiles.

Side-wall layout

With the layout on the back wall established, I could move to the side walls. Since the back wall would be the first surface set with tiles, I needed to subtract the ¼-in. thickness of the tile from the width of the side walls. This meant that the area to be laid out was 33⁵⁄₁₆ in. wide by 82¼ in. high. With a row of surface-bullnose tiles trimming the wall's outside edge, 10 field tiles would fit across the wall's width, while 26 full tiles would be needed along the height, with a 2-in. cut on the bottom and a 2¼-in. cut on the top. Finally, each wall would need 4 full bullnose tiles to fill the 12⅛-in. long by 3-in. wide area running alongside the tub to the floor. The two side walls would thus require a total of 560 field tiles and 64 surface-bullnose tiles.

All in all, then, I would need a total of 993 field tiles and 120 surface-bullnose tiles. Since the owner had ordered only 900 field tiles and 106 trim tiles, I would need another 93 field and 14 trim tiles. To be on the safe side, I added a few tiles to each count for a total of 1,000 field tiles and 130 surface-bullnose tiles. As you can see, only a small number of extras were ordered. If you have any doubt about your ability to cut or trim tiles to fit, you may want to order more extras to account for breakage.

Installing the Waterproofing Membrane

On this job, I planned to install the membrane in seven segments, wrapping each horizontally around the walls and overlapping the rows by at least 2 in. Each segment would be attached directly to the studs, and I would use asphalt roofing cement to seal the overlaps and any other spots that might leak.

Installing the tar-paper membrane would require only a couple of tools: a utility knife, a putty knife or a margin trowel, and a staple gun. Since the asphalt is petroleum-based and not only sticky but also smelly, I would need my charcoal-filter mask and some rubber gloves.

I began installing the membrane by sealing the entire top edge of the tub where it fastened to the blocking with a layer of asphalt roofing cement about ⅛ in. thick and 2 in. wide (see the top drawing at right). This strip of asphalt would anchor the first band of tar paper. Then I proceeded to install each of the seven segments in the order shown in the bottom drawing at right. The box-folded piece at the window sill was required because the sill would be exposed to standing water, but the top of the window did not need this protection.

Because the tar paper should be sharply creased where it wraps the corner of a job, it's a good idea to warm the paper before installing it to make it more pliable. Folding cold tar paper can cause it to split. To warm the tar paper, store the roll under room-temperature conditions before you intend to use it, or put lengths of paper in

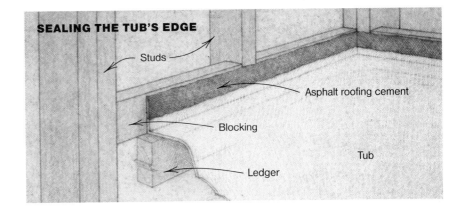

SEALING THE TUB'S EDGE

Studs

Asphalt roofing cement

Blocking

Tub

Ledger

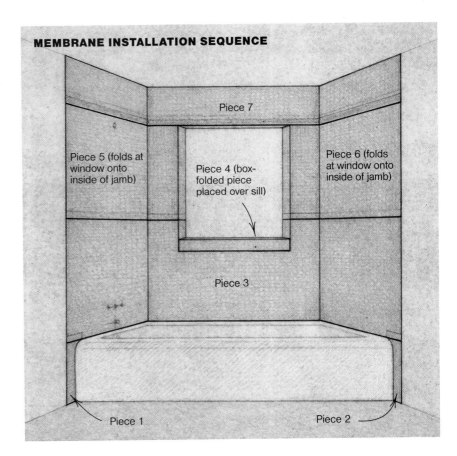

MEMBRANE INSTALLATION SEQUENCE

Piece 7

Piece 5 (folds at window onto inside of jamb)

Piece 4 (box-folded piece placed over sill)

Piece 6 (folds at window onto inside of jamb)

Piece 3

Piece 1

Piece 2

direct sun just before installing it. In any case, make sure that the membrane lies flat against the studs.

After cutting the two pieces for the legs of the side walls (pieces 1 and 2), I pressed them into the asphalt sealing strip at the edge of the tub and stapled through them and the asphalt into the studs to hold them in place. Each piece extended about 2 in. above the top of the tub, and I coated this upper section of each with a ⅛-in. thick layer of asphalt.

To install the first full horizontal band of the membrane (piece 3), I stapled it to the studs and pressed the base of the paper into the asphalt at the top edge of the tub, overlapping the lip of the tub by about 1 in. and overlapping the first two pieces of the membrane by about 2 in. Once the backer board was installed, I could trim any excess tar paper at the edge of the tub. Where the membrane was to pass over a faucet or a control valve, I cut a hole just large enough for the valve to pass through, and sealed the opening between the paper and the valve with asphalt. After piece 3 was positioned, I cut it flush with the sill so that it could be lapped by the box-folded sill piece (4), but left tails at the right and left jambs, which would be folded over each end of piece 4.

Next I coated the top 2 in. of this band with a layer of asphalt, working carefully to avoid tearing the paper between studs. Then I made the box fold to fit on the window sill (piece 4), as shown in the drawing below. After coating the sill and inside of the jambs with asphalt as an additional precaution against water leakage, I positioned the box fold in the window opening and pressed it down into the asphalt all around—the box needn't be stapled to the sill because the asphalt will hold it in place. If the window is already in place, as it was in this case, the tar paper should run right up to the window frame. (If the finished window is not in place, simply run the paper out the opening and lap it down over the outside.)

Next I cut the two sides of the box-folded piece flush with the jambs, covered a 2-in. wide strip below the sill with asphalt and folded the overhanging sill flap onto the face of the wall and into the asphalt. Then I covered the jamb sections of the box fold with asphalt right up to the window frame and folded the tails from piece 3 over the bottom of each side. I made sure that any folds were crisp, not bulky, in order to avoid unnecessary lumps beneath the backer board. Finally, I trimmed the section of the box fold that fit against the window frame (section A in the drawing below).

With the lower portion of the window completed, I installed pieces 5 and 6. I folded each piece inward at the jamb (covering the top 2 in. of the box-folded piece), bedded them in the asphalt and trimmed them with a knife at the window frame. With the window sill and jambs covered, this left the head jamb and area above the window still exposed. I covered

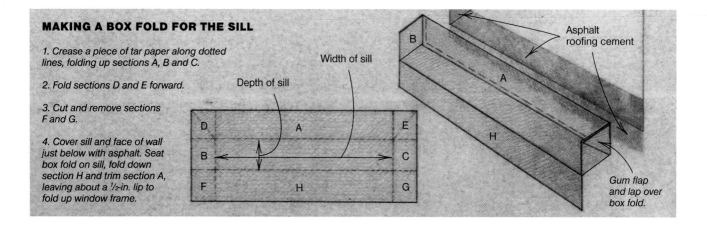

MAKING A BOX FOLD FOR THE SILL

1. Crease a piece of tar paper along dotted lines, folding up sections A, B and C.

2. Fold sections D and E forward.

3. Cut and remove sections F and G.

4. Cover sill and face of wall just below with asphalt. Seat box fold on sill, fold down section H and trim section A, leaving about a ½-in. lip to fold up window frame.

Width of sill

Depth of sill

Asphalt roofing cement

Gum flap and lap over box fold.

these areas with piece 7. I made this piece wide enough so that a flap could be folded inward, toward the window, and bedded in asphalt. I could, of course, have box-folded a single piece of tar paper to cover the head jamb, but I've never found it worth the time, since, again, this area will not be exposed to standing water.

Just before installing the backer board, I coated the membrane with asphalt along each stud. The asphalt sealed the staples and created a gasket between the board and the paper that would help seal the fasteners used to attach the backer board.

As far as I'm concerned, the basic technique for arranging and sealing the tar-paper membrane is the very heart of the tile installation. The proper positioning of the tar paper isn't really as complicated as it may sound. Basically, make sure that there's tar paper behind the entire area to be tiled, and install it as though you were planning to skip the tile and rely solely on the tar paper for waterproofing.

Installing the Backer Board

After measuring and marking the backer board, I cut it with a dry-cutting diamond blade mounted in a power grinder (see the photo on p. 49). This blade left a cut with smooth edges, which made it easy to fit the backer boards together with the recommended ⅛-in. gap. Backer board can also be scored with a carbide-tipped scriber and broken along the scribed line. The technique leaves a fairly rough edge, but because it's sometimes quicker than cutting with the saw, I use the scriber when rough edges won't be a problem (see pp. 74-79 for a complete discussion of installing backer board). After cutting the sheets, I began to install them in the sequence shown in the drawing above.

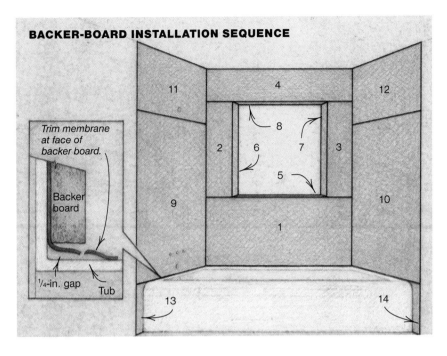

BACKER-BOARD INSTALLATION SEQUENCE

Trim membrane at face of backer board.

Backer board

¼-in. gap   Tub

While backer board used on floors must be laminated as well as screwed (or nailed) to the substrate, it's unnecessary to use an adhesive when fastening it to walls. Although 1½ in. galvanized roofing nails can be used to fasten the backer board, on vertical surfaces I prefer to use special CBU screws, which won't loosen as nails might. Standard drywall screws will not resist corrosion, so use only those screws that are corrosion resistant for wet installations.

Holes in the backer board for the valves and spouts can be made with a carbide-tipped hole saw, or by "punching" them out with a hammer (see pp. 76-77). When using a hammer, first outline the position of the hole with a pencil and then cut through the backer board's reinforcing mesh on both sides with a utility knife. Support the back of the board with one hand and punch through the board at this point with a hammer.

To provide space for caulk and to keep the backer board from wicking water from the edges of the tub, I installed the board ¼ in. above the tub (it should not rest on the shoulder of the tub). Once

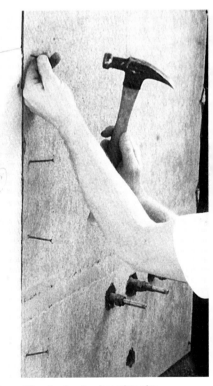

After cutting the backer board to size and 'punching out' holes for the shower valves and spouts, the author started the drywall screws by 'nailing' them partially into place.

all the boards had been fastened in place, I covered the joints between the boards with fiberglass mesh tape and sealed the joints with thinset.

While I had the thinset mixed for sealing the joints between the boards, I troweled a small amount on the top of the sill to create a slight pitch toward the tub. This would prevent shower water from collecting on the sill and possibly penetrating the grout into the backer boards.

Marking Layout Lines

If this shower had had no window and the tiles being used had been uniformly sized, a pair of centered, intersecting layout lines would have probably sufficed for the entire installation. Given the presence of the off-center window in the back wall, however, and the irregularity of the tile, I placed 11 lines to ensure that everything was positioned squarely (see the layout sketch on p. 175).

Rather than using the top of the tub or the ceiling as the starting points for the layout, I preferred to start from a line I knew would be level. Using a 4-ft. spirit level and a pencil, I first marked a horizontal line on the back wall 3 in. below the edge of the window sill. Then I drew a second line parallel to and 45 in. above the first, that is, 15 tiles and grout joints away.

The third line I made was a vertical line centered on the back wall. I measured to the center of the first horizontal line to establish the center of the wall and used the level to scribe an accurate line above and below the window. Then I scribed two other lines on the back wall to mark the grout joint between the field tiles and the surface-bullnose tiles on the window jambs. Again, instead of taking measurements off the existing walls or the window opening, I projected these lines off the centered vertical layout line, 21 in. to each side. (It is my normal practice to disregard existing surfaces and, instead, project my layout lines from reference lines; see Chapter 7 for details.)

Using a spirit level, the author scribed on each side wall a pair of intersecting layout lines and a third vertical line to mark the grout joint between the field and trim tiles.

On the side walls, a pair of centered, intersecting lines would suffice. But to be safe I decided to add a third line to mark the grout joint between the field tile and the trim tile. To establish the first vertical line, I measured $15^5/_{16}$ in. from the corner where the side and back walls met. This point represented the center of the joint at the fifth of the side wall's 10 vertical rows of field tiles plus the $^1/_4$-in. thickness of the tile set on the back wall and the $^1/_{16}$-in. layer of thinset under the tile.

Using the level, I accurately marked and drew in the first line. Then I measured out 15 in. from this line for the second vertical line, which represented the grout joint separating the field and trim tiles. Finally, to make a horizontal line, I measured 15 in. up from the sill line on the back wall, or the space of five tiles. Again using the level, I positioned this line essentially in the center of the wall where it would be the most helpful.

Setting the Tiles

This job was done in the heat of summer in a house that did not have air conditioning. With the temperature hovering around 95°F and no relief in sight, I had to take special precautions to ensure that the temperature of the area at the tub surround was as cool as I could make it while the tiles were being set, and during the grouting portion of the installation. First, I started tiling early and decided to quit before the heat radiating off the walls could prematurely cook the moisture out of the thinset. Second, I chose a thinset powder and a liquid additive that would give me plenty of time for repositioning the tiles (remember, these tiles were quite irregularly sized).

Tiling the window sill

I began setting tile on the window sill, since the grout joints here would locate those for the field tiles below. I spread thinset on the sill and on a small portion of the wall just below it, figuring I would set all these "related" tiles. After I had carefully positioned the bullnose trim tiles on the sill, I started setting the tiles on the wall (I planned to butter and install the $^3/_8$-in. cuts later). It was then that I discovered that I had a problem.

Tiling the back wall

When mixing a thinset powder with a liquid latex additive, there are sometimes a few trade-offs for the advantages gained. Unexpectedly in this case, the adhesive I mixed to be slow-setting also turned out to have less "hang." ("Grip" is the holding power of an adhesive once it has cured; "hang" is its ability to hold tile on a vertical surface before it has cured. Mastics generally have low grip and high hang, while epoxy thinsets have tremendous grip but very low hang.) This hang problem was surprising, since I knew that each of the component thinsets alone would tenaciously hold freshly set tile. But the evidence was easy to spot—the first few tiles I put up on the wall just wouldn't stay up. Tile spacing wedges might have helped matters, but fiddling with them would take too much time. And I didn't want to mix up my normal recipe of thinset because I still needed slow-curing characteristics because of the hot weather.

To solve the problem, I pulled out an old standby—masking tape. The sill tiles weren't going anywhere, so I stuck a length of tape to each one and let the tape cascade down the wall. Then all I had to do was stick the tiles to the wall and stick the tape to the tiles (see the photos on p. 182). Elsewhere on the walls, I supported the topmost row of tiles with small nails partially driven into

To hold tiles in place while the adhesive is curing, it may be necessary to use strips of masking tape, anchoring each vertical row either to a sill tile (above) or a tile supported in place by nails (left).

the backer board. Each of the tiles in this row then served to anchor the tape that would hold the tiles below.

To begin the upper portion of the wall, I first positioned three tiles on each side of the window, 3 in. above the header layout line. Once supported by nails, these tiles would serve to support a 54-in. straightedge, which was held against the wall by nails. The remaining rows of tile on the upper half of the wall could then be aligned with the straightedge and secured with masking tape hung from it. By using a straightedge, I eliminated the time-consuming task of supporting every tile in the top row with nails. After letting the adhesive set up for an hour and a half, I carefully removed the straightedge above the window and set the last row of full tiles and the row of cut tiles at the ceiling, using spacing wedges to hold the cuts in place.

Tiling the jambs

Once I had set the field tiles on the upper wall, I cut the bullnose trim to size and cut the tile for the jambs. Whenever setting bullnose tile at a corner, as in this case, it's a good idea not to begin setting until the tiles for both locations are ready. That outside corner is critical and has to be a nice, smooth transition. If I set one part of the corner ahead of time and let the thinset harden, I wouldn't be able to adjust it when the second part was installed. So once the cuts were complete, I set the bullnose trim around the window and immediately began setting tile on the jambs. After the back wall was done, I quit for the day because the wall was getting warm.

Tiling the side walls

Next day, to speed up the setting process on the side walls, I went back to using nails to support the entire top row of cut tiles, suspending the rows below with masking tape. Although this procedure took time,

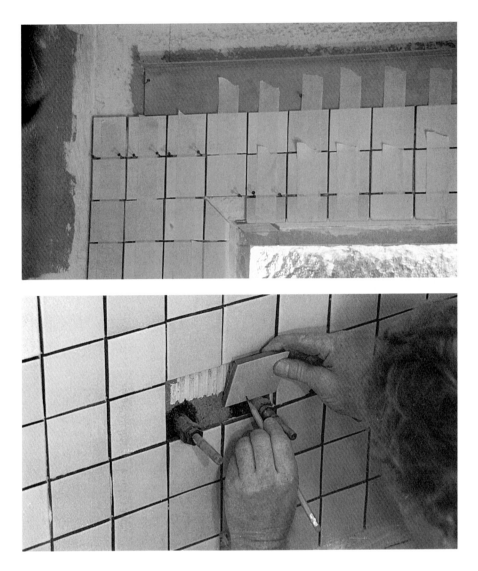

To set the tiles above the window, the author nailed a straightedge in place at the ceiling and anchored on it the strips of masking tape that would hold the tiles (top). Once the adhesive had begun to set up, he removed the straightedge and set the topmost rows, using spacing wedges to hold the tiles in place. The last tiles to be set were those that needed to be cut to accommodate the shower's faucets and valves (bottom).

I didn't have to wait 90 minutes, as I had had to do using the straightedge-bridge system, for the adhesive to harden before setting the top row. When setting the main fields of tile, I had left out those that would require cuts to accommodate the faucets. These I carefully marked, cut and installed last, and then allowed the tiles to set overnight.

Grouting and sealing

The next day I returned to grout the job. Considering the effort I'd spent preparing the walls and setting the tiles, grouting was uneventful. Then, after waiting three days to allow the grout to harden, I caulked the joint between the tub and tiles and the one between the tiles on the inside of the window and the window frame with an elastomeric sealant. Once my work was complete, the owner packed plumber's putty behind the valves. Should the valves ever need maintenance, the plumber's putty can be easily removed, allowing access to tools without harming the surrounding tiles.

Chapter Eleven

Countertop Installations

Installing a tile countertop is much like setting a tile floor, only on a smaller scale. And if the counter includes a backsplash, it is done with the same methods used to apply wall tiles.

There are many setting beds suitable for dry countertops that are not considered functional (a display counter, for example), but for countertops that have to cope with grease, food acids, messy spills and water, the only materials I recommend for ceramic or stone tiles are cement backer boards and mortar beds.

When tiling in the kitchen, because of concerns in food-preparation areas regarding cleanliness, it is very important to meet or exceed industry standards. This means selecting nonporous tiles and latex- or acrylic-modified adhesives and grouts. Porous (nonvitreous) tiles and regular grout and adhesive mortars can easily absorb moisture from food spills and create growth areas for mold, mildew and bacteria that are difficult to clean and maintain.

The example in this chapter demonstrates the use of backer boards to produce a kitchen countertop. While the kitchen is the most obvious room in the house for a countertop installation, tiled counters are also commonly found in bathrooms and laundry rooms. The methods and materials presented here can be used for practically any residential or light-duty commercial application.

Sizing Up the Job

The owner of the house was an accomplished woodworker who planned to remodel his entire kitchen in his spare time. He had begun by moving a few walls to enlarge the kitchen and had built and installed new cabinets. He next wanted to tile the countertops, but realized that he needed help after making the rounds of the local tile shops. Each of the shops had given him conflicting information on how to proceed with the installation, and he called me in the hope that I could sort out the confusion and offer some sound counsel.

When I visited the client's home, I found that only a portion of the kitchen was in fact ready for tiling. The owner explained that he wanted to finish the job in stages over a period of time and asked if I would be willing to tile the first countertop, with him acting as helper. This way he would learn how to tackle the other countertops

LAYOUT SKETCH

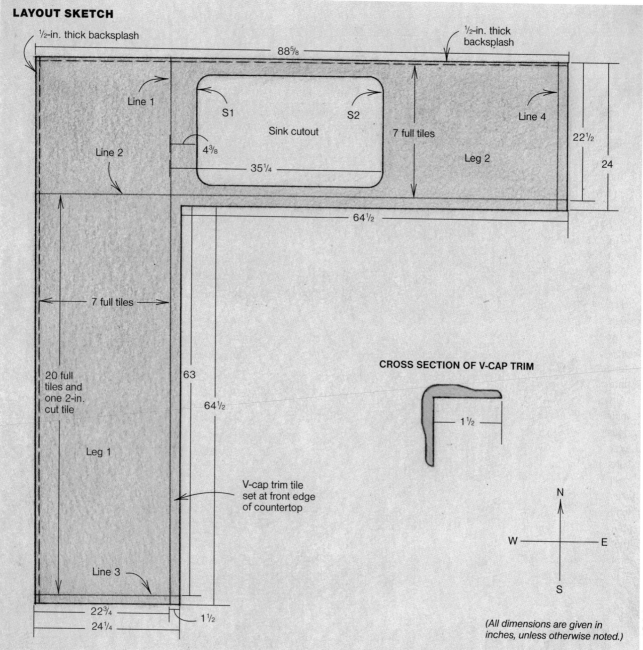

½-in. thick backsplash

½-in. thick backsplash

88⅝

Line 1

S1 Sink cutout S2

Line 4

7 full tiles

22½

24

Line 2

4⅜

35¼

Leg 2

64½

7 full tiles

CROSS SECTION OF V-CAP TRIM

20 full tiles and one 2-in. cut tile

63

64½

Leg 1

1½

V-cap trim tile set at front edge of countertop

Line 3

N

W ——— E

S

22¾

24¼

1½

(All dimensions are given in inches, unless otherwise noted.)

Vincent Babak

A cutting board built into a tiled countertop is a real convenience in a kitchen, provided it's properly installed (see the drawing on p. 100). To produce a handsome and serviceable installation, I suggest that you first buy a board larger than desired and cut it down to fit between full tiles. To prevent damage to the tiles when the board gets wet and swells, leave a $\frac{1}{8}$-in. to $\frac{1}{4}$-in. gap between it and the tiles. This gap also allows for easy removal of the board, should it need replacing. To keep the gap from getting clogged with food particles, fill it as you would a regular expansion joint.

To help prevent knife blades from coming in contact with the tiles and scratching them, I recommend mounting the board so its top sits about $\frac{1}{8}$ in. above the surface of the tiles. When possible, you should also position the board so that its front edge protrudes slightly beyond the edge of the counter, which will make it easier to keep the board clean.

himself. I liked his initiative and enthusiasm and agreed to the plan. As it turned out, we completed the entire first counter from cutting the backer board to grouting the tiles in about six hours.

The countertop we tiled together was on an L-shaped section of cabinets in the corner of the kitchen, and held a sink. The client had chosen vitreous, 3-in. square tiles (about $\frac{3}{16}$ in. thick) with a glossy black glaze for the countertop. They were mounted in 12-tile sheets, and the grout joint was predetermined at $\frac{1}{8}$ in. For the backsplash, he had picked lipstick-red 3-in. by 6-in. tiles that were $\frac{1}{2}$ in. thick. These tiles would be set in a single "soldier course" row—that is, standing upright instead of horizontally (the completed countertop is shown on p. 195).

Although the finished job would be stunning, I immediately discovered a serious problem with the countertop tiles: they scratched very easily. The client assured me that this counter would receive very little wear and that he planned to make cutting boards to protect the tiles when using the top (cutting boards can also be built into the countertop, as explained in the sidebar above). He insisted that he had always wanted a black countertop, and that was that.

Planning the installation

With regard to the specifics of the job, I needed to use an installation method that the owner could duplicate by himself on the other countertops. I decided to set the tile on backer board, since it makes an excellent setting bed and is relatively easy to install (see pp. 74-79). Also, the client had already covered the tops of the cabinets with a layer of $\frac{3}{4}$-in. AC exterior plywood, unwittingly accommodating the requirement that backer board used for countertops should be laminated to a plywood substrate at least $\frac{3}{4}$ in. thick. The backer board would need to be laminated to the substrate with either a latex or an epoxy thinset and further secured with $1\frac{1}{2}$-in. screws or $1\frac{1}{2}$-in. roofing nails. Since a latex thinset suitable for use with plywood was not available locally, I opted to go with the epoxy for laminating the backer board.

Because the countertop would see limited service, I decided that no waterproofing membrane was needed. Had this been a heavily used countertop, however, a waterproofing membrane would have been mandatory. I would have recommended a sheet membrane and positioned it to extend from the lowest point of the counter's front edge, across the full width of the top, and up onto the entire height of the backsplash.

On this job, both the combined width of an entire sheet (12⅜ in.) and its grout joint (⅛ in.) and the combined width of a single tile (3 in.) and its grout joint (⅛ in.) were figured:

TILE SHEETS	SINGLE TILES
1 = 12½ in.	*1 = 3⅛ in.*
2 = 25 in.	*2 = 6¼ in.*
3 = 37½ in.	*3 = 9⅜ in.*
4 = 50 in.	*4 = 12½ in.*
5 = 62½ in.	*5 = 15⅝ in.*
6 = 75 in.	*6 = 18¾ in.*
7 = 87½ in.	*7 = 21⅞ in.*
8 = 100 in.	*8 = 25 in.*
	9 = 28⅛ in.
	10 = 31¼ in.

V-cap depth = 1½ in.

The sink the client had purchased was of the self-rimming variety, meaning that it was designed to be installed on top of the tiled counter. Although this type of sink makes life easy for the tilesetter, I think it proves a real nuisance for the owner, because food particles often get jammed beneath the sink's lip during cleaning. For this reason, I suggested that the sink be installed under the tiles to produce a neatly finished, sanitary edge. To do this, the top of the sink would need to be kept nearly flush with the top of the backer board (see the bottom photo on p. 190).

Estimating Materials

The customer had taken advantage of a sale at a local tile store and had ordered more than enough tiles for all the kitchen countertops, including trim pieces. I began the job by determining the exact dimensions of the tiles and making up a tile/grout-joint list (shown at left).

Tile

Ordinarily when I compile a tile/grout-joint list, I determine the width of the basic tile-and-grout-joint unit and then calculate the total number of tiles needed to cover the job (see pp. 119-121). Because the black tiles were sheet-mounted, however, the list had to include not only the combined width of a single tile and grout joint but also the combined width of an entire sheet and grout joint. I could, of course, have just made a list that included enough single tiles to stretch the longest length of the countertop. But instead, I worked up a quick list composed of the tile dimensions in a single sheet, and a list of sheet dimensions that would cover the longest length of the counter.

In figuring the amount of tile that would fit, I consulted the first list to discover how many full sheets would fit down the length of the countertop, then found out how many single tiles would fill in the remainder of the countertop by looking at the single-tile list. For the width of the countertop, I used my single-tile list. I added to the end of the list the interior depth of the V-cap trim that would finish off the front edge of the countertop (see the drawing on p. 186). Each sheet of tiles was approximately 12⅜ in. square.

With this information, I'll usually proceed to doing a trial tile layout on paper. One of the reasons for a trial layout is to suggest changes in the structure of the job, such as making the run of cabinets a little bit longer or shorter to accommodate full tiles. That's possible when cabinet construction has not yet begun, but in this case the cabinets were already built and in place and there wasn't anything to change about them. I therefore skipped the paper layout, and instead waited until the backer board was installed to do an actual full-size layout.

Backer board

Figuring the amount of backer board needed wasn't difficult, but because the material isn't particularly cheap, I wanted to minimize any waste. I had a stock of 3-ft. by 4-ft. sheets already on hand, so I decided to use these. Cutting them lengthwise and carefully using the offcuts, I found that three full sheets would be sufficient to cover the countertop. It's perfectly fine to use small, scrap pieces of backer board to fill in small areas (as long as you don't overdo it). Sometimes this saves having to buy an additional sheet, and it's often just easier to do. Had I cut a large, sink-sized hole in a single sheet of backer board, the sheet would have been too fragile to handle. So instead, I cut the backer board for the large open areas on either side of the sink, then cut smaller pieces to fit the narrow areas just in front of and behind the sink.

Setting materials

With regard to the amount of setting materials needed, I checked the manufacturer's coverage tables for the adhesive I planned to use. In order to laminate the backer board to the plywood substrate and backsplash area, I would need enough epoxy thinset to cover about 22 sq. ft. of countertop with a ¼-in. square-notched trowel, that is, roughly ½ gal. of epoxy liquid and about 2 gal. of filler powder. While the same epoxy thinset could be used to set the tiles, for economy's sake I would switch to a latex thinset. Since I planned to use the same-size trowel to apply the latex thinset, the amount of this adhesive needed was roughly the same as for the epoxy.

To calculate the amount of grout needed, I consulted the manufacturer's grout tables and figured that the job would require a 10-lb. sack of dry grout. Before mixing any grout, I set aside two cups of dry grout for the owner for any future repairs, wrapping up this grout in a plastic bag taped tightly shut to keep moisture out. Two cups will more than suffice if a few tiles have to be replaced or regrouted later on. Then I mixed up the remaining ingredients, which yielded a pound or two more grout than I would actually need on the job. It is possible to mix only enough to fill the joints, but I like to mix extra for ease of working the grout into the joints. Also, coming up short in the midst of a job is more than just a nuisance—sometimes it is almost impossible to eliminate a line between two batches of colored grout.

Because the grout joint is the place where moisture can penetrate the installation and reach the other layers of the tile sandwich, I always mix an additive with grout to increase its effectiveness against water seepage (or use a grout with a dry additive already in the mix). On this job, I would need between one and two quarts of additive for the 10 lb. of grout.

Preparing and Installing the Backer Board

To make sure that all the backer board fit the job, I cut all the pieces and positioned them dry on the plywood substrate before laminating any of them. With the backer board in place, but not laminated to the substrate, I dropped the sink into the hole, let it rest on the backer board and with a pencil traced on the board the outline of the sink and the position of the reinforcing bars under its lip. I then removed the sink and the backer board and cut a groove for the reinforcing bars with a dry-cutting diamond blade. (If you don't have a diamond blade, use a ¼-in. carbide router bit.) The groove had to be deep enough to allow the lip of the sink to sit directly on the backer board, yet not so deep that it cut entirely through.

The author uses a dry-cutting diamond blade to cut the backer board to size and to create the groove for the sink. Shimming up the blade with a scrap piece of backer board controls the depth of the groove.

The first step in laminating the backer board to the plywood substrate is to spread and comb epoxy thinset on the plywood (top). Next the backer board is positioned in the adhesive (above), 'beat' in with a hammer and beating block, and secured with nails.

Before I mixed the epoxy for laminating the backer board to the plywood, I wanted to make sure that the cabinets themselves wouldn't become casualties of the process. So I draped an apron of sheet plastic over the faces and ends of the cabinets, and taped it in place. Working with tile adhesive is messy business, and a few moments spent preparing for the worst will keep you from having to clean up later on. It's a good idea to protect anything within splash, drip or splatter range with plastic sheet, a canvas tarp or kraft paper.

Working on one leg of the countertop at a time, after mixing the epoxy thinset I spread and combed it on the plywood with a ¼-in. square notched trowel. Then I positioned each piece of backer board, leaving an ⅛-in. gap between the boards. To bed the backer board firmly in the epoxy, I used a hammer and an 8-in. square of ¾-in. plywood to "beat" each piece into the adhesive. Then I secured the board to the plywood with 1½-in. roofing nails spaced 8 in. on center (on floor installations that will have to carry heavy loads and foot traffic, I upgrade to CBU screws).

To laminate the boards with the sink groove, I tentatively placed them in the adhesive and then slipped the sink into position to make sure that it was accurately seated before nailing any of the boards in place. Once I had nailed the grooved sections, I removed the sink, buttered the underside of its lip with epoxy and put it back in place. Buttering the lip would prevent the sink from moving around underneath the tiles.

To keep the bottom edges of the backsplash boards from resting directly on the backer board of the countertop, I used shims to create an expansion-joint gap no larger than ¼ in. While backer board used for walls need not be laminated but only nailed to the studs, it was easy enough to laminate the narrow strips for the backsplash anyway. When doing this, it's much simpler to apply and comb the thinset directly on the strips rather than on the wall. In this case, I used 2-in. long nails to secure the strips because the nails had to penetrate the backer board and the drywall to reach the studs.

The author positioned the backer board surrounding the sink in the adhesive, but waited to nail it until he had dropped the sink in place and made sure that the reinforcing bars on the sink's underside rode correctly in the grooves.

The author combed thinset directly on the backer-board strips for the backsplash (above) and laminated them to the wall before nailing them to the studs behind the drywall (right).

Once the backer board was laminated, the author taped all the joints with fiberglass-mesh tape and edge-glued the boards with thinset adhesive to prevent any movement in the substrate from telegraphing through the joints and cracking the tile.

For the same reason, he also taped and edge-glued the countertop's front edge.

Because the countertop was small, layout lines were needed only around its front edge for the grout joint between the V-cap trim tiles and the field tiles.

Once all the backer board had been nailed in place, I covered the joints with fiberglass-mesh reinforcing tape and forced thinset through the tape into the joints to edge-glue the sections of backer board (see the lower two photos on the previous page). I treated all the joints this way and ran tape around the front edge of the boards so that it lapped over the edge of the plywood top as well (which helps to hold the thinset in place).

Layout

Because this countertop was relatively small, I needed to snap only the four layout lines representing the ones I had marked on the layout sketch (see the drawing on p. 186). Corresponding to the grout joint between the V-cap trim tiles and the field tiles, these lines were placed 1½ in. from and parallel to the front and side edges of the countertop. But rather than confine the lines to the V-cap area, I ran them into the space for the field tiles at the back corner of the cabinets. Here they would help align the tiles on both legs.

My solution to the layout problems in this project involved some compromises, but that's not uncommon when you're faced with fitting tiles to an existing surface. Layout began at the intersection of lines 1 and 2. The distance from that point to the rear of the countertop on the west wall was 22¾ in. This gave me enough room for seven rows of full tiles, with a ⅞-in. space left over. But a cut this narrow would not look attractive. The usual thing to do in this case would be to adjust the layout to put cuts larger than half-size at the front and the back of the counter. This layout would lend some symmetry to the cuts, but it would also mean that a cut edge of field tile would be next to the V-cap, and this should be avoided wherever possible. Because tiles often have a rounded, or "cushioned," edge, the cut edge of such a

tile is higher than the edges of other tiles, and is prone to damage or collecting dirt. So we decided that the solution to this layout problem was to shim out the back-splash with a layer of backer board. With a layer of thinset behind it, the ½-in. thick backer board would reduce the width of the counter by about ⅝ in., and once the ½-in. thick backsplash tiles were set, that awkward little ⅞-in. cut would no longer be needed.

On the other leg of the countertop, the distance from line 2 to the north wall was 22½ in. This gave me enough room to set seven rows of full tiles with a ½-in. space left over. Once again, we decided to absorb that space by installing backer board at the backsplash. The extra thickness of the backsplash would actually be an advantage, since the client wanted to cap the red tiles with a wooden ledge to hold spice jars.

Along the length of the cabinets, I found that I could set 20 full tiles with a 2-in. cut against the V-cap at the south end of leg 1. I didn't like it, but there wasn't much I could do. The counter couldn't be shortened or lengthened, and shifting the layout to the north would result in cuts all along the front of leg 2. I'd just have to live with the cut tiles here. A similar compromise was necessary on the other end of the countertop.

The next thing to check was the position of the sink in relation to the tiles. To see how the tiles would fall, I measured the distance from the sink edges (S1 and S2 in the drawing on p. 186) to line 1. Consulting the tile/grout-joint list, I saw that I would need a 1¼-in. cut tile on the left side of the sink and a 2⅛-in. cut tile on the right (I planned to use surface-bullnose tiles all around the sink). I didn't like the visual imbalance of the cuts, but on the whole the layout was a good one. Nothing was glaringly out of place, and the thickness of the backer-board backsplash would make the spice ledge a bit more stable.

Setting the Tiles

Because it would take much longer to set the tiles than it did to laminate the backer board, I mixed only half the latex thinset needed. Since I planned to begin setting against the layout line at the inside corner of the L and work my way down the first leg, I would apply the first batch of thinset to this leg only. In order to keep from leaning on the V-cap trim tiles as I positioned the field tiles, I left setting the V-caps on both legs until last. After I had finished the first leg, I next set the tiles around the sink and finally addressed the balance of field tiles on the second leg.

Sheet-mounted tiles often need a little more coaxing than individual tiles to line up straight, in part because the additional expanse of tile has more grip than a single tile does. Another reason is that every sheet-mounted tile isn't always perfectly aligned with its neighbors, and the occasional oddball tile must be prodded and pushed to conform, which, of course, is resisted by the backing. Using a straight-edge or even the straight side of the notched trowel makes the alignment process considerably easier, as shown in the bottom photo at right. If you wait about five minutes after initially positioning the sheet in the thinset, the backing (because its glue is usually water-soluble), will often lose its grip on the tiles and allow the offending tile to be easily repositioned. If you're in a hurry, of course, you can always cut through the backing with a utility knife and move the tile.

Tiling around the sink

When I had finished setting field tiles on the first leg, I moved on to trimming out the sink, where surface-bullnose tiles would overlap the metal lip by about ¼ in. To make sure that these tiles adhered, I back-buttered each piece before positioning it in the adhesive on the setting bed. Instead of wiping off the excess adhesive that squeezed out between these trim tiles, I waited until the adhesive had set up and then cut it away with a knife—I didn't want to risk disturbing the tiles until the adhesive had set up somewhat. But I did want to make sure that any globs of thinset were cleared from the joints.

To keep the grout joints of the surface bullnose consistently sized across the front and rear edges of the sink, I checked the position of the tiles against the tile/grout-joint list. The novice setter might find it helpful instead to strike layout lines to identify the positions of the bullnose tiles around the sink. At each corner of the sink, the surface-bullnose tiles were cut to a 45° angle as a decorative solution to the problem of turning the corner while keeping a bullnose edge toward the sink (see the photo on p. 194). This kind of cut is easiest on the wet saw, but, with practice, it can also be made with the snap cutter (and a tile rubbing stone to smooth the edge over). It's important to remember that the width of the angled grout joint between the corner tiles has to be the same as that used elsewhere. This grout width should be consistent and must be allowed for when the cuts are made.

Tiling the backsplash

Once I had set the countertop field and bullnose tiles, I combed thinset over the backsplash and positioned the red tiles. I made sure to align their joints with those on the countertop, and I inserted a spacing wedge under each tile to hold it in place until the adhesive had set up. Backsplash tiles shouldn't rest directly on the counter-top tiles; instead, they should be raised above the countertop by the thickness of a grout joint and the gap later filled with a sealant or caulk color-matched to the grout. Once the thinset on the backsplash had begun to set up, I cleaned the excess thinset out of the joints.

The author began setting the tile on the L-shaped countertop at the inside corner of the L.

Using the smooth side of a notched trowel as a short straightedge lessens some of the difficulty of properly aligning sheet-mounted tile.

While factory-made V-cap and bullnose outside corners were available, inside corners had to be created by mitering cuts on the wet saw.

Setting the V-caps

Having set the countertop and backsplash tiles and cleaned the joints, I no longer needed to lean over the counter and could begin setting the V-caps. These trim tiles needed to be bedded in thinset on both the top and the edge of the counter. To cover both surfaces, I spread thinset with the notched trowel on the countertop, and back-buttered the inside lower portion of each V-cap (see the drawing below).

Trim tiles like surface bullnose and V-cap often tend to be slightly smaller or larger than the field tiles they accompany, probably because trim and field tiles are usually fired separately. Whenever I find that the trim tiles I'm using in an installation are different in size from the field tiles, I simply center the trim piece in relation to the field tile. This means that the grout joints between trim tiles may run a little wider or narrower than those between field tiles, but the slight difference usually isn't apparent to the casual observer.

On this job, factory-made V-cap outside corners were available, but I had to miter two standard V-cap tiles to produce the inside corner (as shown in the photo at left). While it's possible to create these miters with the biters and a rubbing stone, it's more practical to use the wet saw. The latter tool does the job quickly and produces a smooth cut whose edge can be rounded over with a rubbing stone. To hold the V-caps up straight against the miter gauge of the wet saw and ensure an accurate cut, I supported the V-cap with a small wooden block.

Because V-caps often come out of the kiln slightly distorted, I always take time after setting each section of trim to sight along the top and front faces of the V-caps to see that they're aligned. Once I had set all the V-caps, I went over all the tiles again, looking for any that were out of place and checking to see that all the excess thinset had been cleaned off the tiles and from the joints.

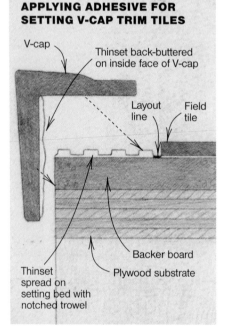

APPLYING ADHESIVE FOR SETTING V-CAP TRIM TILES

V-cap

Thinset back-buttered on inside face of V-cap

Layout line

Field tile

Thinset spread on setting bed with notched trowel

Backer board

Plywood substrate

Grouting the Tiles

The customer's choice of white grout was no accident. He wanted to see the tiles, and there is no greater contrast than between black and white. A grouting situation like this, however, calls for precise work. If the grout is not evenly and thoroughly mixed to begin with, or if the joints are not uniformly filled, inconsistencies will be very apparent against the backdrop of black tiles.

Usually I can spread quite a bit of grout before I have to go back and begin cleaning up. With slick, black tiles like these, though, whose surface scratched easily, I had to work and clean up a small area at a time to keep the residual grout from hardening on the surface of the tiles and requiring heavy scrubbing. I used my regular technique for cleaning up the excess grout (see Chapter 8), but paid particular attention to shaping the joints uniformly with the sponge.

White grout used with black and red tile produces a handsome effect, but the stark contrast in colors meant that the author had to use extra care in grouting, and work and clean up a very small area at a time.

Occasionally, I found that I had wiped away too much grout with the sponge and then had to repack these spots with fresh grout, making sure in each case to reshape the joint before the grout hardened.

Grouting the lower edge of the V-cap tiles that extended about ½ in. below the level of the plywood base was a little tricky. Because packing this area with grout would have been a little impractical with the grout trowel alone, I used my rubber-gloved hand as a second grouting tool, as I often do to grout an awkwardly positioned joint. In this case, I backed up the rear of the joint with one hand (using my thumb as a "fence" to keep grout within the joint) and packed the joint with the grout trowel held in the other hand.

Once I had cleaned off the grout residue and the grout had begun to set up, I went back over the entire surface looking for sloppy joints. There always seems to be a high or low spot here and there that was missed the first time around. The time to make any last-minute adjustments in the joints is while the grout is firm but not yet hard.

Caulking the expansion joints

Finally, I used the tip of a utility knife to cut out the grout from the joints where the bullnose tiles meet the sink, and from the joint between the deck and backsplash tiles. These two joints, which would be prone to cracking, needed to be filled with a bead of caulk or sealant color-matched to the grout (see the Resource Guide for the name of a reliable supplier of color-matched caulks and sealants). To save me an extra trip, the owner agreed to caulk the joint himself after giving the grout a couple of days to dry out. I also suggested that he wait at least 48 hours before installing the plumbing fixtures. After the effort spent setting the tiles, neither one of us wanted to risk damaging them by wrenching on the fixtures before the thinset was solid.

Chapter Twelve

■ ■ ■

Special Installations

If you're new to tilesetting, you'll probably consider every installation a special one, and in a real sense you'll be right. No two residential installations are ever exactly alike. Each has its own set of unique characteristics and problems, and each requires its own individual strategy and layout. Nonetheless, with several installations under your belt, you'll begin to realize that the fundamental principles of tilesetting remain the same from job to job, and that most tile installations fall into three generic categories: floors, walls and countertops.

If your tilesetting plans are a bit more exotic, or if you just haven't found a detail or two you need for a particular project, you should find it here. This chapter serves as a catchall for special installation information that ranges from how to put in a soap dish to how to set cleft slate and other rough-split paving stones. In some cases, what distinguishes the installation

from an "ordinary" job may be only a single special requirement—for example, the need for extra heavy-duty waterproofing protection or a heat-resistant adhesive— with the balance of the tiling procedure the same as for a similar wet or dry job on a comparable setting bed. In other cases, such as the sloped mortar-bed shower floor at the end of this chapter, the entire installation should be regarded as special since the work involves different techniques and requires considerably more skill than the thinbed methods discussed elsewhere in this book.

Mosaic Tile

In the past, most sheets of mosaic tile were face-mounted, that is, the individual tiles were held together in sheet form by a piece of paper or cloth glued to the faces of all the tiles in the sheet. Once the tiles were positioned over the bond or adhesive coat, the paper or cloth sheet was moistened, which softened the glue and released its grip on the tiles. It was a very tedious (and messy) process.

Today, most mosaic tiles are back-mounted onto a punched paper sheet or onto plastic netting (see p. 10). Tiles can also be assembled into sheet form by sticking the individual tiles together with small adhesive dots between each tile and its neighbor (known as dot-mounted tiles). These sheets are a distinct improvement over face-mounted tiles since the installer can always see each piece of mosaic and make sure it is aligned with its neighbors.

As with any back-mounted tile, however, the backing material on mosaic tile can interfere with the bond of the adhesive. If the tiles are dot-mounted, an oily residue left on the backs of the tiles during manufacturing may cause additional bonding problems. When purchasing dot-mounted tile, be sure to check the back of several sheets in two or three boxes before taking the tile from the store. If you can wipe oil from the back of the sheets with a paper towel, ask for another lot of the tile or consider choosing different tile altogether. If you've already bought the tile and find oil on the sheets, try exchanging it. If you can't, clean the backs of the sheets with a mild detergent and water (wiping the backs "clean" with a rag won't suffice). Then allow the tile to dry fully before setting it.

Whatever the type of backing material, its interference with the adhesive is a particular problem with 1-in. mosaic tiles. With the already small surface area of the individual tiles largely covered by the backing material, the issue is how to apply enough adhesive to bond each tile firmly to the setting bed and at the same time avoid the next-to-impossible cleanup of adhesive that will ooze up into all the grout joints.

Most setters quickly clean as much adhesive as possible from the surface of the tiles and the tops of the grout joints and then simply use a white grout over white adhesive or a grey grout over grey adhesive. This approach can reduce the mottling that sometimes occurs in colored grouts at the thin spots that lie over globs of adhesive. But the drawback to this system is that the color of the grout and adhesive may not be identical, and with time both may change and still produce a mottled effect. In addition, the setter has only two grout colors to choose from.

Setting mosaic tile

To avoid these problems, I draw upon the thick-bed setting method used by the ancient Romans and combine their approach with modern materials. (This method required the setter to "beat" tiles down into a wet mortar bed, which forced some of the mortar up through the joints. The excess mortar was then compacted between the joints to serve as a grout.) Nowadays when I install mosaic tiles, I use 100% solids epoxy as both the adhesive and the grout. I begin the installation by making sure that the setting bed is hard and completely flat, since even the slightest depression or high spot becomes glaring when covered with small mosaic tiles. Then, with a ¼-in. square-notched trowel, I spread and comb the adhesive/grout mixture on a small area of the bed. After setting the sheet on the bed, I force it into the epoxy with a beating block and hammer (see the photo at left on the facing page).

To check the coverage, I remove the test sheet and examine the back. There should be a distinct impression of the sheet in the epoxy, and the back of all the tiles in the sheet should also be fully covered. If the coverage is inadequate, I place the sheet face down and give its back a skim coat of the epoxy with a flat trowel. Then I bed the treated sheet in the epoxy (recombed with

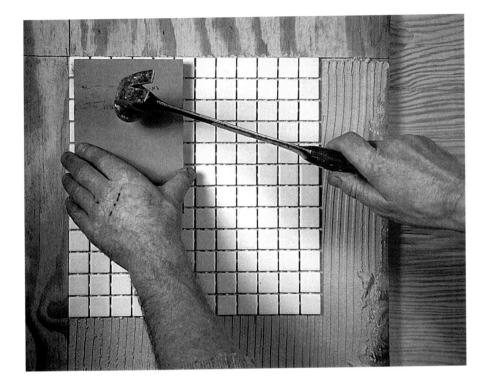

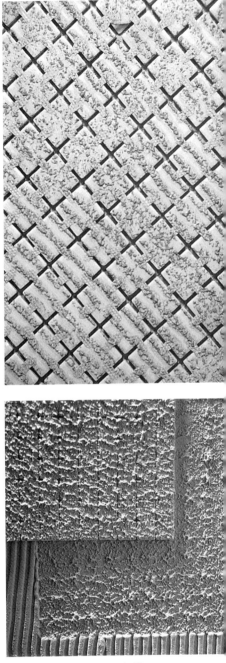

the ¼-in. notched trowel to create a new setting bed of adhesive), work the sheet with the beating block and hammer, and check the coverage again. Though many installers feel that the bond is sufficient with 75% coverage of the tiles, I disagree. In my experience, if the job gets normal wear, a lot of the tiles will eventually break or become loose unless they're fully bedded in and surrounded by the epoxy adhesive/grout. To achieve the full coverage shown on the sample sheet in the photo at bottom right, I switched to an even larger trowel with notches ¼ in. wide by ⅜ in. deep.

When I actually begin setting the sheets, I beat them level with their neighbors and check all the joints to see that they're lined up. It is not important if some of the epoxy oozes up through the joints, because the same material will be used as the grout after the adhesive has hardened. However, it is important to remove any excess epoxy and treat it as if it were the actual grout joint; so, before

moving out of arm's reach, I use a Scotch-Brite pad and water to pare down the excess, and then follow this with a wipe of a dampened sponge to remove any residue on the surface.

It's especially crucial with this setting technique to use as little water as possible when cleaning the tiles. Too much water can wash away the epoxy resin in the adhesive/grout at the top of the joint, thereby weakening it. After initially cleaning off the surface of the tiles, I check all the sheets to see if any need slight repositioning. Then I shape the joints and do the final cleanup. It's important to do a thorough job of cleaning the tiles, because hardened epoxy resins are extremely difficult to remove.

Once all the sheets have been installed and the epoxy has been given a chance to harden (check the manufacturer's instructions), I can go back with a fresh batch of the same epoxy and grout the tiles.

Before beginning a mosaic-tile installation, set a sample sheet of tiles to check the adhesive's coverage. After setting and beating in the sheet (top left), remove it and look at the back. If the adhesive coverage is insufficient (top right), switch to a larger-notched trowel to achieve full coverage (above).

Tiles Exposed to Heat

Setting tile around fireplaces and wood-stoves (and sometimes around ranges) involves some special considerations, the foremost of which is heat. Fireplaces and stoves can generate enough heat to destroy the bond of many adhesives. Organic mastics, for example, should never be used for these installations, and even some thinset adhesives should be avoided. Choose instead a heat-resistant adhesive that can withstand sustained temperatures of up to 400°F (see the Resource Guide).

Before proceeding to install tile near any appliance that generates lots of heat, however, you *must* consult your local building inspector for installation details. Local codes vary, but some are very strict about such things. Depending on the circumstances of the job and your local codes, you may have to incorporate an airspace or some fire-resistant material between the tilework and any combustible walls.

Creating an airspace

If you must incorporate an air channel behind the tilework—maybe you're tiling a woodstove surround, for example—the task isn't too difficult. The idea is to build up a slender wall of noncombustible material, set the tile on that, and then separate this assembly from any combustible wall with noncombustible spacers. Let's assume you want to put your woodstove near a combustible wall (some ⅝-in. thick gypsum drywall, by the way, fits into this category). One noncombustible spacer that's easy to work with is called "hat channel." It's just a light-gauge sheet-metal track about ⅞ in. deep, which in cross section resembles, well, a fedora. First, snip the hat channel into lengths appropriate for the size of surround you want and screw them to the wall (and into the studs) through their "brim." Next fasten at least two layers of backer board to the "crown" of the hat channel with drywall screws. Then simply set tile on the backer board using a heat-resistant adhesive.

The resulting installation will use air to carry heat away before it can reach the combustible wall. Be sure, though, to use enough hat channel to give the backer board adequate support. And don't figure on saving money by using 2x4s as spacers instead of hat channel—remember, they're combustible, and I wouldn't want to bet *my* house on their suitability.

Surface preparation

The face of a fireplace requires preparation before tiling. Scrupulously clean off all traces of soot, which would prevent the adhesive from bonding properly. Also check to make sure that the surface is reasonably smooth and flat. If not, knock down the high spots with a masonry rubbing stone. If the front of the fireplace is composed of bricks and their surface is too irregular for setting tiles, clean the bricks, coat them with a thin layer of thinset and fill the irregularities with mortar, as shown in the drawing on the facing page.

If the fireplace has a metal face, like those on some "zero-clearance" fireplaces, do not set tires directly on this surface. Most of these faces are too flimsy to support the weight of tiles. Instead, I recommend laminating backer board to the surface. Before laminating the board, grind or sand off any paint and then use a heat-resistant epoxy adhesive for both lamination and tilesetting. Be sure not to tile over any intake or exhaust vents. After the face tiles have been set, the inside edge between the tiles and the firebox can be trimmed in one of several ways, as shown in the drawing at left on p. 202. To support the tiles until the

FLOATING AN EVEN SETTING BED OVER AN IRREGULAR FIREPLACE FRONT

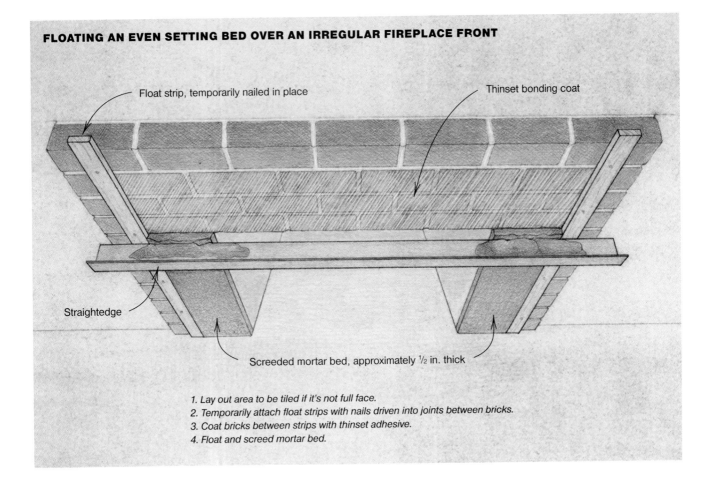

Float strip, temporarily nailed in place

Thinset bonding coat

Straightedge

Screeded mortar bed, approximately ½ in. thick

1. Lay out area to be tiled if it's not full face.
2. Temporarily attach float strips with nails driven into joints between bricks.
3. Coat bricks between strips with thinset adhesive.
4. Float and screed mortar bed.

adhesive sets up, either tape them in place or use a bridge like the one shown in the drawing at right on p. 202. The bridge is simply propped in place—it's not necessary to fasten it.

Tiling a hearth

If you're tiling only the hearth of a fireplace, the major concern is not so much heat damage as it is the pounding that most hearths have to endure. Even if you're horrified at the idea of using your hearth as a chopping block for wood, it will take a beating from logs that get dropped on it and fireplace tools that fall out of their rack. For this reason, you need to provide a setting bed for the tiles that's at least

1¼ in. thick. Since I'm a fan of mortar beds, I'd suggest floating a mortar bed over the hearth, but you could also laminate a couple of pieces of backer board together with thinset and a layer of galvanized expanded mesh between the two boards to achieve this thickness.

To use backer board as a setting bed for the hearth, cut the boards to size and coat one side of each with a layer of thinset mortar spread with a ¼-in. square-notched trowel (work on a flat section of flooring or a workbench). Then position the piece of galvanized mesh over one of the boards and nest it into the thinset mortar. Align the other piece (mortared side down) to

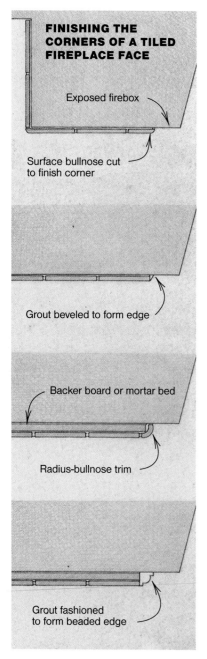

FINISHING THE CORNERS OF A TILED FIREPLACE FACE

Exposed firebox

Surface bullnose cut to finish corner

Grout beveled to form edge

Backer board or mortar bed

Radius-bullnose trim

Grout fashioned to form beaded edge

HOLDING TILES IN PLACE

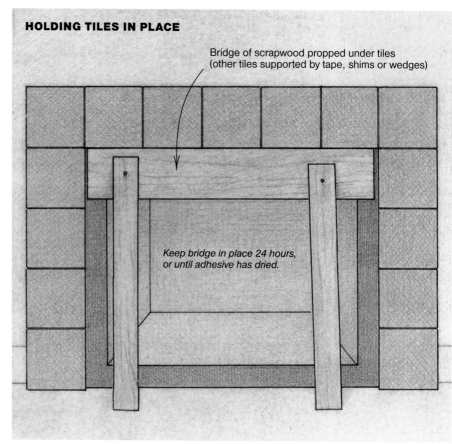

Bridge of scrapwood propped under tiles (other tiles supported by tape, shims or wedges)

Keep bridge in place 24 hours, or until adhesive has dried.

the first and allow the thinset mortar about 48 hours to harden and dry. When dry, this assembly can then be laminated to the subflooring with another layer of thinset mortar (see pp. 77-78).

The hearth will get its share of heat, so a heat-resistant thinset wouldn't be a bad idea. Consult your local building inspector, though. If the hearth borders wood flooring (whether finished or subflooring), leave a ⅛-in. to ¼-in. gap between the tiles and the wood (the open joint should match the width of the grout joints but be no less than ⅛ in.). Caulk the joint with a sealant color-matched to the grout to prevent seasonal or heat expansion from destroying either surface.

Soap Dishes

Both metal and ceramic-tile soap dishes can be installed in showers. I don't care for metal soap dishes because they're difficult to keep clean and because installing them requires cutting a hole in the setting bed and the waterproofing membrane. Instead, I always urge customers to choose ceramic soap dishes, which come in two types: one that's mounted to the setting bed like a regular tile and protrudes out from the wall, and one that's recessed into the wall.

While these two types of soap dishes are installed differently, they should both be positioned after the rest of the tile has been set on the wall or backsplash. This, of course, means that as you're setting the main field of tile, you'll need to omit or cut tiles to accommodate the dish. Also, although many manufacturers of soap dishes state in their installation instructions that the dishes can be installed with grout, they should be adhered with a thinset adhesive—*not* grout and certainly *never* an organic mastic.

Surface-mounted soap dishes

The surface-mounted dish is bonded directly to the setting bed. There's usually a mounting pad on the back side that spaces the dish slightly away from the wall. Depending on the size of the dish, the pad allows it to be inset either with a grout joint surrounding it, or to overlap the surrounding tiles partially or completely, eclipsing one or more grout joints.

Installing a surface-mounted soap dish is simple. Cover both the setting bed and the mounting pad on the back of the dish with a layer of thinset about ⅛ in. thick, and press the dish firmly into position. To maintain even joint spacing around the perimeter of the dish, use tile wedges or chips of tile to shim up the dish and support its weight until the adhesive sets up. Clean off any thinset that oozes out of the joints and temporarily anchor the dish in position with a couple of strips of masking tape. Allow the thinset to harden overnight before grouting the joint.

Recessed soap dishes

If you prefer the look of a recessed soap dish, be ready to tackle a more complex job. You'll first need to fasten 2x blocking to the framing to create support around the approximate mounting position of the dish. The space within the blocked area should be about 1 in. wider and higher than the actual size of the dish. Next install the substrate and the waterproofing membrane (I prefer to use CPE sheet membrane, see pp. 106-107), cutting a hole in the membrane corresponding to the position of the dish.

Then fashion a small "pocket" out of the membrane, using the box-fold technique described in making a shower pan (see p. 212) to fit into the recess created by the

blocking. Spread thinset adhesive around the wall opening, then press the pocket into place and seal its folds and the flaps overlapping the wall membrane with solvent. (If you're using tar paper as the waterproofing membrane, which is installed under the substrate, use asphalt roofing cement to seal the laps; with plastic film, use silicone. For trowel-applied membranes, simply cover the blocking and substrate with the liquid membrane and reinforcing fabric.)

Next set the wall tiles up to the opening and let them sit overnight. Then lightly coat the recessed pocket with thinset and stuff it with wall mud, shaping it approximately to fit the back of the soap dish. Once this has dried, coat its surface and the mounting sides of the dish with a ¹⁄₁₆-in. thick layer of thinset and press the dish into place. Clean off any excess thinset and allow the adhesive to harden before grouting.

Soap dishes often have a handle molded into the body of the dish. Since the dish is designed to hold soap, not the weight of a person, *never use this handle as a grab bar!* You risk serious injury, or, at the very least, you're liable to break the dish or pull it away from the wall. If you want a grab bar on your tiled wall, buy hardware specially designed for this purpose, and fasten it securely to the wall framing behind the tile.

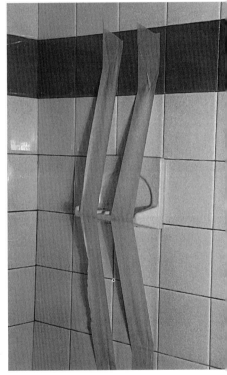

After applying adhesive to the setting bed and the back of the soap dish (top), position the dish, shimming it with tile chips, and secure it with masking tape until the thinset has dried (above).

Nonceramic Alternatives to Trim Tiles

If ceramic trim tiles are not available to accompany the tiles you're setting, you may want to consider some alternatives to ceramic trim. Any number of materials can be used. Wood is probably the most common alternative, but I've fashioned trim out of everything from sculptured marble and stone to old decorative bricks, glass wine bottles, broken pieces of pottery, shells and even ceramic drainpipe (cut lengthwise into four pieces to create a massive quarter-round).

Plastic trim

Another substitute for ceramic trim, when the job calls just for surface bullnose, is one of the plastic strips made especially to finish off glazed tile installations. These strips come in a variety of colors and sizes for the most popular sizes of tile. The strips are anchored by the tiles they trim off and are held in place with regular thin-set adhesive.

This type of trim has several limitations. The material itself is not as durable as most ceramic tiles. When used where it will be subject to lots of wear (to trim the step of a tiled stairway, for example), the strip will wear out. Unless the plastic is immediately replaced when it begins to show signs of wear, the edges of the tiles on the steps may in turn get damaged. Replacing this strip is difficult, however, since the trim is embedded in the adhesive anchoring the neighboring tiles. For these reasons, I suggest reserving plastic trim for locations where it will receive minimal wear.

Wood trim

Wood is increasingly popular for trimming off tile installations. The only problem with using wood trim is that it expands when it gets wet and tile does not, and the resulting gaps aren't exactly attractive. In some instances, the expanding wood may even damage the tile. Even if the planned installation will not get wet, the wood trim will nonetheless expand and contract with seasonal changes in humidity. Therefore, I recommend completely sealing the wood used for trim, firmly attaching it with screws and isolating it from the tiles and the setting bed with a bead of caulk or sealant.

When installing wood trim, screw it to something solid, like a stud or a plywood substrate. The trim should be positioned about $\frac{1}{8}$ in. away from the tiles and setting bed to allow for expansion and contraction in both the bed and the wood. Use silicone or color-matched caulk to fill this gap.

Wooden stair nosing is often used to trim off tiled steps. Even though it's usually nailed in place, I think the nosing should be glued and screwed in position. Although water isn't usually a problem here, the nosing should nonetheless be given at least two coats of sealer before being installed.

Countertop installations

On most kitchen countertops, water is a constant problem. Before attaching any trim to a countertop, I recommend sealing the front of the trim and giving the back two or more extra coats of sealer. While wood trim can be installed flush with the surface of the tiles, I prefer to set it $\frac{1}{16}$ in. to $\frac{1}{8}$ in. higher than the tiles to create a lip that will keep spills on the countertop (see the drawing on the facing page). The trim should be drilled and counterbored every 6 in. to 8 in. to accept screws. Be sure to bore the holes deep enough so that you'll be able to cover the head of the screw with a wooden plug.

On a thinset countertop, the sealed wood trim should be installed after the tiles have been set. Bed the trim in caulk and attach it to the plywood with screws long enough to offer secure attachment to the plywood. Again, keep the tiles $\frac{1}{8}$ in. from the trim.

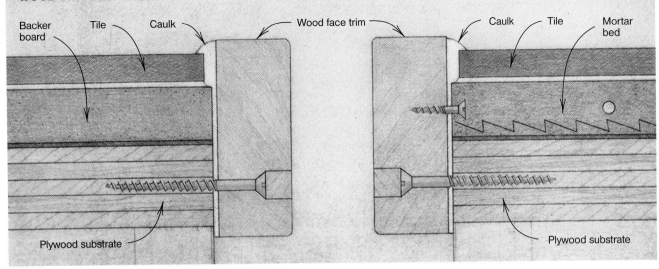

WOOD TRIM ON THINSET AND THICK-BED COUNTERTOPS

Backer board | Tile | Caulk | Wood face trim | Caulk | Tile | Mortar bed

Plywood substrate

Plywood substrate

If the trim is to finish off a thick-bed countertop, I suggest attaching it before floating any mortar. First, run short screws partway into the back side of the trim, so that the protruding screw heads will key into the mortar when it's floated and lock the trim into place. Coat the wood trim with caulk, and then install with screws as explained above. Caulk the gap between the tiles and the trim after the tiles have been installed.

Once the installation is in use, keep an eye out for any dark streaking on the trim, which would indicate water penetrating the wood. The amount of maintenance required for the sealer will depend on how much wear the installation receives, but you can expect the need for a periodic touchup.

Paving Stones

As much as I like ceramic tile, I am easily seduced by the natural beauty of paving stone, and I thoroughly enjoy the challenge of its installation. Stone is usually purchased in gauged form, that is, cut to a uniform thickness and dimension, but some is

available in cleft form, meaning that it has been split rather than sawn from large chunks of stone. Gauged stone is set more or less like regular ceramic tile (see pp. 25-27), while the very irregular shapes and sizes of cleft stone require that it be set quite differently.

Cleft paving stones

Because of the highly irregular shape and size of cleft stone, installing it is like working a jigsaw puzzle: Each piece is contoured to fit its neighbor. Let's look at the special procedures for installing cleft stone in the context of an entryway I set with slate from mainland China.

Cleft slate should be set only on a bed of mortar or concrete, twice as thick as the average thickness of the slate being set (in this case, the thickness ranged from $\frac{1}{4}$ in. to almost 3 in.). In no case, however, should the setting bed be less than $1\frac{1}{2}$ in. thick.

Whether the installation is interior or exterior, I recommend using a latex additive with the mortar or concrete to prevent efflorescence, which is a whitish deposit of soluble salts on masonry

Tile set outdoors, as for a patio, should have a concrete slab as its setting bed. I recommend floating this slab so it slopes to a drain, or with enough of a crown to allow water to drain from the surface of the tiles (and away from the house!). Choose only vitreous tiles for this installation to prevent freeze/thaw damage, and use additives with both the thinset adhesive and the grout (or use an adhesive and grout with the dry additive premixed).

surfaces. With either mortar or concrete, the bed should be allowed to harden before any of the stones are actually installed.

The organizing principle in setting a cleft-stone floor is to position the largest and thickest pieces first and then build the rest of the floor around these anchoring stones—a procedure that needs to be done in overlapping stages. I began this job, as I always do when working with cleft stone, by grouping the stones in piles according to

size. Once I had arranged all the pieces of slate into about a dozen piles, I was ready to begin the first round of setting.

After first installing the largest pieces, distributing them evenly throughout the entryway, I would set progressively smaller sizes of stones until the entire area had been covered. At the point when the stones began to touch or overlap one another, I would have to begin trimming them to make them fit together. To do this, I would

After grouping the cleft stones according to size, the author distributed the largest ones throughout the entryway (top right). Then he set the slate, progressing from the largest to the smallest pieces and placing the pieces randomly throughout the foyer. When the stones being set overlapped one another, he marked trimming lines on them and chipped them to shape with a mason's hammer (bottom right).

slip a new stone into the fresh mortar supporting one already set and then scribe a trimming line on the new stone to guide me in chipping it to shape with a mason's hammer. While this may sound like a tedious way to proceed, this setting pattern actually saves a lot of work. If I had simply started in one corner of the entryway and worked my way across the floor, I would have needed to trim almost every piece of stone to fit its neighbor.

Setting the stones

To set the stones on this entryway, I used a combination of thinset adhesive and a slightly wet mixture of deck mud (see p. 217). I applied a thin layer of the adhesive to both the setting bed and the back of the slate, and then troweled deck mud over the thinset on the setting bed to shim up the

stone and make its top surface level with that of its neighbor. To ensure accuracy and to speed up the lengthy procedure of leveling the large stones set first, I made a height gauge, like that shown in the drawing below, from a couple of scraps of 2x4s.

After positioning each of these large pieces of slate in the mortar, I placed the gauge over each stone and tapped it with a hammer until the gauge's "legs" made contact with the setting bed. I then removed the gauge and cut away the mud that had oozed beyond the edge of the slate. By repeating this procedure with each new piece of slate, I ensured that it was set at the correct height.

Once I had set the largest stones randomly over the entryway, I no longer needed the height gauge. Instead, I could

FOUNTAINS AND SWIMMING POOLS

For installations where the tile will be continuously submerged in water, choose only vitreous tile. And because such installations tend to move slightly when filled with water, I strongly recommend using only thinset adhesives and grouts to which a latex additive has been added. While many of the details of tiling swimming pools and fountains will be familiar to anyone who has studied earlier chapters, many others are unusual, and beyond the scope of this book.

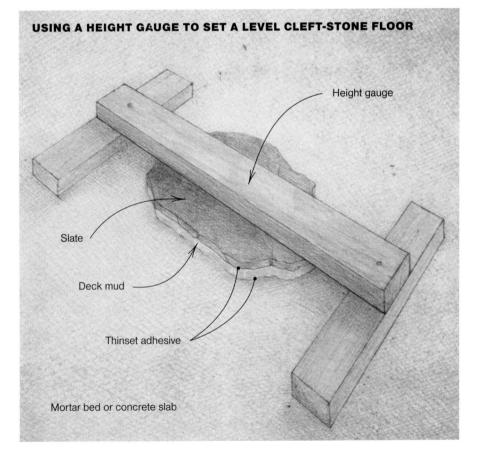

USING A HEIGHT GAUGE TO SET A LEVEL CLEFT-STONE FLOOR

Height gauge

Slate

Deck mud

Thinset adhesive

Mortar bed or concrete slab

While grout joints up to 1 in. wide are not uncommon on informal slate floors, the author chose ¼-in. wide joints for this formal foyer, which meant many hours of chipping with the mason's hammer to produce these narrow joints.

gauge the height of each new stone with a straightedge bridging two pieces of slate already set in mortar. When I had gotten the largest pieces of slate set, I stopped to let the mortar supporting the slate set up overnight.

I set the remaining stones just as I had the larger pieces of slate, using a straightedge held against the surface of neighboring stones to adjust the height of each new piece. When I had set a "community" of stones, I raked the deck mud from between them with the tip of a narrow margin trowel, cutting the mud down to a depth of about ½ in. to leave room for the grout. Then I cleaned off the surface of the slate with a damp sponge.

The process for grouting cleft stone is about the same as that for ceramic tile (although on very coarse, porous or highly irregular stones, you might want to use a grout bag; see pp. 149-150). More care, however, must be taken to clean up the grout and to do it quickly, since the uneven surface of the stone can easily trap the grout.

Mortar-Bed Shower Floors

With the development of shower floors (known as "receptors") made from synthetic materials and the availability of cement backer boards for shower walls, the all-mortar-bed shower stall is rapidly becoming a symbol of the past. Nevertheless, because of the inherent size limitations of factory-made receptors, the mortar-bed shower floor still has a while to go before it too is retired for good.

In my opinion, there is nothing so luxurious as stepping onto a beautifully tiled shower floor. The instructions you will find here represent a mix of methods and materials that have served me well for 25 years. Although I generally frown on beginners tackling a mortar-bed project, a sloped mortar-bed shower floor, in spite of its apparent complexity, is well suited to the accomplished amateur willing to go the extra mile for quality.

Anatomy of a mortar-bed shower

Before addressing the actual installation procedure, let's look first at the anatomy of a mortar-bed shower. The three key elements are the subdrain, the shower pan and the sloped subfloor.

THE SUBDRAIN At the center of a sloped mortar-bed shower floor is the subdrain (or clamping drain), whose open upper half is covered by a chrome screen and whose lower half connects to the waste or drain line (see the bottom drawing on the facing page). Around the circumference of the top half are six small holes. Three of the holes accommodate the bolts that clamp the drain halves together, with the shower-pan membrane sandwiched between. The other three are weep holes to let any moisture that gets into the mortar bed escape into the drain. If this residual moisture were trapped, it might promote the growth of fungus and bacteria in the bed. The subdrain should be located right in the center of the shower floor, with the split between the two halves positioned flush with the sloped subfloor.

THE SHOWER PAN Unlike waterproofing membranes that need only shed water, a shower pan is a heavy-duty membrane designed and built to hold water until it can find its way to the drain pipe. Shower pans have been made from a variety of materials, including copper, lead and galvanized sheet metal, tar paper slathered with hot tar (known as "hot-mopped pans"), fiberglass cloth and resin, trowel-applied materials and synthetic sheets.

During the course of my early tile career, I removed countless metal, hot-mopped, fiberglass and trowel-applied pans. After experimenting with a number of synthetic sheet materials and rejecting

CROSS SECTION OF SHOWER FLOOR

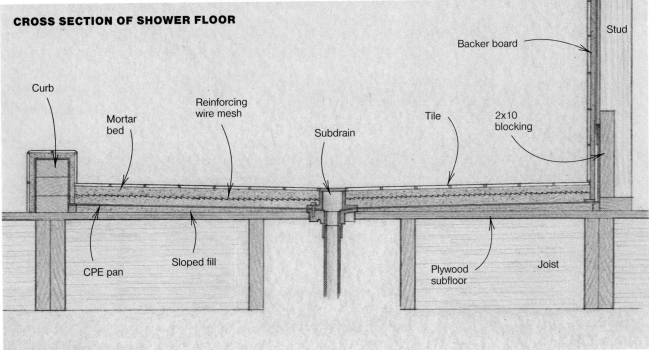

Curb

Mortar bed

Reinforcing wire mesh

Subdrain

Tile

2x10 blocking

Backer board

Stud

CPE pan

Sloped fill

Plywood subfloor

Joist

Vincent Babak

all but one because of cracking, splitting or other problems, I settled on a pan material made from chlorinated polyethylene (CPE). It is thick, tough and flexible, and I have never had to remove or repair a pan made from this material.

For the shower pan to perform properly, it must sit on a sloped subfloor, extend up the surrounding walls and lap over the threshold (curb) of the shower stall. Where the pan extends up the walls (at least 2 in. to 3 in. higher than the top of the curb), it must be fully supported by 2x blocking installed between the studs.

THE SLOPED SUBFLOOR In any tiled shower, the subfloor below the shower pan must be sloped toward the subdrain to ensure that any water penetrating the tile and mortar above the pan runs to the subdrain. Without a sloped subfloor, residual moisture would stagnate within the floor mortar supporting the tiles and cause

SUBDRAIN ASSEMBLY

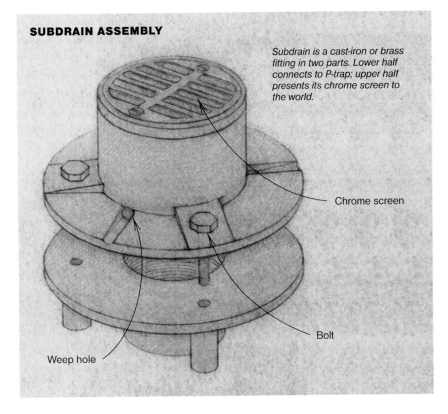

Subdrain is a cast-iron or brass fitting in two parts. Lower half connects to P-trap; upper half presents its chrome screen to the world.

Chrome screen

Bolt

Weep hole

One way to get the necessary drainage to the center of the shower pan is to use pie-shaped sections of plywood over tapered joists or wedges.

chronic maintenance problems (musty smells emanating from the mortar, mildew growing on the tile and grout joints).

The subfloor can be sloped using pie-shaped sections of plywood that pitch toward the drain (see the photo above), but the carpentry skills required to produce this subfloor are beyond the scope of this book. The method I prefer—sloping mortar fill over a flat subfloor—requires a few scraps of wood, enough tar paper and reinforcing mesh to cover the floor, a little mortar and just a moderate amount of skill with a trowel.

Floating the sloped subfloor

The first step in floating the sloped subfloor beneath the shower pan is to locate the center of the subfloor. At this point, cut a hole whose diameter is large enough to allow clearance for the lower half of the clamping drain, but small enough to catch and support the outer flange of the drain (drains can be supported by strapping the drain pipe to something structural, but they will be more stable if the drain housing itself is

supported). These instructions assume that the subfloor on which the drain is to be installed is ³⁄₄-in. thick (minimum) exterior plywood.

With the hole cut, cover the floor with a layer of 15-lb. tar paper and then install the lower half of the subdrain, connecting it to the drain line. Measure from the center of the subdrain to the farthest point of the shower enclosure, and figure out how much slope will be needed over that distance (the subfloor should slope at a rate of ¼ in. per ft.). With the help of a spirit level, extend the height of the top of the lower drain half to the side walls, and add the sloping factor (½ in. of slope for a 2-ft. run, ³⁄₄ in. for a 3-ft. run, etc). Now measure down to determine the height of the wooden screeds you will need. Rip stock down to a square cross section (½x½, ³⁄₄x³⁄₄, etc.), and nail the strips in continuous lengths to the floor around the perimeter of the shower. (These screeds can remain in place after floating the subfloor.)

Next, place a layer of reinforcing mesh over the floor and staple or nail it directly over the tar paper (keeping the mesh about

1 in. away from the drain housing). Then mix a small batch of deck mud to a dry-pack consistency (see p. 217) for the sloped fill. Since the finished slope will be rather thin, use a latex or acrylic additive to strengthen the mud. Trowel the mortar around the floor and pack it tightly with the trowel or a wood float, using the drain flange and the wood strips around the perimeter of the floor as screeding guides (see the photo below). You will need to use a number of different-length straightedges since the distance between the drain flange and the outer walls is constantly changing. Generally, I rough out the surface with a few straightedges and then finish off the rest by eye with a wood float. After the deck mud has hardened overnight, the sloped subfloor will be ready to receive the shower pan.

Making the shower pan

The shower pan for a stall needs to extend several inches up the surrounding walls and lap over the rough curb, which is usually made from three stacked 2x4s (about 4½ in. high). To determine the size of the piece of CPE you need to cut, measure the dimensions of the floor and then add 9 in. for each wall and about 14 in. to 16 in. for the curb. The curb should be completely covered—inside face, top and outer face.

To prepare the pan, unroll the CPE onto a clean, flat surface and cut off a piece that best matches one of the overall dimensions (I buy CPE by the roll for economy, but it is also available by the foot). If a piece cut from the roll is not wide enough, you can expand its effective size by solvent welding another piece of CPE to it (see the sidebar at right). Although this material is much safer to use than hot tar, the chemicals used in the solvents that clean and weld the CPE sheet can be hazardous. Follow the manufacturer's instructions carefully, provide adequate ventilation, restrict sparks or open flames and wear personal safety equipment: latex gloves, eye protection and a charcoal filter mask.

To produce a sloped mortar bed, pack deck mud over a layer of reinforcing mesh and float away the excess using the drain flange and wood screeds around the perimeter of the enclosure as guides.

PAN LAYOUT

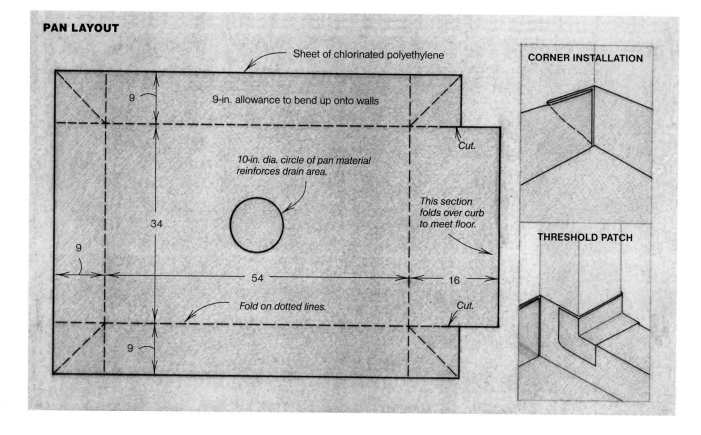

Sheet of chlorinated polyethylene

9-in. allowance to bend up onto walls

9

34

9

54

16

9

9

10-in. dia. circle of pan material reinforces drain area.

Fold on dotted lines.

Cut.

This section folds over curb to meet floor.

Cut.

CORNER INSTALLATION

THRESHOLD PATCH

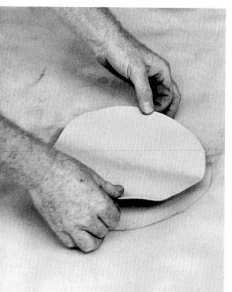

To reinforce the area around the subdrain, cut a circle of CPE slightly larger than the flange on the subdrain and solvent-weld it to the shower pan.

Next, draw the layout of the pan on the CPE with a felt-tipped marker, as shown in the drawing above. The dotted lines show where the material laps up the walls and how the corners are folded. Then cut the pan to its finished size and solvent-weld a circle of pan material about 10 in. in diameter to the area that will end up between the drain halves. Reinforcing this part of the pan makes a thicker gasket for the drain to grip at this potential point of abrasion.

Now crease the material along the four lines representing the perimeter of the floor and fold the diagonal corner lines away from the center of the pan so that the triangular tabs will end up between the pan and the blocking (see the detail at right in the drawing above).

To ensure a watertight seal between the pan and the drain, lay down two beads of sealant (see the Resource Guide) on the

bottom half of the drain, one inside and one outside the bolt circle. Then partially screw the bolts into the lower half of the drain. After the pan has been installed, you'll be able to feel where the bolt heads are and cut precise holes through the pan material.

To help keep the pan material flat against the blocking, subfloor and curb, coat these surfaces with an even layer of asphalt roofing cement spread with an 1/8 in. V-notched trowel. Now the pan is ready to install.

Installing the shower pan

Roll the prefolded pan into a bundle and position it over the subfloor, as shown in the bottom left photo on the facing page. Starting at the drain, smooth the air bubbles out toward the walls and press the material into the corners. To flatten the

After cutting and marking the pan layout on the CPE, crease the material along the fold lines.

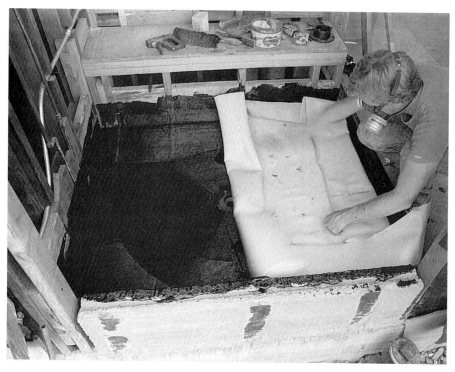

After coating the blocking, sloped subfloor and curb with asphalt roofing cement, unfold the bundled pan into position on the shower floor (left). Once the pan has been positioned, it can be stapled to the blocking along the top inch of the material. The corners of the pan are folded so that the triangular-shaped tabs end up against the blocking (above).

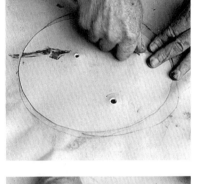

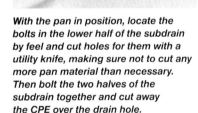

With the pan in position, locate the bolts in the lower half of the subdrain by feel and cut holes for them with a utility knife, making sure not to cut any more pan material than necessary. Then bolt the two halves of the subdrain together and cut away the CPE over the drain hole.

folds in the corners, drizzle some CPE solvent onto the mating faces, allow the CPE to soften and then press the layers together.

When you're satisfied that the pan is snug, staple along the top edges of the CPE, except at the curb. Here, slit the pan material next to the jamb openings and lap the CPE over the curb. The junction of the jamb and the curb can be difficult to seal and often leaks, but the manufacturer of the CPE material also makes an accessory piece, called a dam corner, that you can use to make this troublesome spot water-proof (see the detail at right in the drawing on p. 212). After it is solvent-welded in place, staple the top of the pan at the curb wall. All that is needed to complete the pan is to install the top half of the drain.

To put the drain halves together, feel around for the bolts and press the CPE down over the head of each with one hand (see the photos at left). With the other hand, use a sharp knife to cut small holes in the pan so it can slip over the bolts (be careful not to cut any more pan material than is necessary). Then stretch the CPE over the bolts, unscrew them from the lower half and position the upper half over the bolt holes. Don't put any sealant under the top half of the drain since this would clog the weep holes. Reinsert the bolts and tighten them evenly with a socket wrench. Finally, cut away the disc of CPE covering the drain hole.

Water testing the shower pan for leaks

Before going any further in the installation, the pan should be tested for leaks. To test for leaks, plug the drainpipe with an expandable stopper (you can buy one at a plumbing supply store or borrow one from your plumber) and fill the pan with water nearly to the top of the curb. Mark the level of the water and then let the pan sit undisturbed for 24 hours. The next day, check the water level. If there is no change, the pan holds water and the installation can proceed.

If the water level has gone down, you'll have to locate and fix the leak. Look for signs of water on surrounding surfaces, and, if possible, below the pan as well. If you see nothing to indicate a leak, chances are the plug used to stop the drain may have been leaking. If this is your guess, refit the plug and repeat the test.

If the water has completely drained from the pan, the leak probably occurred around the drain flange—either the drain halves were not bolted tightly enough, or they were bolted too tightly and the pan material tore. For the former, retighten the bolts and water test again. For the latter, cut away the tear and enough pan material so that a patch can be solvent-welded to the pan.

If the water level has dropped only an inch or two, the leak may be around an errant staple near the top of the pan or it may be behind one of the corner envelope folds. If you find a hole or a tear, drain the water from the pan, dry off the CPE and solvent-weld a patch to the material, making sure to overlap the puncture by at least 2 in. all around. If you determine that the leak is located within one of the corner folds, cut a bandage of CPE 4 in. wide and long enough to cover the crease and overlap it around all sides by a minimum of 2 in.

Preparing the walls

After the water test, work can begin on the wall surfaces. While the traditional method is to float mortar beds for shower-stall walls, a good alternative is to use cement backer boards (CBUs) as the setting bed. As explained in Chapter 5, CBUs are relatively easy to install, but they do require some special detailing when used in a stall shower.

There are two main problems to overcome when using CBUs on shower walls: first, how to maintain a smooth, plumb line where the CBUs overlap the

Steam heat is notorious for the cracks it causes in mortar beds (the usual backing for steam applications) and tile. Steamrooms are extra-heavy-duty stall showers that require sloped floors, sloped tiled ceilings, tight-fitting doors and controls to regulate the steam.

Unlike conventional waterproofing techniques used for ordinary shower stalls, steamroom environments require con-siderable detailing to contain not only moisture but also water vapor. In addition, industry standards call for insulation as part of a steamroom construction. If your tile plans call for a steamroom, I would recommend that you contact a qualified tile installer with a good track record of steamroom installa-tions. (For more information about steamrooms, refer to the TCA *Handbook* SR613.)

shower pan and, second, how to secure the lower edge of the CBUs without puncturing the shower pan. I solve the first problem by shimming out the CBUs far enough to clear the pan (see the drawing at right). The mortar bed floated over the shower pan takes care of the second problem, locking the lower edges of the boards in place. Here's an overview of how to install CBUs on shower walls.

The first step is to nail ¼-in. lattice strips to the face of each exposed stud above the top of the pan. These strips will shim out the CBUs past the pan. Next, install the waterproofing membrane—in this case polyethylene film, whose thickness is negligible compare to tar paper. Run a bead of silicone caulk down each stud and across the top edge of the shower pan to hold the film in place. The lower edge of the polyethylene should overlap the shower pan by 2 in. to 3 in. Now you're ready to install the CBUs.

To maintain a solid wall, the empty space between the back of the CBUs and the face of the shower pan should be filled with thinset mortar. Mark the location of the top of the shower pan on the back of the CBU and trowel and comb the contact area with thinset mortar. Next, place a couple of temporary shims on the floor of the shower (to keep the CBU from digging into or tearing the pan material) and position the coated CBU over the studs. Screw the board to the studs, making sure not to run any screws into the pan area.

Once all the CBUs are installed, scribe layout lines around the perimeter of the walls to guide the finished height of the sloped mortar-bed floor, using the ¼-in.-per-ft. sloping factor, as explained on p. 210. (Note that when I am working with mortar-bed walls, the "layout line" I use to help float the sloped floor is usually the bottom edge of a row of tiles.) Before floating the floor, however, turn your attention to the shower curb.

Floating a curb

Although the walls of a stall shower can be made from CBUs, the curb of the shower must be floated with mortar since fasteners cannot be used below the top level of the curb (except on the outside face, the side away from direct contact with water). The mortar used to float the curb is anchored in three ways: by reinforcing mesh bent over the inside, top and outside faces of the curb; by the mortar-bed floor of the shower, which locks the inside face of the curb in place (just as it does the CBUs); and by conventional fasteners (nails or staples) on the outside face of the curb.

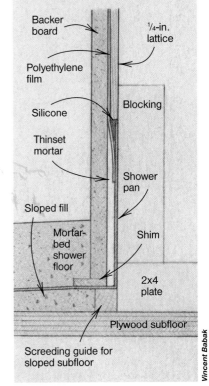

CROSS SECTION OF SHOWER-STALL WALL

Backer board

¼-in. lattice

Polyethylene film

Blocking

Silicone

Thinset mortar

Shower pan

Sloped fill

Mortar-bed shower floor

Shim

2x4 plate

Plywood subfloor

Screeding guide for sloped subfloor

Vincent Babak

To float the curb, trowel mud over the reinforcing mesh (top right) and then screed it with the body of a carpenter's square held against the floor (bottom right).

The first step is to determine the width of the mesh needed to cover the three faces of the curb. Cut the mesh to size, and then prefold it, slightly exaggerating the fold so that it will hug the curb tightly. Next, slip the mesh over the curb and, while pressing down with a straightedge on top of the curb, staple the front portion to the outside face.

Once the mesh has been fastened, mix up only enough prepackaged thick-bed mortar to cover the inside and outside faces of the curb. Position a straightedge parallel to the curb and hanging over the inside face about $5/8$ in. (or flush with the CBU or wall) to gauge the thickness of the mortar. You can do this working alone, but a helper makes the job a lot easier (see the photos above). Press a thin layer of mortar into the mesh with a margin trowel, and then build up more mortar until slightly more than the desired thickness has been attained. Next, use a flat trowel to pare down the excess mortar. Use a small level to check for plumb and make corrections as needed.

The face of the curb is done in the same fashion, but instead of paring off the mortar with a flat trowel by eye, use a framing square held against the floor to cut away the excess. The top of the curb could be floated with the inside and outside faces, but I prefer to wait until these planes are covered with tiles. That way, I can use the tiles themselves to guide the floating of the sloped top.

Mixing floor mortar

For a small area like a stall-shower floor, it is more convenient to use a prepackaged thick-bed mortar mix rather than mess with separate bags of sand and cement (see the Resource Guide). Unlike wall mortar, which has a shortening-like consistency so it can be spread over (and stick to) wall surfaces, floor mortar, or "deck mud," should be somewhat dry and crumbly—just moist enough so that all the ingredients stick together, but not so moist that it is pasty. For ease of mixing, use a mortar mixing box and a mason's hoe.

First, dump the dry ingredients into the box, spread the mix evenly and then punch holes in the mix with the handle of the hoe (see the photo at left below). The holes allow more of the mix to be wetted by the liquid, cutting back slightly on mixing time. Follow the manufacturer's mixing instructions to determine how much liquid to add to the mix, but initially add only 75% of the liquid required. Distribute the liquid over the entire box (not just at one end) and then begin mixing with the hoe.

The method that works best for me is to start at one end, take small bites out of the mix with the hoe and keep chopping until I have worked the entire contents of the box. Once all the mix is piled up at one end, I reverse my position and chop through the mix again—still taking small bites with the hoe. I repeat this three times until all the ingredients—wet and dry—have been homogenized. Then I check to see if the mortar has reached the right consistency. To test the consistency, I take a handful of the mix and squeeze it into a ball. If the

After spreading the dry ingredients in the mixing box, the author pokes a series of holes in the mix and pours in three-quarters of the liquid needed (left). When properly mixed, deck mud neither crumbles nor oozes from your hand when squeezed but rather holds together firmly (above).

ball stays together (see the photo at right on p. 217), the mortar is ready to float. If the ball crumbles, it requires the addition of a little more liquid and more mixing.

Floating the sloped shower floor

Floating a thick mortar-bed floor is a three-step process: floating a bottom layer of deck mud, installing a layer of reinforcing mesh and floating a top layer.

To build up the bottom layer of mud, spread out enough mortar to cover the pan, using the layout line around the perimeter of the floor as a guide. To keep mortar from clogging the weep holes, cover the drain flange with a small handful of pea gravel, tile chips or tile spacers (see the bottom left photo below). Deck mud gets much of its strength from being packed, but for the first layer simply distribute the mortar evenly with a wood float until its depth is just a bit over half the required thickness—it doesn't need to be perfect, but the slope of the first layer should approximate the slope of the pan.

Next, place the layer of mesh over the mud and hold it tight against the first layer with more mortar (see the photo below). Then dump more mortar over the mesh. This time, use the wood float to pack the mud, not just move it around. The idea is to

To float the shower floor, first build up half the thickness of the floor (top left), placing tile spacers around the bolting flange to allow any water that enters the floor to flow freely around the weep holes (bottom left). Then cover the first layer of mortar with reinforcing mesh (above).

Float the second layer of mortar with a wood float, using the base of the wall tiles (or a layout line on the backerboard setting bed) and the top of the subdrain as guides. Check the slope with the level as you work.

build up a layer of mortar slightly higher than what is needed and then to pare it down with straightedges, the wood float or a steel flat trowel. I use the three in combination: the wood float to pack and pare down the bed, the straightedge to ensure that the slope is smooth and flat, and the steel trowel to finish up.

Begin at the layout line and work the float around the perimeter of the floor. Then angle the float toward the drain and begin paring down the slope. Next, use the front of the float to pare down around the drain housing; the mortar here should be lower than the top of the drain by an amount equal to the thickness of the tiles that will be set on the floor. At this point, the floor is still rough. Use a straightedge or short level to check progress and ensure

that you're not paring away too much mortar. If this is the case, simply pack some mortar around the low spot and refloat.

I find the work goes much easier if I work in stages—focusing on the perimeter first, then the middle ground, and finally around the drain—smoothing the surface of the floor a bit more with each pass. When I am satisfied with the floor, I go over it again with the straightedge to make sure the surface is smooth with no dips or high spots. If any corrections have to be made, I take care of them right away; otherwise, I let the mortar bed sit overnight to harden before I install the tiles.

Chapter Thirteen

■ ■ ■

Troubleshooting and Repairs

Tiles can be damaged in many ways. Improper installation, insufficient backing or water damage in the substrate are the most common culprits, but falling objects and normal wear and tear can also do tile harm. Before making any repairs, you need to determine whether the damage is being caused by internal forces within the setting bed or by external forces.

Damage caused by external forces—usually falling objects—is generally confined to one or two tiles, which can be replaced without needing any repair to the setting bed. Damage caused by internal forces requires that the setting bed or substrate be repaired before any tiles are replaced. In some cases, this may mean replacing the entire installation.

The first step in troubleshooting a tile problem is to make an accurate diagnosis so you can decide whether to rip out everything and start from scratch, make spot repairs or simply ignore the problem. To my eye, a few minor cracks in a

venerable tile installation in an old house or public building hardly detract from an otherwise beautiful and sturdy installation. Unfortunately, though, even a tiny opening in the tilework can be a problem if the tiles were installed to protect the structure from water.

Many ceramic-tile problems are readily apparent to the careful observer. Knowing what to look for and where to look is half the battle. Regular cleaning of tile surfaces should include an inspection for cracks, loose tiles, falling or crumbling grout, worn-out sealant in expansion joints and water stains. Caught early on, most problems can be dealt with easily and inexpensively, especially in wet areas where damage costs can be substantial. Besides telling you how to recognize problems, in this chapter I'll describe some useful techniques that can help you salvage an otherwise sound installation and also explain how to recognize when the entire installation must be replaced.

Diagnosing Problems

The three most common symptoms of a troubled ceramic or stone tile installation are cracks in the joints or the tiles, broken tiles or tiles that have parted from the setting bed, and water stains below or around tiles installed in a wet area. Troubleshooting any tile installation begins with looking for any of these three problems; you need to check all horizontal planes, all vertical planes, wherever any plane changes direction, and at the margins of the installation where the tiles meet other materials.

Cracked joints

Cracks in the joints or the tiles are the most common problem on tile installations. In my opinion, most of these cracks are caused by failure to include expansion joints in the installation (see Chapter 6). The drawing below shows potential problem areas in a residential bathroom, including the inside corners of a tiled tub surround, where the tiles meet the rim of the tub, where floor tiles meet the face of the tub and where floor tiles meet the walls. If hard grout is used to fill the joints in these transition areas, cracks are very likely to appear. If they do, the only long-range solution is to remove the grout and

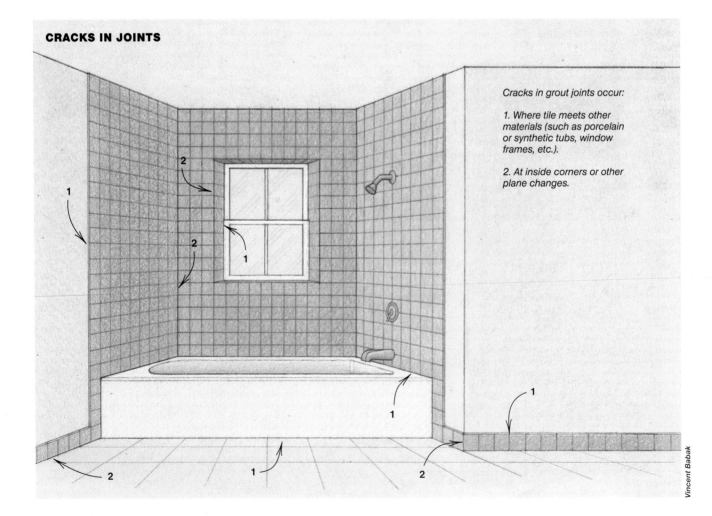

CRACKS IN JOINTS

Cracks in grout joints occur:

1. Where tile meets other materials (such as porcelain or synthetic tubs, window frames, etc.).

2. At inside corners or other plane changes.

Vincent Babak

replace it with a flexible caulk or sealant. Filling the cracks with more grout will only result in another crack. Before excavating the grout and filling with a flexible material, however, it is very important to determine whether the cracks have allowed water to damage the setting bed (see below).

Cracked or crumbling grout joints in the main field of tile are often the result of an improperly mixed grout, in which case the joints should be cleaned out and regrouted, as explained on p. 228.

Cracked tiles

Cracks appearing in grout joints that should have been filled with a resilient material are inevitable and easily corrected as long as there is no other damage. If cracks run through the body of the tiles, however, there may be a more serious structural problem.

Cracks can be expected to appear in the tiles if they are installed over expansion joints or control joints in the setting bed, over dissimilar materials (a concrete slab used to extend an existing wood subfloor, for example) or over a setting bed that is too flexible for the tiles (in which case, the cracks usually appear over a more rigid part of the structure, such as a floor joist, as shown in the drawing below). In all these cases, the only effective solution is to remove the damaged tiles (or all the tiles in the case of the too-flexible setting bed) and correct the underlying structural problem.

Cracking problems caused by underlying construction joints or dissimilar materials can sometimes be minimized by installing an isolation membrane "bandage" over the affected area (see pp. 109-111) and by filling the surrounding grout joints with a resilient caulk or sealant. The drawing on p. 224 shows a typical application. Although this method cannot be used to eliminate cracks completely, it is usually the best approach when no other finishing material can be found. Before proceeding with this kind of repair, check first with the manufacturer of the membrane (see the Resource Guide).

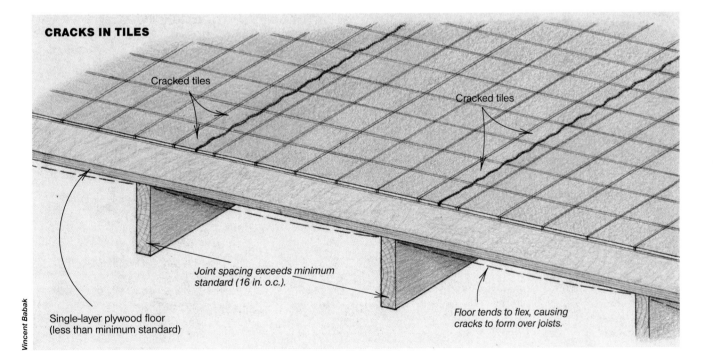

CRACKS IN TILES

Cracked tiles

Cracked tiles

Joint spacing exceeds minimum standard (16 in. o.c.).

Single-layer plywood floor (less than minimum standard)

Floor tends to flex, causing cracks to form over joists.

Vincent Babak

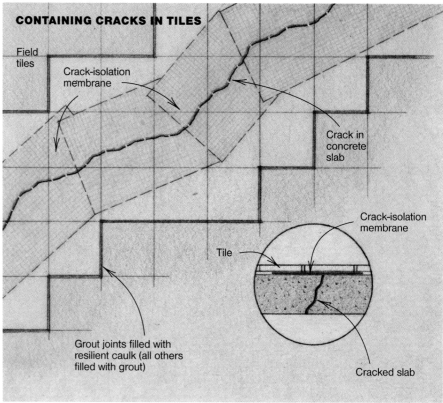

CONTAINING CRACKS IN TILES

Field tiles

Crack-isolation membrane

Crack in concrete slab

Crack-isolation membrane

Tile

Grout joints filled with resilient caulk (all others filled with grout)

Cracked slab

Vincent Babak

Broken tiles

Tiles typically break or come loose because of a problem with the setting bed (it may be soft or disintegrating) or failure of the adhesive bond. If the setting bed appears to be sound, old grout and adhesive can be removed from the affected area and a new tile can be installed with fresh adhesive and grout (see p. 226). If the setting bed appears to be damaged, it must be repaired before replacement tiles can be installed. If many tiles are broken or loose (more than about 5% of the total), you'll have to investigate further to determine the cause of the problem and the extent of the repairs.

The first step is to remove all the affected tiles (see pp. 225-227) and examine the adhesive residue left on the back of the tile and the setting bed. There should be an equal amount of adhesive on both surfaces. If the adhesive is mostly on the tile and there is little or none on the

setting bed, something on the surface of the setting bed (most likely a thin film of dust) prevented a good bond. In this case, the remaining tiles may also be ready to come loose. If, on the other hand, the adhesive is stuck mostly to the setting bed, it's an indication that the adhesive skinned over before the tiles were installed, the adhesive was too dry to adhere to the tiles, or something on the back of the tiles interfered with the bond. Many tiles break or work loose simply because they are not supported by enough adhesive in the first place—coverage should be 95% to 100%.

The condition of the adhesive bond can also be determined by sound (without having to remove any tiles). On tile floors, I use the "chain-drag" method. I simply drag a short length of chain with links about 2 in. long over the floor tiles and listen for a hollow sound, which indicates a broken adhesive bond. For wall tiles, I give each tile a light tap with the rounded end of a ½-in. box wrench. If the wrench "rings," chances are the tile is firmly attached; a hollow sound usually indicates a loss of bond. These test methods are not 100% accurate, but they give a good indication of the condition of the adhesive bond without having to remove or destroy any more tiles than necessary.

Water stains

Water stains are usually the first symptom of a problem with tiles installed in a wet area. In many cases, the hidden structure of a building may become thoroughly soaked long before water stains appear to indicate that a problem exists.

The place to look for water stains is usually next to or directly below the wet area, although this is not always where you'll find them. In many buildings, I have seen water enter tilework through a penetration in the tiles (a pipe opening or a screw hole for a shower door, for example), drip down to the subfloor, and then travel sideways—sometimes the entire length of the building—before making a noticeable stain.

If you find stains around a wet area, begin by checking the obvious sources of leaks. Make sure that all expansion joints are filled with caulk or sealant and that all enclosures (shower doors, tub sliders, etc.) are properly caulked. Check the gaskets or packing behind faucet valve covers or shower heads; these areas should be packed with plumber's putty to prevent the passage of water. Make sure the setting bed is sound and that the tiles themselves are firmly attached. If you find a loose tile, lift it off and check to see whether the installation includes a waterproofing membrane. If it doesn't, or the setting bed appears "spongy" when you push on the tile, there's trouble behind the tilework, and you'll have to rip out the tile to make the necessary repairs.

If the tile installation itself appears sound, the water stains may be caused by leaks in the water-supply or drain lines. Open up any access panels (or remove some drywall) to check for leaks in the hot and cold supply lines. To check for drain-line leaks in a tub/shower, fill the tub until water enters the overflow. If this does not appear to leak, open the drain plug and check for leaks in the drain lines.

For a stall shower, remove the drain screen and plug the drain pipe. Fill the shower up to the top of the curb and then go to an access area (or cut through water-stained drywall below the shower) to look for leaks. If you spot drops of water, try to determine if the water is coming from the subdrain or the shower pan. If there's no water visible after an hour, remove the plug and observe the drain pipe as the water drains away. If leaks are detected in the plumbing, make the necessary repairs and repeat the water test before reinstalling any drywall. If the shower pan is the source of the leak, the tiles must be removed and the pan replaced.

Removing Tiles for Repair or Replacement

Removing tiles for repair or replacement is not a particularly difficult job, but it does involve some hard work. For most residential and small commercial installations, a hammer, a few chisels and a lot of elbow grease are what get the job done. (If you have more than 1,000 sq. ft. of tile to remove, you may want to check the Resource Guide for power-tool rentals appropriate for tile removal.)

Whether you're removing a single tile or an entire field, always wear safety glasses. And when taking out an entire field, I recommend wearing gloves, too, since it's easy to get cut. Also, whenever removing an entire field of tile, always begin the job by disconnecting any tub spouts, shower heads or plumbing valves present, and protecting tubs, preformed shower floors, carpeting and other finished surfaces with tarps.

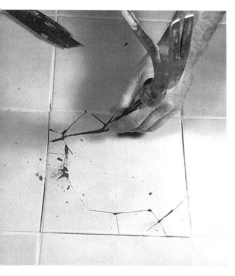

Removing a single tile

The first step in removing a single tile (or only a few tiles) is to dig out the grout from the joints surrounding the tile. Removing the grout prevents the hammer blows to the problem tile from "telegraphing" through the grout and damaging neighboring tiles. (If you're replacing several tiles, you need only remove grout from the perimeter of the area being repaired—not from around each tile.) Remove the grout with a short piece of hacksaw blade, a utility knife, a grout saw or, if the joints are wide enough, a dry-cutting diamond blade.

Once the grout has been removed, deliver a sharp blow to the offending tile with a relatively light hammer, or with a hammer and cold chisel. Some tiles may shatter throughout with only one blow; others may require several hits. Whatever the number, the blows should be short and sharp rather than earth-shaking. The idea is to be able to remove the tile in small chunks. If you use a chisel, try alternately holding it perpendicular to the tile when

you hammer it and then at an angle. The latter position may enable you to wedge the chisel under the tile and pry sections away from the substrate.

Next, with a utility knife, a putty knife or a margin trowel, remove any traces of tile adhesive left on the setting bed. After scraping away all the adhesive, remove any grout remaining on the edges of the adjacent tiles and vacuum away the chips and dust. If all the original adhesive is not removed, the replacement tile will sit higher than the surrounding tiles.

With the adhesive and grout removed, the replacement tile can be set. You'll get the best results by using the same adhesive as that used to attach the original tiles. If you don't know what that was, at least use the same type of adhesive—that is, organic mastic or a thinset adhesive. Apply adhesive both to the setting bed and to the back of the tile, then press the tile firmly into place and clean up the adhesive that oozes up through the joints. If you're replacing a tile on a vertical surface, tape it in place until the adhesive has dried.

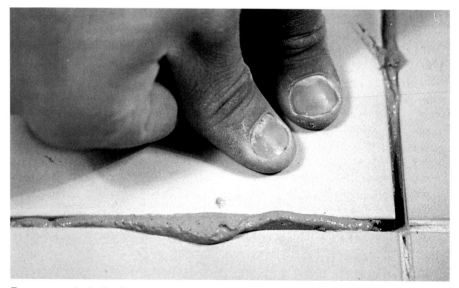

To remove a single tile, first remove the grout surrounding it and then crack the tile with a hammer and cold chisel (top left). After removing the chunks of tile, scrape off the adhesive on the setting bed (center and bottom left). With fresh adhesive applied to the bed and the back of the new tile, press the tile firmly into place and clean up the excess adhesive (above).

Finally, grout the tile in the regular fashion, making sure to dampen the area being grouted so that the setting bed doesn't suck moisture out of the grout.

Removing a field of tiles set over drywall

To protect the surrounding walls, first use a utility knife or a drywall saw to cut through the drywall around the field of tiles. Be sure to cut only through the drywall—any deeper and you might cut through plumbing or wiring behind. Then punch through the tiles with a hammer to create a hole, and grab the edge of the hole with both hands. Give it a few sharp jerks, wiggling the tile and drywall away from the studs. Unless the drywall has been badly damaged by water, the entire installation should come out in moderately large sections. (Some of the sections may be quite large, so it's a good idea to have some help on hand.) Use a pry bar if necessary to get leverage, but be sure not to put a strain on the surrounding walls. After the sections of tiled drywall have been removed, pull out all the nails from the studs before installing a new substrate for the tiles.

Removing a field of tiles set over plywood

There are two ways to remove tiles set over a plywood or particleboard underlayment—one at a time or in sections. Try ripping out a couple of individual tiles to see how good the original adhesive's bond is. If the grip of the adhesive is weak, you may want to remove the field tile by tile and then remove the underlayment. (Because plywood is not an ideal setting bed for tile, it should be removed along with the old tile.)

If you decide to remove the tiles and underlayment together (the fastest approach), first cut through both layers around the perimeter of the installation with either a carborundum or a dry-cutting diamond blade. Then make a second cut, parallel to and about 3 ft. to 4 ft. away from the perimeter cut. Next make perpendicular cuts every 4 ft. to 5 ft. to connect the first two cuts. Pound the hook of a pry bar into one of the cuts and lift out one of the sections of tile and substrate. Once the perimeter of the tile and substrate has been removed, the remainder of the installation may be removable with the pry bar alone.

Removing a field of tiles set over a concrete slab

Before removing any tiles set on a slab, determine if the tiles actually have to be removed. If they're being removed solely for aesthetic reasons and not to correct structural problems, you'll save yourself a lot of work by simply setting the new tiles over the old ones. This methods works as long as the new height does not interfere with the structure or any of its parts. If not, grab your hammer and chisel and have at it. Once the tiles have been removed, scrape or sand away the remaining adhesive. If the tiles were set with an organic mastic, avoid using chemical strippers to remove the residue, as this could interfere with bonding the new tiles.

Removing a field of tiles set over a mortar bed

As with concrete slabs, removing a field of tiles set over a mortar bed is tough work. For this reason, I again suggest considering setting tile over an existing thick-bed installation, unless, of course, there's structural damage in the substrate and framing. If you want to remove the tiles, don't expect to be able to reuse the mortar setting bed. You'll have to rip up the bed, too.

You can remove the tiles in one of two ways. First, you can attack the wall, floor or countertop with a hammer, chisel and pry bar. I recommend that you start hammering along the full length or width of the installation at its midpoint and then follow up with more blows to crumble the underlying mortar. Then cut through the reinforcing mesh with wire snips and use the pry bar to remove portions of the tile and bed.

An alternative method, and the one I find easier, is to use a carborundum or dry-cutting diamond blade to make a grid of cuts in the installation, spaced from 12 in. to 36 in. apart. Adjust the depth of the blade to cut through, but no deeper than, the thickness of the tile and bed. Then insert the tip of the pry bar into the saw-kerf (enlarge the kerf with the sawblade if necessary) and pry away each section. Once the debris has been cleared away, you can float a new bed in place of the old.

Regrouting an Installation

Although cracked or crumbling grout joints are often the first sign of structural problems, they sometimes signal nothing more than the fact that the grout itself was improperly mixed, contained too much liquid ingredient, was mixed without an additive or was weakened by using too much water during cleanup. If you suspect that the grout itself is the problem, you should be able to regrout the joints with a bit of preparation. Just bear in mind that grout gets much of its strength from having a relatively thick cross section that is reinforced by the sides of the tiles. If you simply cover the existing grout with a thin layer of new grout, it is unlikely that the new application will last.

Removing the grout

Use a grout saw, hacksaw blade or utility knife to remove the old grout down to the setting bed (being careful not to cut through any membrane if one was used). If some of the grout is very difficult to remove, it is probably in good shape and can remain. Vacuum away the dust and debris, clean the surface of the tiles with a vinegar/water solution (see below) or a recommended cleaner (see the Resource Guide) and allow the area to dry completely before applying the new grout (following the steps outlined in Chapter 8).

Where some of the old grout is to remain in place, you will of course want to match the new grout with the old. Making a perfect match may be difficult or impossible, even if you use grout saved from the original for the repair. Take a chunk of the grout you have removed and compare it to color samples available from local tile suppliers. If you cannot find a perfect match, you'll either have to pick the closest shade and live with the difference or remove all the original grout and install the new color over the entire area.

One final, and very important, point when regrouting: Always use a latex or acrylic additive with the grout. The additive will both help waterproof the grout and increase its resistance to cracking.

Maintaining an Installation

For routine cleaning of a tile installation, I recommend using a solution of one cup vinegar to a gallon of water. Although there are many good products on the market specifically designed to clean tile, this mildly acidic solution works well to cut through light oil and dirt, leaves no residue on the tile and is inexpensive.

If you find that the grout joints in an installation routinely get very dirty, give them a thorough cleaning with one of the special tile-cleaning products, let them dry for a full three to four days, and apply an impregnator to the entire surface of the installation. (Make sure you choose an appropriate tile sealer for food-service areas.) Impregnators are generally more expensive to apply and maintain than silicone sealers, but they provide greater resistance to dirt and staining. Depending on use, impregnators will have to be reapplied from time to time.

Cleaning grout haze

As discussed in Chapter 8, a grout haze or residue is left on the surface of the tiles after initial cleanup of the grout. If this

Use an acid cleaner only as a last resort to remove a stubborn grout haze from the surface of the tiles. Never use acid for routine cleaning—other types of cleaners are available that are safer both to the tiles and to the person doing the cleaning.

SAFETY PRECAUTIONS

The use of acids requires ventilation, eye and skin protection, and a cautious attitude. In addition to the gloves, goggles and charcoal-filter mask needed for protection from acid spills and fumes, keep a bucket of clean water or a running hose nearby to flush your skin or eyes in case of an accident. Since most acids need to be diluted with water before use, the mixing should be done outdoors to dissipate fumes, and the acid should be poured into the water. (Pouring water into acid produces heat and fumes, in direct proportion to the strength of the undiluted acid.) Finally, be sure to follow all instructions on the label.

If there are any painted metal surfaces such as railings in the area where you'll be applying the acid, they should be given a protective coating of petroleum jelly. Since many acids will remove the polish from porcelain fixtures, they, too, should be coated.

APPLICATION

Use an acid cleaner only after the grout has completely cured for 28 days. Because the less acid used the better, begin with full-strength vinegar and a Scotch-Brite pad. Although vinegar is a rather weak acid compared to muriatic acid, it is still quite potent against alkaline deposits like grout haze. If vinegar doesn't work, you'll have to use a stronger acid solution.

Before putting the acid solution on the tiles, flood the entire surface with water. Allow the water to soak in for a few minutes to reduce the amount of acid that will penetrate the tile. (Remember from Chapter 1 that most tiles are not 100% impervious to liquids.) Work the solution into the grout residue with a stiff brush. To keep the surface from drying out and allowing more acid to penetrate, rinse it often with water.

When cleaning natural stone tiles, try the solution you want to use on a scrap piece of stone tile to see what effect it will have on the finish. Apply the solution to half the scrap piece so a comparison can be made. With some stone products, even a small amount of acid, like orange juice or wine, can remove the shine applied at the factory.

Once the area has been cleaned, it must be flushed at least three times with water to remove all traces of the acid. If you're working indoors, you'll have to figure out a way to dam and flood the tiled surface and at the same time protect any surrounding carpeting, wood floors or walls (this is no easy feat and another reason to avoid using acid cleaners). Finally, use hot, soapy water to remove the petroleum-jelly shield on the metal and porcelain fixtures.

Having now explained how to work with an acid cleaner, I repeat what I said at the outset: Acid cleaners should be avoided, which is easily done if you clean up while the grout is still plastic.

---

haze is not removed completely when the tiles are grouted, the hardened glaze may be difficult to remove with conventional cleaners.

If you have a problem with hard grout deposits or stubborn haze on the surface of the tiles, first contact the grout manufacturer and ask for a cleaning-product recommendation. Chances are, the manufacturer will have a solution in stock that will harm neither the tile, the surrounding materials or the user.

If the haze still resists these mild cleaning methods, an acid cleaner may be the only solution. Because of the potential for personal injury (or damage to the tile or surrounding surfaces), I don't like to use acid cleaners, but if you do decide to use them, there are certain precautions you can take to ensure your safety (as explained in the sidebar above).

Resource Guide

Sources of Supply

Much has changed in the tile business since I wrote *Setting Ceramic Tile* in 1987. For one thing, there is a lot more competition among manufacturers of tile, grout, adhesives and other setting materials, which benefits everyone who wants to buy or install tile. And instead of only a few sizes of tile and a limited selection, tiles are readily available in an almost unlimited variety of sizes, shapes, colors and textures.

Grouts used to be available only in white and a few earth tones, but now there are hundreds of different colors to contrast or complement any tile. Adhesive selection was also limited, but today tile installers can choose from many different brands for all kinds of applications.

Manufacturers of tilesetting materials like the concept of single sourcing—the ability to provide installers with all the materials they may need for a particular installation. Today, there are many good brands to choose from that carry the seal of approval of the Tile Council of America or other tile organizations.

I have the opportunity to work with most of the setting materials available today. In many cases, I have to learn about them because they were specified for a particular installation. Professional tile installers usually have favorite brands, and I am no exception. When I am the specifier, I usually choose the products you will find listed in this guide. I use them for a number of reasons: Personal preference rates high, but I demand performance, ease of use and personal safety.

If the products I recommend in this guide are not available in your area, check out the inventory in your local tile store.

Chances are you will be able to find suitable materials close to home without having to search far and wide for my personal favorites.

Ceramic and natural stone tiles are available from a variety of sources, including stores that sell only tiles and those that sell a variety of finishing materials. If you are looking for very distinctive tiles, ask your local dealer for the name of a local tile artisan who can create custom tiles to order.

Ceramic tile

American Olean
1000 Cannon Ave.
P.O. Box 271
Lansdale, PA 19446
(215) 855-1111
(Glazed wall, floor, mosaic, porcelain and ADA tiles)

Laufen International
P.O. Box 6600
4942 E. 66th St. North
Tulsa, OK 74156
(800) 331-3651
(Glazed wall and floor tiles)

Summitville Tiles
P.O. Box 73
Summitville, OH 43962
(216) 223-1511
(Glazed wall, floor, mosaic, porcelain and ADA tiles)

Italian Tile Center
Division of the Italian Trade Commission
499 Park Ave.
New York, NY 10022
(212) 980-1500
(Provides information on Italian tile manufacturers)

Japan Ceramic Mosaic Tile Manufacturers Association
No. 39-18 Daikan-Cho
Higashi-Ku
Nagoya, 461 Japan
(052) 935-7235
(Provides information on Japanese tile manufacturers)

Trade Commission of Spain
2655 Le Jeune Rd.
Coral Gables, FL 33134
(305) 446-4387
(Provides information on Spanish tile manufacturers)

Installation tools

L.S. Starrett
121 Crescent St.
Athol, MA 01331
(617) 249-3551
(Measuring tools)

MK Diamond Products
1315 Storm Parkway
Torrance, CA 90509
(800) 845-3729
(Wet saws and blades)

Risso Machine Shop
8310 Amelia St.
Oakland, CA 94621
(510) 569-2145
(Wet saws)

Superior Tile Cutter
1556 W. 134th St.
Gardena, CA 90249
(310) 324-3771
(Snap cutters, biters and other installation tools)

Vic Industrial
P.O. Drawer 12610
Knoxville, TN 37912
(800) 423-1634
(Complete line of ceramic and stone tile fabrication, installation, repair and maintenance tools, equipment and materials; geared toward the professional)

Walton Tool Company
517 W. 17th St.
Long Beach, CA 90813
(800) 421-7562
(Full line of tile installation tools)

Surface-preparation equipment

Edco Rental Tough
100 Thomas Johnson Drive
Frederick, MD 21702
(800) 638 3326
(Shot blasters, self-propelled abrasive wheels and other tools for preparing concrete slabs)

Miracle Sealants and Abrasives
12806 Schabarum Ave.
Irwindale, CA 91706
(800) 350-1901
(Mirastrip chemical stripper for concrete slabs)

Vic Industrial
P.O. Drawer 12610
Knoxville, TN 37912
(800) 423-1634
(Grinders and other tools for surface preparation)

Safety equipment

GATEWAY AmSafe
4722 Spring Rd.
Cleveland, OH 44131
(800) 822-5347
(Full line of personal safety equipment)

Backer board

ITW Buildex
1349 W. Bryn Mawr
Itasca, IL 60143
(800) 323-0720
(Hi-Lo S Rock-On backer-board screws)

James Hardie Building Products
10901 Elm Ave.
Fontana, CA 92337
(800) 942-7343
(Hardibacker Square Edge, Hardibacker Multilay backer board)

U.S. Gypsum Industries
101 S. Wacker Drive
Chicago, IL 60606
(800) 621-9622
(Durock backer board, Durock screws, Imperial Type P reinforcing mesh tape)

Membranes

Laticrete International
1 Laticrete Park North
Bethany, CT 06525
(800) 243-4788
(9235, 9236 trowel-applied membranes)

The Noble Company
614 Monroe St.
Grand Haven, MI 49417
(616) 842-7844
(Nobleseal TS, Chloraloy 240 sheet membranes, and companion sealants)

Adhesives, grouts, mortars and mortar additives

Custom Building Products
13001 Seal Beach Blvd.
Seal Beach, CA 90740
(800) 272-8786
(Adhesives, grouts, additives)

H.B. Fuller
Building Products Division
315 S. Hicks Rd.
Palatine, IL 60067
(800) 323-7407
(Adhesive remover)

Laticrete International
1 Laticrete Park North
Bethany, CT 06525
(800) 243-4788
(Complete line of adhesives—including Latapoxy 2000 heat-resistant epoxy thinset—grouts, mortars and mortar additives)

Tile and grout cleaners and grout releases

American Olean
1000 Cannon Ave.
P.O. Box 271
Lansdale, PA 19446
(215) 855-1111
(Full line of grout installation and maintenance products, including Grout Away cleaner)

Laticrete International
1 Laticrete Park North
Bethany, CT 06525
(800) 243-4788
(TC-500 and TC-50 mild tile and grout cleaners, grout release)

Summitville Tiles
P.O. Box 73
Summitville, OH 43962
(216) 223-1511
(SL-44 grout cleaner and mildew remover)

Stone-tile cleaners, sealers and maintenance products

Miracle Sealants and Abrasives
12806 Schabarum Ave.
Irwindale, CA 91706
(800) 350-1901

Vic Industrial
P.O. Drawer 12610
Knoxville, TN 37912
(800) 423-1634

Caulks, sealants and impregnators

Aqua Mix
P.O. Box 4127
Santa Fe Springs, CA 90670
(310) 946-6877
(Paver sealers)

Color Caulk
723 W. Mill St.
San Bernardino, CA 92410
(909) 888-6225
(Color-matched caulks and sealants)

Miracle Sealants and Abrasives
12806 Schabarum Ave.
Irwindale, CA 91706
(800) 350-1901
(511 Impregnator)

Self-leveling compounds and services

Custom Building Products
13001 Seal Beach Blvd.
Seal Beach, CA 90740
(800) 272-8786
(Level-Quik site-mixed leveling compound)

Gyp-Crete
920 Hamel Rd.
Hamel, MN 55340
(800) 356-7887
(Provides self-leveling underlayment services for the flooring industry)

Laticrete International
1 Laticrete Park North
Bethany, CT 06525
(800) 243-4788
(#86 Self-Leveling Underlayment site-mixed leveling compound)

Testing laboratory

Tile Council of America
P.O. Box 1787
Clemson, SC 29633
(803) 646-4021
(Conducts ASTM, ANSI and other tests on tile and related products)

Miscellaneous supplies

General Plumbing & Supply
P.O. Box 4666
Walnut Creek, CA 94596
(510) 939-4622
(E-Z Test cast-iron shower drains)

3M Center
St. Paul, MN 55144-1000
(800) 364-3577
(8440 white Scotch-Brite pads—available through tile or cleaning supply distributors)

Organizations

American National Standards Institute
1430 Broadway
New York, NY 10018
(212) 642-4900
(Promotes knowledge and voluntary use of approved standards for industry, engineering and safety design in all industries, including the tile industry)

Ceramic Tile Distributors Association
800 Roosevelt Rd.
Building C, Suite 20
Glen Ellyn, IL 60137
(708) 545-9415
(Association of distributors, manufacturers and allied professionals)

Marble Institute of America
33505 State St.
Farmington, MI 48335
(810) 476-5559
(Provides information on all aspects of natural and manufactured stone products)

Materials and Methods Standards Association
614 Monroe St.
Grand Haven, MI 49417
(616) 842-7844
(Shares nonsecret, technical tilesetting data and encourages the free exchange of information on tiling problems and solutions)

National Association of Home Builders of the U.S.
15th and M Streets, N.W.
Washington, DC 20005
(202) 822-0200
(Disseminates information on all phases of homebuilding, including tile installation)

National Tile Contractors Association
P.O. Box 13629
Jackson, MI 39236
(601) 939-2071
(Serves every level of the tile industry with publications, seminars and technical assistance)

Tile Council of America
P.O. Box 1787
Clemson, SC 29633
(803) 646-4021
(Composed of members from various companies and organizations involved in producing and installing tile and related products, this group is dedicated to maintaining a high standard of quality for tile installations.)

Tile Heritage Foundation
P.O. Box 1850
Healdsburg, CA 95448
(707) 431-8453
(Member-supported group dedicated to the research and preservation of ceramic surfaces in the U.S.—good folks to know)

Education and training

The Tile Shop
(Newsletter published monthly by CTA Press for professional installers)

Mortar Bed Floors
Mortar Bed Walls
Mortar Bed Countertops
Grouting and Finishing
Installing Glass Block Panels
(Training manuals published by CTA Press for contractors, apprentices and helpers)

CTA Press publications are written by Michael Byrne and are available from:
Ceramic Tile Associates
P.O. Box 1773
Burlington, VT 05402-1773
(802) 865-0445

E-mail:
mbyrnetile@aol.com
glassblock@aol.com

Bibliography

Tile design

Coyle, Carolyn. *Designing with Tile.* New York: Van Nostrand Reinhold, 1995.
(If you are an architect, designer or tile retailer, this book should be on your shelf.)

Tile history

Austwick, Jill and Brian Austwick. *The Decorated Tile: An Illustrated History of English Tile-making and Design.* New York: Charles Scribner's Sons, 1981.

Berendsen, Anne. *Tiles, A General History.* New York: The Viking Press, 1967.

Catleugh, Jon. *William de Morgan Tiles.* New York: Van Nostrand Reinhold, 1983.

de Solà-Morales, Ignasi. *Gaudí.* New York: Rizzoli International, 1983.

Descharnes, Robert and Clovis Prévost. *Gaudí: The Visionary.* New York: Viking Penguin, 1982.

Gonzalez-Palacios, Alvar and Steffi Röttgen. *The Art of Mosaics.* Catalog with essays by Steffi Röttgen and Claudia Pryzyborowski. Los Angeles: Los Angeles County Museum of Art, 1982.

Haswell, J. Mellentin. *Van Nostrand Reinhold Manual of Mosaic.* New York: Van Nostrand Reinhold, 1973.

Hutton, Helen. *Mosaic Making Techniques.* New York: Charles Scribner's Sons, 1977.

Schaap, Ella, with Robert L.H. Chambers, Marjorie Lee Hendrix and Joan Pierpoline. *Dutch Tiles in the Philadelphia Museum of Art.* Catalog with essays and technical notes. Philadelphia: Philadelphia Museum of Art, 1984.

Sherman, Anthony C. *The Gilbert Mosaic Collection.* West Haven, Conn.: Pendulum Press, 1971.

Zerbst, Rainer. *Antoni Gaudí.* Cologne: Benedikt Taschen Verlag, 1991.

Tile installation

For tips on installing or working with particular materials (for example, backer board, CPE membranes or thinset adhesive), write the product's manufacturer for the relevant brochure.

American National Standards Institute. *Standard Specifications for the Installation of Ceramic Tile* (ANSI A108-1992). New York, 1992.
(Lists and defines setting materials and installations)

Materials and Methods Standards Association. *MMSA Bulletin.* Palatine, Ill., 1984.
(Provides specific recommendations for problem installations)

Tile Council of America. *1995 Handbook for Ceramic Tile Installation.* Clemson, S.C., 1995.
(Describes various setting materials and installation methods)

Tools, health and safety

American National Standards Institute. *Practice for Occupational and Educational Eye and Face Protection* (ANSI Z87.1-1992). New York, 1968.

———. *Practices for Respiratory Protection* (ANSI Z88.2-1969). New York, 1969.

———. *Safety Requirements for Ceramic Tile, Terrazzo and Marble Work* (A10.20-1988). New York, 1988.

Jackson, Albert and David Day. *Tools and How to Use Them.* New York: Alfred A. Knopf, 1981.

McMann, Michael. *Artist Beware.* New York: Watson-Guptill, 1979.

Occupational Safety and Health Association. *All about OSHA* (OSHA 2056). Washington, D.C., 1992.

———. *Chemical Hazard Communication* (OSHA 3084). Washington, D.C., 1992.

———. *Construction Industry Digest* (OSHA 2202). Washington, D.C., 1992.

OSHA handbooks are available from:
Superintendent of Documents
Government Printing Office
Washington, DC 20402-9325
(202) 275-0019

General construction

Hemp, Peter. *Installing and Repairing Plumbing Fixtures.* Newtown, Conn.: The Taunton Press, 1994.

———. *Plumbing a House.* Newtown, Conn.: The Taunton Press, 1994.

The Journal of Light Construction. *Kitchens and Baths.* Richmond, Vt., 1994.

Love, T.W. *Construction Manual: Concrete and Formwork.* Carlsbad, Calif.: Craftsman, 1973.

Portland Cement Association. *Design and Control of Concrete Mixtures.* Skokie, Ill., 1988.

Safford, Edward L., Jr. *Electrical Wiring Handbook.* Blue Ridge Summit, Pa.: Tab Books, 1980.

Glossary

acrylic thinset adhesive
See *latex thinset adhesive.*

ANSI
American National Standards Institute. This organization was established in 1918 to promote knowledge and voluntary use of approved standards in industry, including engineering and safety design.

back-butter
To apply adhesive on the back of a tile to supplement the adhesive spread on the setting bed. All button-backed tiles, sheet-mounted mosaic tiles, small cut tiles and any tile with an uneven back require back-buttering to ensure a strong bond between them and the setting bed.

backer board
Nail- or screw-on substrate manufactured specifically for ceramic or stone tiles. Made from sand and portland cement and reinforced with an external skin of fiberglass mesh, or internally with mineral fibers. Unaffected by water.

back-mounted tile
Tile packaged in sheet format, with the mounting material applied to the back of the tile.

beating block
Wood or composition board used to level the surface of tiles and increase contact between the tiles and the adhesive layer.

bisque
The refined mixture of clay, water and additives that has been shaped into the body of the tile.

bond strength
A tile adhesive's ability to resist separating from the tile and setting bed after curing (see *grip).*

brick-veneer tile
Tile produced by several methods that simulates the appearance of real brick.

button-backed tile
Tile manufactured with raised dots or squares on the back, which serve to separate the individual tiles when they are stacked in the kiln and ensure that heat circulates uniformly among them.

caulk
A soft, putty-like, flexible and waterproof material used in tiling primarily to cap off expansion joints and to seal seams around plumbing valves and faucets.

cement-bodied tile
Tile made of mortar rather than clay. This tile has the appearance of stone or paver tile, is very durable and is less expensive than ceramic tile.

chlorinated polyethylene (CPE) membrane
A covering made of chlorinated polyethylene in sheet form, which is applied to a setting bed or substrate to serve as a waterproofing, curing or isolation membrane.

cleft stone
Stone tile split, rather than sawn, from a large block of stone and consequently uneven in thickness and dimensions.

cold joint
A poorly bonded joint formed in a mortar surface when one area of mortar hardens before the next batch is placed against it.

compressive strength
A tile adhesive's ability to withstand a heavy load without fracturing.

control joint
A partial interruption in a concrete slab, formed or cut with a saw. Used to direct or control cracks in the slab.

cove trim
Trim tile with one concave edge that serves to form the juncture between a floor or countertop and a wall.

crystallization
A proprietary method of increasing the surface hardness of natural stone.

CTI
Ceramic Tile Institute of America. Established in 1954, this organization works to upgrade installation standards and test new materials.

curing membrane
A covering applied to a substrate over which a mortar setting bed is to be floated in order to prevent the substrate from sucking moisture from the mortar and causing it to cure prematurely.

deck mud
See *mortar, mud.*

dot-mounted tile
Tile packaged in sheet format and held together by plastic or rubber dots between the joints.

down angle
Trim tile with two rounded or curved edges that serves to finish off an outside corner.

efflorescence
The whitish deposit of soluble salts on the surface of grout or mortar. Carried to the surface by moisture that evaporates, the salts can come from the water used to mix the grout or mortar, the bisque of the tiles, or any salt-bearing water that enters the installation from an outside source.

embossed-back tile
Tile whose back is embossed with marks to identify manufacturing specifications for a particular production run.

epoxy thinset adhesive
One of the three types of sand-and-cement-based, thinset tile adhesives, which must be mixed with liquid epoxy resin before use. See also *thinset adhesive.*

expansion joint
An intentional interruption in a field of tile to prevent damage to the tiles from seasonal movement in the setting bed.

extruded tile
Tile formed when green bisque is pressed through a die and cut to specified lengths.

face-mounted tile
Tile packaged in sheet format, with the mounting paper applied to the face of the tile.

fat mud
See *mortar, mud.*

field tile
Tile set in the main field of an installation.

float strips
Wooden strips used in pairs when floating a mortar bed to gauge the depth of the bed and provide a guide for screeding away the excess mortar on the surface. Sometimes called screeds.

floated bed
A bed of mortar applied to a floor, wall or countertop to serve as the setting surface for tile.

freeze/thaw stability
The ability of a tile installed outdoors to withstand, without cracking, the cycle of freezing and thawing in colder climates. Porous, nonvitreous tiles, which readily absorb water, are less freeze/thaw stable than nonporous, vitreous tiles.

gauged stone
Stone tile cut to uniform thickness and dimensions and sometimes polished.

ghosting
A noticeable change in the color of grout caused by foreign material (such as excess adhesive or tile spacers) left in a grout joint.

glaze
The protective, decorative coating, usually made of lead silicates and pigment, that is fired on the face (and sometimes edges) of many tiles.

green bisque
The unfired bisque, or body, of a tile.

grip
A tile adhesive's ability to hold a tile in place once the adhesive has cured (see *bond strength).*

grout
A sand-and-cement-based powder, mixed with a liquid before use, that serves to fill in the joints between tiles and finish off an installation.

grout, plain and sanded
Cement-based material used to fill in the joints between tiles. Plain grout is used for joints less than $1/16$ in. wide, while grout to which sand has been added for strength is used for wider joints.

hang
A tile adhesive's ability to hold a tile in place on a vertical surface before the adhesive has cured.

hot-mopped pan
An old-fashioned type of shower pan made of alternating layers of hot asphalt and tar paper.

impervious tile
An extremely dense-bodied tile that, by comparison with nonvitreous tile, is fired at a very high temperature for a long period of time. The bisque of this tile contains less than 0.5% air pockets, is therefore almost waterproof and is freeze/thaw stable. Some impervious tiles have high compressive strength, while others are very fragile.

inside corner
The joint at the internal angle of two intersecting surfaces.

isolation membrane
A covering used on top of a setting bed to prevent seasonal movement in the bed from cracking the tiles.

jury stick (story pole)
A measuring stick created for a particular tile installation whose unit of measure, rather than inches or centimeters, is the width of a single tile and grout joint used for that job. This tool gives the setter a quick, efficient means of determining how many tiles will fit in a given area and where to position layout lines.

latex or acrylic thinset adhesive
One of the three types of sand-and-cement-based, thinset tile adhesives, which must be mixed with a liquid latex or acrylic additive before use. See also *thinset adhesive.*

layout lines
Lines chalked on a setting bed to guide in accurately setting tile.

leather-hardened tile
Bisque ready for firing in a kiln, which has dried sufficiently to lose its pliability.

level (adjective and noun)
Flat or horizontally straight; a tool used to check for level.

lipping/lippage
A condition on floor or wall tiles where one or more tile edges protrudes above the desired surface plane.

margin
The perimeter of an installation. In the case of a floated mortar bed, the margin refers both to the bed's entire outside edge and also to the narrow side areas of the bed falling beyond the farthest float strips (see drawing, p. 88).

medium-bed thinset mortar
A special adhesive mortar designed to be applied in a thicker cross section than regular thinset mortar. Used for irregularly shaped tiles or to compensate for a less-than-perfect setting bed. Used primarily for floor tiles.

mesh
See *sand*.

monopressatura
A premium-quality, large-size porcelain tile produced on high-speed equipment. The *monopressatura* process was developed specifically for large porcelain tiles.

mortar
The mixture of sand, cement and water used for floating mortar beds, often referred to as mud by professional tilesetters. Mortar is prepared either as deck mud or as wall mud. Used on floors and countertops, deck mud is a stiff mixture that can support heavy loads when dry. Wall mud, also called fat mud, is a thinner, more spreadable mixture to which lime has been added to make it sticky so that it will cling to walls.

mosaic tile
Glass or vitreous porcelain or clay tiles that are 2 in. square or smaller, usually unglazed and generally packaged in sheet-mounted format.

mud
The term professional tilesetters often use for the mortar floated over a floor, wall or countertop as a setting bed for tile. See also *mortar*.

nonvitreous tile
A soft-bodied, very porous tile that, by comparison with vitreous tile, is fired at a low temperature for a short period of time. With about 7% of its bisque made of air pockets, nonvitreous tile is very absorbent and hence not freeze/thaw stable.

open time
The time exposed adhesive spread on a surface takes to begin to "skin over," or lose its bonding ability.

organic mastic
A ready-to-use petroleum- or latex-based tilesetting adhesive, which, by comparison with any of the thinset adhesives, has less bond and compressive strength, is more readily damaged by water and is less flexible when cured.

outside corner
The joint at the external angle of two intersecting surfaces.

paver tile
Clay, shale or porcelain tile, either formed in frames by hand or mechanically rammed into a die, which is usually at least ½ in. thick, occasionally glazed and principally used on floors. Most paver tiles are produced in Mexico and in the Mediterranean countries.

penetrating oil
A type of sealer used to protect the surface of unglazed tile, which penetrates the bisque of the tile.

penny rounds
Small mosaic tiles shaped like thick pennies.

perimeter joint
An expansion joint placed at the margin of an interior floor between 16 ft. square and 24 ft. square or a wall 12 ft. to 24 ft. long. This joint allows for seasonal expansion in the floor or wall while preventing damage to the tiles.

plumb
A surface or line perpendicular to a level surface or line (see *level*).

polymer-modified adhesive, grout and mortar
Polymer-modified identifies any mortar mixed with a latex or acrylic additive. The additive may be added in dry form by the manufacturer, or in liquid form by the user.

porcelain tile
A high-quality vitreous tile that is usually manufactured unglazed. On some porcelain tiles, the surface color runs through the entire body of the tile, making it ideal for high traffic areas that are subject to wear.

quarry tile
Extruded, unglazed, vitreous or semi-vitreous clay tile, usually ½ in. to ¾ in. thick, which, because of its density, is often used on floors.

radius trim (radius bullnose)
Curved tile used to border and complete a field of tile installed on a raised setting bed.

reference lines
Two lines chalked on a setting bed that intersect at a 90° angle and establish the starting point for plotting a grid of layout lines to guide in accurately setting tile.

reinforcing mesh
Wire mesh used over a mortar substrate being floated or at the midpoint in a mortar bed to strengthen the bed.

retarder additive
An ingredient found in adhesive and grout additives that slows down the evaporation of liquid from the setting material, retarding the rate at which the setting material cures and enabling it to achieve a higher bond strength.

ridge-backed tile
Tile manufactured with a series of ridges on the back, which increase the surface area contacting the tile adhesive and thus improve the adhesive's grip.

sand
The fine aggregate used to increase the strength of mortar and concrete and reduce shrinkage tendencies. The grade, or size, of sand particles is determined by passing the sand through various mesh materials called sieves, which are given a designation based on the number of holes per inch in the material.

screed (noun and verb)
The straight-edged tool used to straddle a pair of float strips and cut away, or screed, the excess mud on the surface of a floated bed of mortar.

sealant
A high-quality resilient joint filler available in a limited range of colors. Generally speaking, sealants are more durable than caulks.

semi-vitreous tile
Somewhat porous tile fired at approximately the same temperature as nonvitreous tile but for a slightly longer time. Because air pockets make up from 3% to 7% of its bisque, this tile is absorbent and not particularly freeze/thaw stable.

set-up time
The time adhesive spread on a surface takes to begin curing, or hardening.

setting bed
The surface on which tile is set.

shower and tub pan
A heavy-duty type of waterproofing membrane used on installations below the waterline (for example, shower floors and tubs), which is installed below the setting bed and which must be able to hold water.

slake
In tilesetting, to allow the mixture of mortar, thinset adhesive or grout to "rest" for a brief period after its ingredients have been thoroughly combined and before the final mixing occurs. Slaking enables the moisture in the mix to penetrate any lumps in the dry components, making it easier to complete the mixing procedure.

spacer
See *tile spacer.*

spacing lugs
Built-in projections on the edges of a tile that, like tile spacers, enable the setter to install tiles with a consistently sized grout joint.

speed-cap trim
Two-piece trim tile that, like V-cap trim, is used on the front edge of a countertop and has a top surface curved slightly upward to prevent water from running onto the floor.

spots
Small, glazed paver tiles used as accent tiles with larger pavers.

square
Having corners that are 90°.

story pole
See *jury stick.*

subfloor
A rough floor, whether plywood or boards, which is laid over joists and on which an underlayment, or substrate, is installed.

substrate
The backing to which another material is applied or attached.

surface trim (surface bullnose)
Field tile with one rounded edge used to border and complete an installation.

TCA
Tile Council of America. Established in 1945 and composed of companies producing tile and related products, this organization promotes the industry and sets installation specifications.

thick-bed installation
An installation using a floated bed of mortar as its setting bed.

thinbed, or thinset, installation
An installation using a non-mortar setting bed, which may or may not use a thinset adhesive.

thinset adhesive
One of three types of powdered, cement-based tilesetting adhesives that must be mixed with a liquid before use. Whether a water-mixed thinset, a latex or acrylic thinset, or an epoxy thinset, this type of adhesive, by comparison with an organic mastic, has greater bond and compressive strength, sets up more quickly, is more flexible when dry and is more water- and heat-resistant.

thinset installation
See *thinbed installation.*

thinset mortar
The generic term tilesetters use to refer to mortar-based tilesetting adhesives.

3-4-5 triangle
A triangle with sides in the proportion of 3:4:5, which produces one 90° corner. Plotting a 3-4-5 triangle is a method many tilesetters use to establish a pair of square reference lines on a large surface. These lines can be used both to determine if the installation site is square and to create a grid of layout lines for setting tile.

tile spacer
A plastic device sold in various shapes and widths that is used to ensure a consistently sized grout joint when setting tile.

tolerance limits
Acceptable deviations in the level, plumb and square conditions of the framing whose effect on a tile installation will be negligible. The TCA guidelines, for example, state that walls no more than ⅛ in. out of square in 10 ft. can be tiled with minor adjustments in the layout.

top-coat sealer
A product that seals and protects the surfaces of unglazed tile.

trim tile
Tile glazed on one or more edges and produced in a variety of shapes to border and finish off the main field of an installation.

trowel-applied membrane
A three-part waterproofing membrane applied on top of the setting bed and consisting of a layer of fabric sandwiched between two layers of liquid latex.

tub pan
See *shower and tub pan.*

underlayment
On floors, a smooth surface applied over a subfloor, on which tile is set.

up angle
Trim tile with one rounded or curved corner that serves to finish off an inside corner.

V-cap trim
V-shaped trim tile used on the front edge of a countertop. The tile's top surface is gently curved upward at the front edge to prevent water from running onto the floor.

vitreous tile
Dense-bodied, nonporous tile that, by comparison with nonvitreous tile, is fired at a high temperature for a long period of time. Because the ingredients in the resulting bisque have fused together like glass, this tile contains only from 0.5% to 3% air pockets, absorbs very little water, is freeze/thaw stable and has a high compressive strength.

wall mud
See *mortar, mud.*

water-mixed thinset adhesive
One of the three types of sand-and-cement-based, thinset tile adhesives, which must be mixed with water before use. See also *thinset adhesive.*

waterproofing membrane
A covering applied to a substrate or on top of the setting bed before tiling to protect the substrate and framing beneath from damage by water that may penetrate the installation.

Index

Ground-fault circuit interrupters (GFCIs), need for, 63, 66
Grout:
    acid cleaners for,
        disadvised, 66
        precautions with, 229
    additives for, 44, 170, 189, 228
    amount needed, estimating, 189
    applying, 148-149, 170-171
    cleanup of, 170-171
        dry, 149
        wet, 150-152
    colored, 44
        and tile compatibility, 44-45
    for contrast, 44-45, 194
    coverage, table for, 44
    discussed, 43
    haze-cleaning solutions for, 153, 228-229
    impregnators for, 153
    and joint width, 44
    making, 44
    mixing, 147-148
    plain vs. sanded, 44
    polymer-modified, 44
    removing, 226, 228
    safety precautions with, 68
    sealers for, 153
    sequence for, 170-171
    setup time for, 150
    tools for, 65-66
Grout bags:
    for porous tiles, 15
    using, 66, 149-150
Grout joints:
    cleaning, 228
    cracks in, causes of, 222-223
    impregnator for, 228
    layout lines for, 126
    regrouting, 228
    shaping, 151-152, 170
    spacing, 64
    and tile list, 119-121
    width of, 148
Grout release, as coating for tiles, 45
Grout saw, using, 48, 146
Grouting tools. *See* specific tools.

H

Handbook for Ceramic Tile Installation
    (Tile Council of America):
    discussed, 71, 72
    substrate caution of, 156
Hawks, uses for, 55
Hearths:
    tiling, 201-202
    See also Fireplaces.

Heat:
    effect of, on setting materials, 139, 140-141, 145, 150, 181
    setting tiles exposed to, 200-202
Heating pipes, tiling around, 94
Hole saws:
    applications for, 62
    heat shock with, 63
    using, 63, 76
Humidity, effect of, on setting materials, 139, 150

I

Impervious tile:
    adhesives for, 9
    water-absorption rate of, 7, 8
Impregnators:
    for grout, 153, 228
    for stone tile, 31

J

Joints. *See* Cold joints. Control joints.
    Expansion joints. Grout joints.
Jury stick, making, 125-126

L

Latex thinset adhesive. *See* Thinset adhesives.
Layout:
    adjusting, for out-of-square condition, 123-125
    for countertops, 131-133, 192
    drawings for, preliminary, 118-119
    estimating for, 121-122, 161-164, 176-177
    for floors, 122-130, 164-166
    importance of, 113-115
    of irregular patterns, 134-135
    of irregular tiles, 133
    jury stick for, 116, 125-126
    layout lines for, 126-127, 165-166
    preparing for, 116-122
    principles of, 115-116
    reference lines for, 122-125, 164
    tile/grout-joint list for, 119-121, 161, 162, 188
    tools for, 50-53, 116
    for tub surround, 175-176, 180-181
    for walls, 130-131
    around window, 174-176, 180
Level, checking for, 73
Levels. *See* Spirit levels.
Linoleum:
    as setting bed, 85
        adhesives for, 43
Lipping, and stone-tile installations, 29-30
Lumber, dimensional, as setting bed, disadvised, 82

M

Maintenance, of tilework, 30-31, 228
Marble Institute of America, tile-grading system of, 24-25
Marble tile. *See* Stone tile.
Marking, tools for, 53
Masking tape, for wall installations, 181-182
Mason's hoe, as mixing tool, 54
Masonry:
    cracks in, containing, 84
    depressions in, leveling, 83-84
    as setting surface, 82-84
Mastics. *See* Organic mastics.
Material Safety Data Sheets (MSDSs), discussed, 68, 69
Measuring, tools for, 50-53
Membranes:
    curing, need for, 89, 111
    isolation, 109-111
        over concrete slabs, 110
        need for, 84, 85, 86, 110
        repair with, 223, 224
        trowel-applied, 111
    purpose of, 104
    sound control, need for, 111
    waterproofing,
        and backer-board installation, 35
        need for, 84, 86, 104
        with plywood, 36, 43
        polyethylene film as, 215
        sheet, 106-107
        tar-paper, 105-106, 177-179
        trowel-applied, 107-109
        See also Chlorinated polyethylene.
            Shower pans.
Metal. *See* Sheet metal.
Mexican pavers. *See* Paver tiles.
Mixing boxes, described, 54
Mixing paddles, using, 54, 139, 147
Monopressatura (porcelain tile), discussed, 14
Mortar:
    additives for, 89, 211
    floor, 87
        mixing, 217-218
        sloped subfloor, 210-211
    safety precautions with, 68
    types of, defined, 39
    wall, 87
    See also Grout. Thinset adhesives.
Mortar beds:
    adhesives for, 40, 43
    applications for, 38
    curing, 88-89
    efflorescence in, additives against, 205
    floating, 88-89
    membrane for, 106

Editor: Peter Chapman
Designer/Layout Artist: Suzanna Yannes
Illustrator, except where noted: Elizabeth Eaton

Typeface: Symbol
Paper: Warren Patina Matte, 70 lb., neutral pH
Printer: Quebecor Printing/Hawkins, New Canton, Tennessee